Redistributing Happiness

Redistributing Happiness

How Social Policies Shape Life Satisfaction

Hiroshi Ono and Kristen Schultz Lee

PRAEGER™

An Imprint of ABC-CLIO, LLC

Santa Barbara, California • Denver, Colorado

Library of Congress Cataloging-in-Publication Data

Names: Ono, Hiroshi, 1966– author. | Lee, Kristen Schultz, author.
Title: Redistributing happiness : how social policies shape life satisfaction /
   Hiroshi Ono and Kristen Schultz Lee.
Description: Santa Barbara : Praeger, 2016. | Includes bibliographical references
   and index.
Identifiers: LCCN 2016017826 (print) | LCCN 2016032728 (ebook) |
   ISBN 9781440832970 (alk. paper) | ISBN 9781440832987 (ebook)
Subjects: LCSH: Happiness—Social aspects.
Classification: LCC BF575.H27 .O56 2016 (print) | LCC BF575.H27 (ebook) |
   DDC 302—dc23
LC record available at https://lccn.loc.gov/2016017826

ISBN: 978-1-4408-3297-0
EISBN: 978-1-4408-3298-7

20   19   18   17   16   1   2   3   4   5

This book is also available as an eBook.

Praeger
An Imprint of ABC-CLIO, LLC

ABC-CLIO, LLC
130 Cremona Drive, P.O. Box 1911
Santa Barbara, California 93116–1911
www.abc-clio.com

This book is printed on acid-free paper ∞

Manufactured in the United States of America

Some figures within the book are reprinted with kind permission from the following sources:

Figures 3.1, 3.3, and 8.1: Diener, Edward, and Eunkook M. Suh, eds., *Culture and Subjective Well-Being*; Figures 7.2, 7.3, and 7.4, © 2000 Massachusetts Institute of Technology, by permission of The MIT Press.

Figure 4.1: Lee, Kristen Schultz and Hiroshi Ono. 2008. "Specialization and Marital Happiness: A U.S.-Japan Comparison." *Social Science Research* 37(4): 1216–1234.

Figure 8.2: Guriev, Sergei and Ekaterina Zhuravskaya. 2009. "(Un)Happiness in Transition." *Journal of Economic Perspectives* 23: 143–168.

Contents

Illustrations

FIGURES

BOXES

TABLES

1

Introduction: The Science of Happiness

What makes people happy? A basic assumption underlying the study of human behavior is that we all want to be happy. The pursuit of happiness is a fundamental right written into the founding documents of many countries, East and West.[1] And yet, it is only in recent years that scholars have become seriously engaged in "happiness science." The study of what makes people happy is far from complete. Despite the accumulation of wealth and higher standards of living in richer societies, people claim to be no happier today than they did 50 years ago. The disconnect between economic well-being and subjective well-being has led to a renewed interest in the study of happiness. Happiness research is now discussed widely in policy circles, academia, and the popular media. Across the social sciences, it is flourishing, with each discipline making its own contribution toward the discovery of what makes us happy or unhappy.

Our research showcases the sociologist's contribution: *What makes people happy depends on the social context.* Accounting for social context allows us to observe that what makes people happy in one social setting may not do so in another. And, that happiness found usually owes to the right mix of social context and individual factors. While economists search for a universal model of happiness, sociologists seek answers that are specific to the social-institutional context.

WHAT IS HAPPINESS AND HOW DO WE STUDY IT?

Our study starts with a simple yet bold assumption: Happiness can be measured. Although this may seem like a trivial issue to some, the treatment of happiness as a measurable outcome has been (and continues to be) the cause for great controversy in the social sciences. Indeed, some may argue that the issue remains unresolved. To this day, when we lecture about happiness or present our research findings on happiness, there is usually at least one skeptic in the audience who objects to treating happiness as a measurable outcome.

The controversy is understandable because of the subjective nature of happiness. To begin with, happiness is a measure of well-being. In general, well-being has an objective and subjective component.[2] Objective well-being includes measures such as personal income, wealth, and educational attainment, which do not rely on people's perceptions. Happiness, on the other hand, is a form of subjective well-being, which is an affective state that requires self-evaluation and reflection. Unlike objective "hard" outcomes such as money income and years of education, happiness is hard to capture and even harder to quantify. We can say that Julie is richer than John by simply reporting how much more money Julie has compared to John. But how do we establish, objectively and scientifically, that Julie is *happier* than John?

Like other sciences, social science must be an objective science. Is there a way to treat happiness scientifically, so that we can deepen our knowledge of what makes people happy? It took many years, actually decades, to convince the scientific community that happiness can be measured. The progress toward measurability was a significant first step in solidifying its empirical foundations and in advancing the science of happiness overall.

An important point to clarify early on is what exactly we mean by happiness. Subjective well-being can be separated into life satisfaction, positive experiences, and negative experiences. Life satisfaction refers to an individual's evaluation and appreciation of his or her life (rather than fleeting emotional reactions or moods). Our use of the term *happiness* comes closest to the idea of life satisfaction.

In the social sciences, the most common way to measure happiness is through self-reported questions collected through social surveys. The survey method is very straightforward in that we simply *ask* the respondents about their level of happiness. The underlying assumption is that "people are reckoned to be the best judges of the overall quality of their lives" (Frey and Stutzer 2002, p. 405).

Of course, this is not the only way to think about happiness. It does not, for example, capture moments of joy, nor does it necessarily capture what Aristotle referred to as *eudemonia*, or the fulfillment of one's potential. However, these other forms of happiness do not lend themselves as well to social scientific study. Empirical research has demonstrated the validity of self-reports in capturing happiness as we define it. For example, an individual's self-reported happiness is highly correlated with his or her friends' and family's reports of happiness (Layard 2005) and also corresponds to predicted results of MRI brain scans (Bartram 2012). And for our purposes it is important to note that self-reports of happiness can reliably be compared across countries, so long as the objective is to compare predictors of happiness in different countries rather than to compare absolute levels of happiness (Diener and Suh 2003). It is quite possible that the citizens of certain nations may have a cultural tendency to rate their happiness as higher than the citizens of another nation (see discussion in Chapter 3). This can prove problematic for analyses attempting to compare the overall level of happiness in one country versus another. We, however, are less interested in these country-level comparisons of overall happiness than in studying how the predictors of happiness interact with the social beliefs and policies of different countries, resulting in different accounts of happiness cross-nationally.

A common critique in self-reported responses to happiness is that bias may arise because of the subjective nature of happiness.[3] Not all individuals may perceive the questions in the same way. Responses may vary depending on how the happiness question is phrased, where the happiness question is asked in the survey (e.g., beginning, middle, or the end), or if the respondent just happened to have a very good (or bad) day at the time of the survey. However, although we cannot rule out the possibility of reporting bias in survey responses, scholars have discovered "remarkably consistent patterns in the determinants of happiness" (Graham 2005, p. 44) in studies across countries and over time. We hereby acknowledge the caveats regarding the empirical treatment of happiness, but proceed with the assumption that the shortcomings do not systematically influence our results.

We would like to add one final note on measurements. In empirical research, happiness and life satisfaction are two closely related measures of subjective well-being. While some critics may not agree on their precise definitions or their theoretical distinctions, studies have shown that it matters little in empirical research. The form of the well-being equation is nearly identical whether one uses happiness or satisfaction as the outcome variable (Blanchflower and Oswald 2004). For clarity and consistency, we will use the expression *happiness* throughout our book unless otherwise noted.

HAPPINESS DATA

The growing interest in happiness studies has been greatly facilitated by the availability of high-quality microdata. The data come in many forms such as repeated cross-sectional surveys, international/ comparative surveys, and longitudinal/ panel surveys, which we briefly review next.

In our research, we use data collected from large-scale surveys consisting of thousands of respondents, and try to find patterns in the data. Most surveys are designed to look at a whole range of outcomes, and not just happiness. So happiness is just one of the many questions that are asked in the survey along with, for example, job status, marital status, presence of children, educational attainment, current income, and current household income.

The typical happiness question asks the respondent about his or her state of happiness. For example, in the General Social Survey (GSS), which is a long-standing large-scale survey administered in the United States, the happiness question is: "Taken all together, how would you say things are these days? Would you say that you are not too happy, pretty happy or very happy?" The responses are then coded 1, 2, and 3 respectively. The researchers can then tabulate the results and assign numerical values to happiness, such as the mean value of happiness, the proportion who responded "very happy" or "not too happy," and so on.

The most common form of survey is the cross-sectional survey, so named because the data are collected at one point in time, to represent a cross-section of the population. The GSS, for example, is a cross-sectional survey with a sampling scheme that is carefully designed to collect a representative cross-section of the American population. More interestingly, the GSS has been asking the same happiness question using the same sampling design every year or every other year since 1972, making it a special type of data known as repeated cross-sectional data. We can, therefore, plot a trendline of happiness over the past 40+ years to see how happiness has changed over time in the United States (see, e.g., Figure 1.1a).

There are also international surveys, such as the International Social Survey Programme (ISSP), that include survey responses from 30+ countries. The ISSP started in 1984 in just four countries (Australia, Germany, Britain, and the United States) and has expanded to include 48 countries in the 2013 wave of data collection. The ISSP does not ask the happiness question in every wave but does so only periodically. In our study, we analyze data from the 2002 Family and Changing Gender Roles Module of the ISSP in Chapters 5 and 6. Since the identical happiness question was asked, using the same sampling design, we can compare how happiness differs across the 34 countries included in this module.

And most importantly for our research purpose, the ISSP is hierarchically structured. Individual observations are collected within a country. In statistical terms, the data are hierarchically ordered because individuals (who occupy the lower hierarchy) are nested within countries (which occupy the higher hierarchy). Hierarchically structured data allow us to estimate hierarchical linear models (or multilevel models), which we discuss in the methods section.

Other datasets that collect happiness data across countries include the World Values Survey, which covers some 70+ countries (see, e.g., Bjørnskov et al. 2007), and the Gallup World Poll that covers 130+ countries (see, e.g., Deaton 2008). The GSS, which originated in the United States, is now available in Europe as the European Social Survey and covers 30 European countries. There is also an East Asian equivalent called the East Asian Social Survey, which includes China, Japan, South Korea, and Taiwan.

Panel (or longitudinal) surveys are designed to track individuals over time. Panel data are especially useful because they allow researchers to examine how a person's happiness can change in response to particular events in the life course, such as marriage (or divorce), childbirth, job loss, or change in income. For example, VanLaningham et al. (2001) use panel data from the Marital Instability over the Life Course study to illustrate changes in marital happiness over the life course.

And finally, there are rare and highly specialized datasets that allow researchers to apply advanced statistical techniques. An example of this is the twin study—that is, a dataset that includes a sample of identical twins. Twins data are very precious and useful because we can isolate the effects of the environment and social surroundings from genetic effects. We will discuss the twin study design in greater detail in Chapter 2.

STATISTICAL METHODS AND TECHNIQUES TO EXAMINE HAPPINESS

The rich collection of survey data allows researchers to apply a diverse array of analytical methods, such as fixed effects models, hierarchical linear models, social network analysis, and tests for age-period-cohort effects. Each of these methods is a tool for the social scientist to analyze how individual-level characteristics and societal-level factors interact to shape happiness.

Fixed effects models can be used when analyzing panel data as a way of controlling for unobserved individual characteristics. By comparing an individual to himself or herself over time, the researcher can connect changes in the individual's happiness to other changes (or events) in his or her life, such as changes in marital status or employment status, rather than to fixed characteristics such as gender or race. For example, fixed effects models can be used to examine the relationship between marriage and happiness. With cross-sectional data such as the GSS, we compare the happiness of a married person to the happiness of an unmarried person. If the former is greater than the latter, then the interpretation is that marriage and happiness are positively correlated. But with panel data, we can compare the happiness level of the same person before and after marriage, which brings us closer to understanding causation, rather than just correlation. If his or her happiness is greater after marriage, then we can surmise that marriage has a positive effect on happiness.

Multilevel models (see discussion under the section "The Sociological Approach to Happiness") allow the researcher to partition out how much of the variation in reported happiness we observe is between individuals in a particular context (e.g., a country) and how much is between contexts. This method also allows the researcher to examine the interplay of individual and context effects on happiness.

Social network analysis allows the researcher to analyze an individual's reported happiness as a function of not just his or her own characteristics but as a function of the characteristics (including the happiness) of those around him or her. The key assumption is that individuals are embedded in social networks. We derive the sources of our happiness (and unhappiness), at least in part, from our structural positioning within social networks. Special data are required because the analysis requires estimating network characteristics such as density, closure, and centrality.

And finally, age-period-cohort models are used by researchers to examine the role of historical context in shaping an individual's happiness. These models are particularly useful for determining if individuals born and raised in different time periods have different average levels of happiness.

In spite of considerable advances in survey design and methods, the limitations of measuring happiness remain a key challenge in happiness studies. Time diary methods (see, e.g., Kahneman et al. 2004; Kahneman and Krueger 2006) ask respondents to either record their happiness throughout the day or to reconstruct their happiness on the previous day do a better job of capturing fluctuations in happiness but the data are generally not available cross-nationally. Measuring true happiness may require a more biological approach—for example, wiring human subjects with instruments to measure how their brainwaves respond to different stimuli. Nevertheless, we believe that self-reported survey measures of happiness are more suited to measuring the individual's perception of their happiness, rather than their physical or emotional response to a specific stimulus.

As scientists, we are keenly interested in understanding what influences an individual's assessment of his or her happiness, measured through self-reported surveys. Applying statistical methods and discovering how social and economic factors influence happiness are important contributions to this cause. We can use our statistical models to make predictions and to conduct simulations to explore counterfactual conditions (although we have to be very careful with our assumptions). We can thus answer pressing questions—for example, if people are not happy, under what conditions would they be?

THE HAPPINESS EQUATION

Estimating happiness starts with the basic model where we assume that happiness (U) is a function of observable characteristics (x):

$$U = f(x_1, x_2, x_3, \ldots, x_n)$$

Statistically, this function can be expressed in regression form as:

$$U = \alpha + \beta_1 x_1 + \beta_2 x_2 + \beta_3 x_3 + \ldots + \beta_n x_n + \varepsilon$$

We refer to this equation as the happiness equation. Our mission, then, is to come up with a set of explanatory variables (x) that raise the predictive power of U. Because we are social scientists, each explanatory variable that we test must be motivated by theory. We may discover x's that are significantly correlated with U. But the association may be dismissed as spurious, unless the inclusion of the variables can be backed with solid theory. We draw on theories developed by psychologists, economists, and sociologists in deciding which explanatory variables to include in our own analyses.

The explanatory variables can be categorized into several groups. In our research, we make the big distinction between individual- (or micro-) level variables, such as demographic characteristics and socioeconomic status, and societal- (or macro-) level characteristics such as national income and economic inequality. Chapters 2 and 3 are largely dedicated to explaining how these characteristics are related to happiness.

Describing and reporting the results of statistical models require great caution and care. If we estimate a happiness equation that looks like the one we see here, then for the most part, we are dealing with correlations and not causation. For example, suppose that one of the x's in the happiness equation is whether the respondent is married or not, and its coefficient is positive. We interpret this finding to mean that being married (instead of not being married) is associated with higher happiness. But we cannot conclude that marriage causes higher happiness. Causality is a very tricky issue which requires carefully designed survey data, and even then it is difficult to rule out the possibility of reverse causality. For example, does marriage bring greater happiness? Or are happier people more likely to get married? We therefore exercise caution when we describe statistical models and their outcomes.

HAPPINESS AS AN INTERDISCIPLINARY SCIENCE

Happiness science is an exciting area for social science research because it brings together theories from multiple disciplines such as sociology, economics, psychology, philosophy, and political science. We believe that it is not constructive to erect disciplinary barriers, but rather more productive for the multiple perspectives to merge. Each discipline makes a unique contribution. Integrating the multiple perspectives is beneficial, because the theories complement each other. In our research, we integrate sociological and economic approaches to study happiness. We outline similarities, differences, and complementarities of these two approaches next.

THE ECONOMIC APPROACH TO HAPPINESS

First, the economic approach to happiness should be understood as an extension of utility and utility maximization. Students of economics will (hopefully) recall that the concept of utility lies at the very core of microeconomics. The definition of utility can vary, but let us start with the following description from the best-selling textbook *Intermediate Microeconomics* by Hal Varian (2010):

> In Victorian days, philosophers and economists talked blithely of "utility" as an indicator of a person's overall well-being. Utility was thought of as a numeric measure of a person's happiness. Given this idea, it was natural to think of consumers making choices so as to maximize their utility, that is, to make themselves as happy as possible. The trouble is that these classical economists never really described how we were to measure utility. How are we supposed to quantify the "amount" of utility associated with different choices? Is one person's utility the same as another's? What would it mean to say that an extra candy bar would give me twice as much utility as an extra carrot? Does the concept of utility have any independent meaning other than its being what people maximize? Because of these conceptual problems, economists have abandoned the old-fashioned view of utility as being a measure of happiness. Instead, the theory of consumer behavior has been reformulated entirely in terms of consumer preferences, and utility is seen only as a *way to describe preferences*. (p. 54)

So here again we find the tension that we discussed earlier, on the issue of measurability of happiness, or in this case, utility. Consumer choice and utility maximization involve the calculation of cost and benefits. The costs and benefits can be monetary, but whatever is not monetary is treated as psychic. Consequently, the psychic costs and benefits become a black box because they are impossible to quantify.[4] Rather than trying to defend (or debunk) its empirical status, economists started treating utility simply as a "preference representation function" (Deaton and Muellbauer 1994, p. 28). Conventional economics thus assumes that utility functions cannot be directly observed; they can be only *revealed* (or inferred) through preferences.[5]

Treating utility simply as a rank ordering of preferences is an example of ordinal utility. This rather narrow definition of utility as it relates to consumption and preferences is the dominant view of utility in economics. For example, in their best-selling introductory economics textbook, Samuelson and Nordhaus (2005) define utility as "the total satisfaction derived from the consumption of goods or services" (p. 752).

In contrast to ordinal utility, the concept of cardinal utility assumes that utility can be measured and compared across persons. Great tension still remains in economics between ordinal and cardinal utility. As Ng (1997) explains, economists "are very hostile to cardinal utility and interpersonal comparisons. . . (and) prefer to use the more objective concepts like preference and choice" (p. 1848), presumably because choice is more readily observable than is utility. A consumer reveals her preference by, for example, choosing chocolate over vanilla because doing so gives her higher utility. We can observe the choice that she made, but we cannot observe her utility function. Treating utility, happiness, and other subjective matters as a purely theoretical and heuristic apparatus is much easier and safer than trying to transform them into measurable empirical constructs and facing the relentless waves of criticism.

But there are broader interpretations of utility in economics, which depart from the conventional definitions that have been limited to consumption, preferences, and choice. For example, here is Mankiw's (2012) description:

[Utility is] the level of happiness or satisfaction that a person receives from his or her circumstances. Utility is a measure of well-being and, according to utilitarians, is the ultimate objective of all public and private actions. The proper goal of government, they claim, is to maximize the sum of utility achieved by everyone in society. (p. 424)

This definition of utility is closer to how we view happiness and, more broadly, subjective well-being. In a 2002 article featured in the *Journal of Economic Literature*, Frey and Stutzer, two influential economists studying happiness, declared, "Measures of subjective well-being can thus serve as proxies for 'utility'" (p. 405). Happiness economics relies on "more expansive notions of utility" rather than depend on narrow assumptions and definitions (Graham 2005). The broader acceptance of utility, with regard to its theoretical underpinnings and empirical treatment, has opened up immense opportunities for empirical research on happiness in economics.[6]

Second, explaining the relationship between money and happiness remains a primary area of focus for the economists. In a highly influential paper, Richard Easterlin (1974) first showed that individual income and self-reported happiness are closely linked. However, at the aggregate level, the relationship between national income and aggregate happiness across countries is weak or insignificant. Additionally, he showed that aggregate happiness has changed very little in the United States, in spite of significant improvements in income per capita in the postwar period (see Figure 1.1a).[7]

Easterlin's findings came to be known as the Easterlin paradox. The Easterlin paradox has been confirmed in other countries as well, which further

Figure 1.1a Income and Happiness in the United States

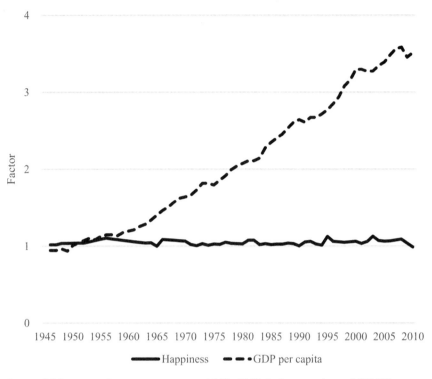

Source: U.S. personal income per capita 1929–2008: Inflation adjusted (2008).

supports his claim. In Japan (see Figure 1.1b), aggregate life satisfaction remained stable between 1958 and 2013 during the same time that real income increased sevenfold (see also Chapter 2). And in post-communist China (see Chapter 8), overall life satisfaction actually declined between 1994 and 2005, during which time average real income rose by 250 percent (Easterlin et al. 2012; Kahneman and Krueger 2006).

Although it has not been short of controversy (see Box 1.1), the Easterlin paradox challenged the conventional wisdom in economics that money and happiness are tightly related.[8] At a broader level, the Easterlin paradox uncovered the disconnect between objective well-being and subjective well-being, leading to serious discussions in macroeconomic policy. What is the point of aiming for high economic growth if more money does not bring more happiness? For researchers, the disconnect between money and happiness led to the acute realization that the two are fundamentally distinct and must be treated separately. Happiness is the ultimate objective of most (if not all) people, whereas money is only the means to increase happiness (Ng 1997).

Figure 1.1b Income and Life Satisfaction in Japan

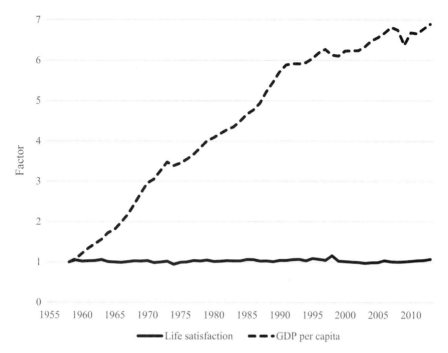

Source: World Database of Happiness and GDP per Capita in 2014 USD—The Conference Board.

Box 1.1 Easterlin Paradox, Revisited

Since its publication in 1974, the Easterlin paradox has been challenged and contested by numerous scholars and critics. In 2008, Stevenson and Wolfers released a 102-page paper titled "Economic Growth and Subjective Well-Being: Reassessing the Easterlin Paradox." The two economists used multiple datasets to reassess the Easterlin paradox and concluded that there is a positive association between subjective well-being and GDP per capita across countries, thereby weakening the paradox. Easterlin et al. (2010) responded with their paper titled "The Happiness-Income Paradox Revisited," in which they defended the paradox. Wolfers (2010) then responded in a blog entry titled "Debunking the Easterlin Paradox, Again," claiming that Easterlin was wrong (again).

Although the controversy continues as of this writing, Graham (2010) offers a succinct, if not level-headed, summary in her article "More on the Easterlin Paradox: A Response to Wolfers." While not taking position of yay or nay, Graham explains that whether the Easterlin paradox remains true or not depends on many factors, such as how the happiness question was phrased, which countries are included in the comparisons, and which time periods are considered. She cautions against dismissing the paradox as being "plain wrong," and concludes with a message giving credit to Easterlin.

> [T]here is the simpler question of giving credit where credit is due. We would not be having this debate, nor would we have a host of analysis on well-being beyond what is measured by income, had Easterlin not triggered our thinking on this with his original study of happiness and income over three decades ago. . . . In the big picture of things, Easterlin had the idea.

References

Easterlin, Richard A., Laura Angelescu McVey, Malgorzata Switek, Onnicha Sawangfa, and Jacqueline Smith Zweig. 2010. "The Happiness–Income Paradox Revisited." *Proceedings of the National Academy of the Sciences* 107(52): 22463–22468.

Graham, Carol. 2010. "More on the Easterlin Paradox: A Response to Wolfers." *Brookings Institute Blog*. (December 15, 2010).

Stevenson, Betsey and Justin Wolfers. 2008. "Economic Growth and Subjective Well-Being: Reassessing the Easterlin Paradox." *Brookings Paper on Economic Activity* 39: 1–102.

Wolfers, Justin. 2010. "Debunking the Easterlin Paradox, Again." *Freakonomics Blog*. (December 13, 2010).

Although recent happiness research conducted by economists is more diverse, uncovering the linkages between income and happiness remains a strong tradition in the economic approach, whether it be at the macroeconomic level (e.g., Di Tella et al. 2003) or at the micro-individual level (e.g., Blanchflower and Oswald 2004). One key area of contribution has been in the study of absolute versus relative income (Clark and Oswald 1996; Layard 2005). People care less about their absolute income, but care more about how their income compares to other people. Research has also shown that money and happiness are positively correlated, but only up to a point. Once one reaches the saturation point, happiness stops growing regardless of further increases in income (see further discussion in Chapter 2).

And third, the economic approach to happiness is a pursuit to discover the universal model of happiness. This is a fundamental ideological and methodological distinction between economics and sociology. Hirsch et al.

(1987), who are sociologists, explain, with some cynicism and humor, the big differences between sociologists and economists in how they think and solve problems namely, that economists look for "universally acceptable hypothesis. . . which transcend institutional, systematic, and historical variations" (p. 326).[9] The keyword here is *universal*. For economists, what is important is to come up with "clean models," usually steeped in mathematics, which purport to explain all regardless of context.[10] For example, the economic approach to human behavior is based on the model of *homo economicus*, which assumes that individuals are motivated by self-interest and make rational decisions that maximize their benefits (e.g., Becker 1976). Homo economicus is a *universal* model of man. It does not matter where you live or what time period you live in. Individual choice is driven primarily by costs and benefits.

The economic approach to happiness follows a similar tradition. It is a quest for the universal model of happiness. The sources of happiness are devoid of any context. What makes people happy in one context will always make people happy in *any* context. Statistically speaking, this means that there is one universal happiness equation. The explanatory variables in the happiness equation are not context-specific but context-neutral.

THE SOCIOLOGICAL APPROACH TO HAPPINESS

Our study of happiness is grounded in sociological theory. The sociological tradition starts with the position that individuals do not live in isolation, but are socially situated within a broader, social-institutional context. It assumes that the sources of happiness come from both the individual *and* his or her social surroundings.

We can visualize this intuition using the classic framework of contextual-effect models (Anderton and Sellers 1989; Blalock 1984). As Figure 1.2 illustrates, contextual effect models assume that there are two levels of analysis: the macro-contextual level and the micro-individual level. The essence of contextual effect models is to estimate "the influences of context characteristics on individuals or the events experienced by individuals" (Anderton and Sellers 1989, p. 106).

Conventional statistical models are restricted to one level of analyses. For example, following our previous discussion, we can surmise that the primary focus of the economic approach to happiness is to study the relationship strictly at the micro-individual level, that is, to estimate the effects of individual characteristics (c) on an individual outcome (o), which in this case is happiness. The very definition of the universal model of happiness presupposes that happiness can be explained regardless of context. The individual is primary; the context is secondary. Likewise there are studies that have a

Figure 1.2 Contextual Effect Models

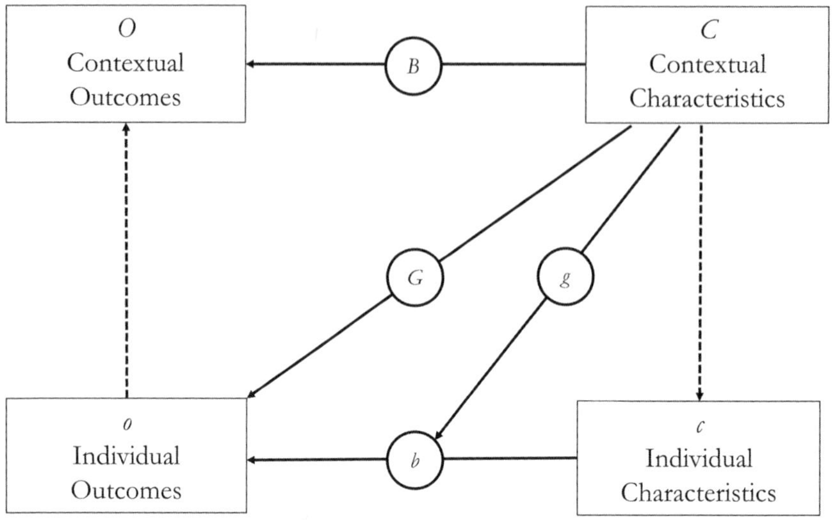

Source: Anderton and Sellers (1989).

strictly macro-level orientation that estimates contextual characteristics (C) on a contextual-level outcome (O), for example, using GDP to estimate aggregate happiness. But such models are also incomplete (at least from a sociologist's position) because they disregard the micro-level foundations of happiness.

The sociological approach presupposes that the individual is embedded in and constrained by the broader social context. The two are inseparable. Happiness is an individual outcome (o) shaped by individual characteristics (c), for example, age, gender, education, and income, as shown by the solid line b. At the same time, an individual is situated in a particular social context. It follows then that her happiness is shaped and constrained by the contextual characteristics (C), for example, religious climate, and economic and social inequality, as shown by the solid line G. And finally, contextual characteristics (C) may also affect the process of transforming individual characteristics to individual outcomes (b), in which case we have a cross-level interaction shown by the solid line g.

Statistically speaking, contextual-effect models belong to the family of cross-level analysis (Blalock 1984) or multilevel modeling because they involve (at least) two levels of analysis.[11] The technique allows us to simultaneously estimate both macro- and micro-level determinants of happiness (and their interactions). We apply multilevel modeling in our own empirical analyses presented in Chapters 5 and 6.

A sociological perspective on happiness is an important contribution to the body of happiness research that has been conducted primarily by psychologists and economists. By making our focus the interplay of the individual and the social context, we address critiques of the happiness literature that it is overly individualistic, biological, and decontextualized (Frawley 2015). We believe that studies that conceptualize happiness as a product of our disposition or personal characteristics or, alternatively, as a measure of progress at the national level, overlook the interplay between individual and society that ultimately shapes our happiness. Individuals with similar characteristics will be more or less happy depending on the social context in which they are living in, and a particular social context will have different implications for the happiness of various groups embedded in the context. The sociological perspective on happiness focuses on this interaction of the personal and the social. Happiness studies in the sociological tradition have thus generated research situated within a particular institutional context—for example, neighborhoods and communities (Firebaugh and Schroeder 2009), social status position (Schnittker 2008), and historical context (Yang 2008).

Sociologists are particularly interested in the study of social problems and often take a critical stance on the existing social order (Bartram 2012). Sociology is rich with analyses of racial, economic, and gender inequality, and of how the social stratification system constrains individual opportunities for socioeconomic advancement. This critical stance on social problems and the attention to social constraints on individual opportunity is apparent in our analysis of happiness. We see happiness as constrained by a variety of social problems—economic inequality, gender inequality, and lack of social cohesion all constrain the opportunity for some groups to achieve happiness.

This is a fundamentally different point of view on happiness than that taken by many positive psychologists. Positive psychology has been criticized as being overly individualistic, as placing the onus for achieving happiness squarely on the individual without paying sufficient attention to the constraints of the social structure in which that individual is living. For example, Frawley (2015, p. 70) criticizes positive psychology as "foster[ing] depoliticized constructions of once contentious issues." She goes on to give the example of unemployment, saying that from the perspective of positive psychologists, unemployment is not seen as a social problem connected to social inequalities but instead as a "character flaw remediable through identifying and fostering 'signature strengths'" (Frawley 2015, p. 70).

As sociologists studying happiness, we focus not on the individual and the individual's success or failure in achieving happiness but on the individual's opportunity to achieve happiness in a particular social-institutional context. While individualistic accounts rooted in positive psychology encourage individual adaptation to the existing social order, our approach highlights inequalities in the status quo, making room for the prospect of larger social change.

OUTLINE OF THE BOOK

The book is organized as follows. In Chapters 2 and 3, we review the micro- and macro-level foundations of happiness. Chapter 2 examines the individual-level sources of happiness. We begin with the psychological perspective, and review such factors as personality, disposition, and genes. We then examine demographic and socioeconomic characteristics such as gender, race, education, and income. Chapter 3 examines the sources of happiness at the societal level. These include macroeconomic indicators such as gross domestic product and inequality, and social-institutional factors such as religious climate and gender beliefs. We also examine the degree of government involvement in social welfare, to explore how the tension between the state and the market affects the well-being of their citizens.

We present our own research findings framed in the sociological tradition in Chapters 4, 5, and 6, showcasing the importance of the institutional context and the interplay between the micro and the macro. In Chapter 4, we focus on the particular case of marriage and happiness in the United States and Japan. What makes people happy in marriage can vary greatly depending on the division of labor between husband and wife (Who works? Who takes care of the kids?), the presence of children, and what the social norms, conventions, and expectations are where you live. To complicate things even more, it also depends on whether you are a man or a woman. We illustrate the complex interactions between gender, marriage, and happiness in two societies that vastly differ in the social-cultural context—the United States and Japan. In Chapter 5, we argue that married people are happier than cohabiting persons in many countries, at least in part because of views toward marriage and gender roles in the society. Some countries espouse more "traditional" gender beliefs relating to marriage, which may lower the happiness of cohabiting persons in those countries. In Chapter 6, we show that social welfare expenditures in social democratic welfare states raise the happiness of the poor but lower the happiness of the wealthy. In other words, happiness is not just an individual characteristic that we can control through positive thinking or by engaging in social activities. Instead, happiness depends largely on the norms, beliefs, and policies of the greater social context in which the individual is situated in.

In Chapter 7, we review the literature relating to the sources of unhappiness. Chapter 8 also examines unhappiness but from the societal level, with special attention to the case of unhappiness in post-communist countries. Chapter 9 concludes.

2

A Happy Person

What is the secret to happiness? What is it that makes one person happy and another miserable, or at least less happy? Is it coded in our genes? Is it our general disposition or world view, our relationships with friends and family, or is it something about our place in society—how much money we have or what kind of neighborhood we live in? In this chapter, we start by exploring the individual characteristics identified primarily by psychologists, such as personality, disposition, and genes as key predictors of happiness. We also look at demographic and socioeconomic characteristics such as gender, age, race, education, income, and the presence of children. We start developing explanations for why one person might be happier than his or her neighbor and why our happiness might change over time.

PERSONALITY, DISPOSITION, AND GENES

Psychologists argue that happiness is intimately connected to personality. In particular, neuroticism has been shown to be predictive of unhappiness whereas extraversion (or a preference for being in the company of others rather than being alone) predicts happiness. Of course, we cannot say with certainty which direction the causal arrow points though. Some scholars have suggested that happiness may actually lead to extraversion, for example (Lucas et al. 2000). In fact, one study conducted an experiment in which participants who were subjected to mood elation showed an interest in social and leisure activities while those who received a depression induction showed an interest in sitting and thinking, being alone, and taking a nap (Cunningham 1988). This makes intuitive sense; when we are happier, we are more likely to enjoy the company of others than when we are feeling down. If happier people are more extraverted and extraverted people are happier, we can see that drawing a single causal arrow from a personality characteristic like extraversion to happiness no longer makes sense.

Other personality characteristics such as self-esteem, agreeableness, and conscientiousness all have been shown to be positively associated with happiness (Diener et al. 2003). Optimism also predicts happiness, perhaps because optimists are more likely to set goals and work toward them, which may lead to more successful accomplishment of goals by optimists compared to others. Making progress toward our goals makes us happy (Fujita and Diener 2005). But, of course, none of these personality characteristics exist in a vacuum. It would be naïve to conclude that the key to happiness is rooted in having a positive outlook or in being more sociable. Instead we have to consider the interaction of personality and the environment in which an individual is living to understand their overall happiness. A sudden onset of severe disability, for example, is likely to negatively affect most people's happiness. How quickly their happiness rebounds or how long they suffer in a state of unhappiness may at least in part be related to their personality characteristics, as well as a host of other factors such as their support network, their social class, and employment status. Similarly, a promotion at work is likely to result in a short-term boost in happiness for everyone but the long-term effect is subject to the influence of our neuroticism, our other sources of meaning and social support, and the relative standing of those around us. Making progress toward our goals overall makes us happy, but the progress made by others around us matters as well—when we judge ourselves to be making less progress, to be achieving less success than those around us, we are generally less happy (Michalos 1985).

But where do different personalities come from? Why are some people more optimistic and why do some struggle with depression? Part of the answer may be found in our genes. Scientists have different methods for evaluating the role played by genes in determining personality and happiness. One commonly used strategy is the twin study. By using a sample of identical (monozygotic) twins, researchers can hold genetics constant while evaluating the effects of environmental influences on an outcome like happiness. You can imagine, for example, in studying happiness, that a researcher could compare identical twins, raised in the same family, with different friendship groups to see if the twin with the greater social support network was happier overall. This design allows us to essentially "remove" the confounding effects of genes and to isolate the effects of the environment and social surroundings on happiness. Twin studies, however, do not allow researchers to identify the specific genes related to behavior. Increasingly, national surveys that include information on people's demographic characteristics, their beliefs and attitudes, their marriage, work, and community involvement, are also collecting genetic information. This advancement is allowing researchers to more carefully examine the interplay of our genes and our environments in predicting our personality characteristics and even our happiness.

When scientists are able to identify different variants of specific genes in their data, they can begin to connect those variants with different personality and happiness outcomes across individuals. DeNeve and colleagues (2012) were able to do this using the genetic information collected by the National Longitudinal Study of Adolescent to Adult Health (or Add Health). They focused on one gene in particular, 5-HTT, that is a serotonin transporter protein that has long and short variants. Other research has found that people with the shorter variant are more likely to become depressed when experiencing life stress, while those with the longer variant are more likely to be optimistic. This means that an optimistic personality may be in part inherited and, as we know, optimistic people are more likely to be happy. DeNeve and colleagues (2012) found some support for the argument that the 5-HTT gene might play a role in explaining happiness, but the evidence was not conclusive. More research is needed to confirm the link between this particular gene and happiness. In general, there is considerable disagreement regarding molecular genetic research and whether there is a true cause and effect relationship between genes and personality or if it is in fact spurious (D'Onofrio and Lahey 2010).

The key to our happiness is not entirely buried in our genetic code. Scholars estimate that between 0 and 64 percent of happiness is heritable—that means there is a lot of uncertainty surrounding the link between genes and happiness. One meta-analysis determined that, overall, about 35 percent of happiness is inherited (Bartels 2015). This is an evolving field with many questions still unanswered but we can say with some confidence that while there is no one "happiness gene," happiness is likely influenced by a set of genes that, combined with environmental factors, influence happiness. Genes are likely part of the story of why some people are, on average, happier than others. Psychologists refer to this average happiness level of an individual as his or her "baseline" or "set point." An individual's level of happiness might fluctuate around that set point but it will eventually return to his or her original, stable level (Lykken and Tellegen 1996). Psychologists argue that this baseline happiness level is influenced by our genes and our environment, including our family context and the socialization that occurs within our families.

But it is important to note that there is not a clear divide between genetic explanations and explanations focusing on the environment in which we live. This is because our environment is partly heritable, and the expression of our genes can be influenced by our environment. The schooling and social support we receive, our propensity to marry and be satisfied in our marriages, our work experiences and our income are all associated with our happiness but they are also likely, at least in part, inherited. Genes can influence the types of environment an individual selects—for example, an individual's genes can influence whether he or she spends more time studying on his or her own or hanging out with friends; individuals may also inherit certain personality traits or proclivities that influence their likelihood of forming and maintaining stable, long-term intimate relationships. Our environment can influence the expression of our genes as well. The field of epigenetics has produced research showing that environmental factors can have an influence, for example, on the hormones that regulate the expression of our genes. Animal studies have even shown the potential for social factors (such as exposure to harsh parenting as small child) to have long-term effects at the cellular level, even across generations (D'Onofrio and Lahey 2010).

We should not, however, conclude that we are doomed to a life of unhappiness or blessed with a happy life at birth. Although our estimates suggest that genes can explain about a third of the variation in happiness across individuals, this means that two-thirds of the variation are attributable to other factors. Even our "baseline" happiness level is not set in stone, and individual actions and decisions seem to have an impact on this baseline happiness level. If we want to understand what makes some people happy and others less so, we have to consider genes in connection with a host of social and economic factors: our relationships with others, our position in society, and our beliefs.

RELATIONSHIPS WITH OTHERS

Perhaps to understand the root of happiness, we need to look beyond individuals and their traits to their relationships with others. Friends and partners are said to be a great source of happiness.

Friends

It is no surprise that our social relationships are an important ingredient to our happiness. In fact, some scholars have said that human connection is not just an important contributor to our happiness but it is a basic human need, a defining element of happiness (Ryan and Deci 2001). But what exactly matters when it comes to friends and happiness? Is it the number of friends we have? How close our relationships with those friends are? And are close friendships enough to ensure our happiness?

Social science research tells us that people who have more friends report higher levels of happiness (Myers 2000) and loneliness is consistently associated with lower levels of happiness (Ryan and Deci 2001). But it is not just the presence of friends that counts, the quality of those friendships matter too.

In fact, in research on young adults, it was found that, above and beyond both the influences of personality (which we already know is a key individual-level predictor of happiness) and the number of friends a person has, the quality of those friendships is an important predictor of happiness (Demir and Weitekamp 2007). Although many of us may prioritize work in our lives, spending time with family and friends is associated with greater happiness in a way that working more is not (Mogilner 2010). Of course, much of the research on friends and happiness is conducted using cross-sectional, or one point-in-time data, and so we cannot say conclusively whether having more high-quality friendships brings us greater happiness or if people who are happier have an easier time making a lot of good friends. It is also not the case that having good friends is enough to make most people happy. Instead, psychologists conclude that good relationships are a necessary, but not sufficient condition for happiness (Diener and Seligman 2002).

So if we want to achieve greater happiness, should we invest all of our time and energy in making and maintaining close relationships? The answer to this question appears to be no. Scholars have found that interactions with even the most peripheral members of our social network increase our happiness. The conversations we have with our neighbors, baristas, and mail carriers matter and contribute to our happiness. People who have more meaningful conversations report greater happiness and people report greater happiness on days they interacted with others, even if those others were just casual acquaintances (Sandstrom and Dunn 2014). The happiness of those other people around us, even if they are not people we would describe as our closest friends, can affect our own happiness. In fact, Fowler and Christakis (2008) found that the effect of an individual's happiness can extend to the friends of a friend's friends. This again suggests that it is not just our closest friends who impact our happiness. Fowler and Christakis go on to show that people who are surrounded by happy people and who are more central in a friendship network are more likely to be happy in the future. It is not just that our friends give us support and make us feel good about ourselves. Their happiness is in a sense contagious. This means that perhaps we should think of happiness at the group-level rather than focusing exclusively on individual experiences. When we are trying to understand how friends affect an individual's happiness, it is not enough to just know how many friends she has and how close they are to her, but we need to understand how she fits into her social network and how the happiness of those around her influences her own happiness.

Marriage and Romantic Relationships

If friendships matter to our happiness, then our most intimate relationships, our romantic relationships, are surely an important source of joy and despair as well. If romantic relationships were not so deeply tied to our happiness, we would have more ballads about work and friends than about romantic love. But how do romantic relationships impact our happiness and does it matter whether the relationship is formalized through marriage or not?

One important way that romantic relationships affect our happiness is through sex (Kahneman et al. 2004; Blanchflower and Oswald 2004; Rosen and Bachmann 2008; Wadsworth 2014). In one time diary study, respondents were asked to record their activities from the previous day and rate how happy they were during each activity. Out of the 19 activities reported, sex was rated most positively (while time spent commuting was rated least positively). Other scholars have found similar associations between sex and happiness—people are happier when they have more sex (but not more sexual partners; the highest level of happiness was reported by those with just one sexual partner in the previous year). There is even some evidence suggesting that how much sex those around us are having influences our own happiness (Wadsworth 2014). While having more sex makes people happier, people are less happy when those in their reference group (those who are about the same age and the same gender) are having more sex. Apparently, not only do people want to have a lot of sex, but they also want to be having a lot more than their peers. Of course, as with the other correlates of happiness we discuss in this chapter, it is unclear whether people are happier when they have more sex or if happier people have more sex. Accurately measuring sex—both frequency and sexual satisfaction—is a real challenge to researchers, which may explain why there is a limited amount of research on the sex-happiness link, despite our widespread understanding that intimacy and sex are important to a happy life.

Formalizing our romantic ties through marriage may also boost our happiness. Many social scientists have found that married people are happier (Hansen and Shapiro 2007; Haring-Hidore et al. 1985; Waite and Gallagher, 2000). But what is it about marriage per se that makes people happy? And why is it that cohabiting partners do not seem to enjoy the same happiness boost, at least in the United States? We discuss this research more extensively in Chapter 5, but we will review some of the key findings about marriage and happiness here.

Some scholars say married people are happier because cohabiters are not as committed to each other; they do not share as strong a bond as married couples do (Popenoe and Whitehead 2002; Waite and Gallagher 2000). If they were more committed, they would be married. Part of the joy that comes from marriage is knowing that you have someone to rely on, in good times and bad. According to these scholars, cohabiters do not have that.

Others have argued that, by being married, you enjoy a safety net—in terms of money, love, and support—that boosts your happiness (Stack and Eshleman 1998). Feeling secure makes us feel happy and cohabiters do not enjoy that same level of security that is found in marriage. Some say it is not the relationship between spouses per se that explains the greater happiness of married couples but rather the social support received by married couples compared to cohabiting couples (Diener et al. 2000). In the United States, married couples are awarded certain rights and privileges not extended to unmarried couples. Beyond the legal recognition of marriage, there is also a certain status given to married couples in social interaction that cohabiting couples may not enjoy. While it is expected that someone bring his or her spouse to work functions and family holidays, the same may not be true for a boyfriend or girlfriend. Because of this special status awarded to married couples in the United States, we see greater happiness associated with marriage than with cohabitation (Diener et al. 2000). Finally, some scholars argue that marriage does not actually make people happier. They argue that we see an association between marriage and happiness because happy people are more likely to get and stay married. In general, most research has found that although part of the association between marriage and happiness may be attributable to this "selection effect," there is still something real about the higher levels of happiness reported by married couples beyond what can be explained by who gets married and who does not (Kim and McKenry 2002; Stack and Eshleman 1998).

Children

Along with our spouses, our relationships with our children may be one of the most important predictors of our happiness. But do children make us happy or does the strain and, at times, drudgery of parenting make us unhappy? And how can we reliably answer these questions using social science research?

Overall, the evidence is that parenting is oftentimes associated with lower levels of happiness. In particular, parents of small children report more unhappiness, and even emotional distress, than parents of older children and childless people (Evenson and Simon 2005; McLanahan and Adams 1987; Umberson and Gove 1989). For many of us, this may go against our understanding of parenthood. We have an expectation that being a parent is supposed to give our life meaning and fill it with the joy of watching our children grow and change. We celebrate the birth of a child as a gift of joy and happiness with baby showers and congratulatory gifts. Perhaps because of this expectation, about 80 percent of adults eventually go on to have biological children. Why, then, do parents report such relatively high levels of unhappiness compared to those without children?

One possibility is that we have unrealistic or overly romantic understandings of parenthood. Although we expect parenting to make us happier, the reality is that it does not. This is a possibility we will consider in more depth in Chapter 7 when we examine the factors associated with unhappiness. But perhaps our measures of happiness are not accurately capturing the true benefits of parenthood. Maybe, as journalist Jennifer Senior has argued, parenthood is "all joy and no fun." Maybe survey measures that are intended to capture an individual's happiness at the time of the survey miss out on the larger picture. Perhaps our surveys do not capture the sense of purpose, the meaning that children contribute to our lives. Parents may not be happier day to day but maybe they experience greater moments of joy than those without children, and may more often report feeling that their life has purpose (Nelson 2014). Pollman-Schult (2014) argues that parenthood does have substantial positive effects on happiness that are rooted in the psychological stimulation and excitement that children bring to our lives and the social connections they foster. It is just that these positive effects are overshadowed by the financial and time costs of parenthood. We should maintain a skeptical perspective in evaluating research that unequivocally claims that children bring unhappiness (see Box 2.1 for an example of one such exaggerated claim). That being said, the finding that parents are no happier, and in many cases less happy, than their childless peers has been found in many different studies using a range of measures. This finding is not just based on general measures of psychological distress or well-being but also measures of loneliness, social activity, and even qualitative measures capturing the tension and ambivalence experienced by parents trying to balance the competing demands of work and family (Blair-Loy 2003).

Or perhaps the happiness associated with parenting is different depending on to whom you are talking. We know that children do not have a uniform effect on everyone's happiness. Children take a greater toll on the well-being of women than men, most likely because women take on the majority of the childcare burden, even when they work outside the home. Some researchers found that even if both men and women experience some strain in trying to manage both work and family demands, this strain leads to psychological distress only for mothers and not for fathers (Nomaguchi, Milkie, and Bianchi 2005). Childcare stress is also greater for those with more limited resources for dealing with it. Low income parents and single parents are particularly susceptible to experiencing stress associated with childcare. Having an extra pair of hands or some extra money to handle childcare crises can make the balancing act of combining work and family more manageable. The effects

---

Box 2.1 Is Parenthood Worse Than the Death of a Spouse?

A 2015 article in the *Washington Post* was titled: "It Turns Out Parenthood Is Worse Than Divorce, Unemployment—Even the Death of a Partner" (Cha, 2015). This striking claim of the depths of unhappiness following childbirth was supposedly based on a 2015 article by Margolis and Myrskyla in the journal *Demography*. However, a little investigation of the link between the claims made in the news report and the actual journal article shows a serious disconnect between the two. In fact, sociologist Aaron Major did just that in a blog post for the blog, *Scatterplot*. In his post, Major raises some questions about the reliability of the claim made that parenthood is associated with a 1.4 point drop in reported happiness on a 10 point scale and goes on to question the comparison between the transition to parenthood with these other major life events—death of a partner, job loss, and divorce. In the case of death of a partner and divorce at least, and probably job loss as well, the transition is most likely preceded by a period of unhappiness as well. Typically, someone will be unhappy in the time leading up to their divorce and a spouse's death is often preceded by an unhappy period of illness. Having a baby on the other hand is typically preceded by a period of happiness—couples often choose to have a baby when they are in a happy, stable relationship, and are financially secure. It should therefore come as no surprise that the *drop* in happiness associated with childbirth would be greater than the *drop* associated with a spouse's death or with divorce. This is not to say that there is no association between parenthood and unhappiness; it just points out how important it is to be a critical consumer of the news media and to ask questions about the meaning of sensational findings.

References

Cha, Ariana Eunjung. 2015. "It Turns Out Parenthood Is Worse Than Divorce, Unemployment—Even the Death of a Partner." *The Washington Post*, August 11. Retrieved August 12, 2015 (http://www.washingtonpost.com/news/to-your-health/wp/2015/08/11/the-most-depressing-statistic-imaginable-about-being-a-new-parent/?tid=pm_pop_b).

Major, Aaron. 2015. "Is Parenthood Really Worse Than Divorce? Demographic clickbait in the *Washington Post*." The Society Pages. *Scatterplot*. Retrieved August 14, 2015. (https://scatter.wordpress.com/2015/08/13/is-parenthood-really-worse-than-divorce-demographic-clickbait-in-the-washington-post/)

---

of parenting on happiness may not be the same everywhere. As sociologists, we are particularly interested in how governments can ease or exacerbate the stress associated with parenting. This is a topic we will discuss more extensively in Chapter 6.

Religion and Social Relationships

Religion is consistently shown to be positively associated with happiness (Argyle 1999; Brooks 2008; Ferris 2002; Stark and Maier 2008). Although some research has pointed to differences between groups in the effect of religion, with African Americans, the elderly, married people, and women particularly enjoying a boost in happiness associated with their religious participation (Argyle 1999; Ferris 2002), there is little debate that religion matters for happiness. But what is it about religion that makes people happy? Is it the sense of meaning and purpose in life that matters? Is it the connection to God? Or is it the connections that religious people form to their fellow congregants?

Questions about why religion is associated with greater happiness are far from settled. Some empirical evidence does in fact point to the sense of meaning and purpose that are derived from religious involvement (Diener et al. 1999; Myers 2000), but other research points to the social support derived from religious participation as most important. Lim and Putnam (2010), for example, argue that it is the connection to others who share your religious beliefs that matters in predicting an individual's happiness. Those friendships formed through religious organizations increase happiness more than friendships formed elsewhere. At the same time, Stark and Maier (2008) argue that even if the benefits of religion for happiness are social rather than doctrinal, those "social" bonds are both to other congregants and to a higher power. It appears that at least part of the happiness benefits of religion is based in social interaction and social support but whether or not this fully accounts for the happiness benefits of religion remains a question to be answered.

DEMOGRAPHIC AND SOCIOECONOMIC CHARACTERISTICS

In order to understand why some people are happier than others, we need to look at an individual's placement in society. It seems to be the case that some of those characteristics that provide social status and privilege in society (higher education and higher income as well as being white) may also be associated with greater happiness.

Race and class are interrelated in U.S. society and so untangling them and attempting to evaluate the independent influence of each is perhaps a fool's errand. Being poor and African American in the United States has different implications for health and well-being and economic opportunity than being poor and white, so in order to understand how our social position affects our happiness, we need to consider both race and class together. Of course, this is not how all social scientists approach the question of social position and happiness and so we will discuss both research that investigates the interplay of race and class and work that examines each independently.

Overall, there is a black-white gap in happiness in the United States that has persisted over time, with whites reporting higher levels of happiness on average. Researchers have analyzed this gap from the 1970s onward and found that, despite progress toward racial equality, this gap in happiness has remained and is much larger than the happiness gap between men and women (Hughes and Thomas 1998; Stevenson and Wolfers 2008; Yang 2008). There is some evidence, however, that the size of the gap has declined in recent decades (Yang 2008). Some scholars explain racial differences in happiness by pointing to the measurable differences between racial groups in socioeconomic standing. African Americans have overall lower educational attainment, have higher unemployment rates, and are more likely to live in poverty (Farmer and Ferraro 2005). Most of our large-scale surveys have measures of socioeconomic status and so researchers have been able to analyze how much of the racial happiness gap can be explained by differences in socioeconomic status between racial groups. Overall, the evidence has been mixed: While some researchers have found that socioeconomic status explains some, or even all, of the racial gap in happiness (Barger et al. 2009; Yang 2008), others have found that this gap is not explained by socioeconomic differences (Hughes and Thomas 1998).

Another explanation for racial differences in happiness focuses on the effects of racial discrimination. These scholars argue that the experience of racism and racial inequality leads to a reduced sense of personal control and greater unhappiness among racial minority groups (Hughes and Thomas 1998). However, little evidence has been found to support this claim, in part because measures of racism are less prevalent in national surveys.

Higher levels of education are also associated with higher levels of happiness, but this association is largely explained by the higher levels of income earned by those with more education. Because of the difficulty of isolating the effect of education, independent from other unobserved characteristics such as personality, we do not have a clear understanding of the nature of the relationship between schooling and happiness. Some find that the happiness associated with higher education cannot be entirely explained by income (Blanchflower and Oswald 2004; Easterlin 2001) while others argue the relationship can be entirely accounted for by the higher income of the more highly educated (Diener et al. 1999). Some have even argued that it is those people with a middle level of education that are happiest, when compared to those with both higher and lower educational attainments (Dolan and White 2008). Perhaps this is because higher levels of education are associated with more intense, demanding jobs that pay more but also demand more of the employee's time, leaving less time left over for leisure.

Although social scientists have statistical methods that allow us to compare individuals with themselves over time, thereby, controlling for unmeasured personality characteristics or motivation and drive that might be associated with both higher education and happiness, these methods do not lend themselves particularly well to the study of education and happiness. In order to use them, we must catch individuals when they have not yet completed their higher education so that we can compare their reported happiness before and after graduation. Few studies have done this and so there is still quite a bit of uncertainty surrounding the exact nature of the relationship between education and happiness.

Over historical time in the United States, we have seen a growing inequality in the reported happiness of people with different levels of education. In particular, inequality in happiness by educational attainment has increased since the 1970s. This growing inequality by educational attainment follows the historical rise in returns to education. As differences in income and benefits have grown between those with the highest and lowest levels of education, so too have differences in reported happiness between these groups. Over this time period, happiness among college graduates has risen while it has fallen among those with some college and fallen sharply among those with a high school degree or less (Stevenson and Wolfers 2008).

Noddings (2003) argues that we should think more carefully about the link between education and happiness. She argues that schooling has become too focused on preparing students for economic success; we should also be preparing students for personal success. We should teach students how to create a happy home life, to nurture relationships with friends and neighbors, to build a sense of community, and to develop their personal character. These lessons, she argues, will foster happiness in the future. So instead of thinking exclusively of the status associated with education and the implications of that status for happiness, Noddings encourages us to consider how education can be a tool for obtaining happiness. This would mean that in the future our educational system would not only serve to further stratify the population in terms of access to desired resources, such as money, good health, and happiness but instead could also serve to provide access to happiness for a wider segment of the population.

An extensive literature, in economics in particular, has examined the association between income and happiness (see also discussion in Chapter 1). As we would expect, when we look at a particular society, at a particular point in time, people with higher incomes are happier. This is not surprising considering the many benefits associated with greater income and wealth: better health, greater longevity, lower rates of infant mortality, fewer stressful life events, and lowered risk of being the victim of a violent crime (Diener and Biswas-Diener 2002). What is puzzling, however, is that if we make comparisons across countries, or across time within a particular country, we do not see the same positive association between overall standard of living and happiness (see Chapter 3 for an extended discussion on income and happiness at the country level). As one example, take the case of changes in the postwar period in Japan. In 1958, Japan had a per capita income that was well below the present poverty line in the United States but by the late 1980s, Japan had risen to become one of the wealthiest nations in the world. However, over this period of remarkable economic growth, the Japanese population showed no discernible change in overall happiness levels. So here again we observe the Easterlin paradox (as we discussed in Chapter 1), and the disconnect between economic and subjective well-being.

How can we explain this paradox? One explanation is referred to as the human needs hypothesis (Diener and Biswas-Diener 2002). This is the idea that income is associated with happiness only insofar as it allows people to meet their basic human needs for food, water, shelter, or even higher order needs like self-respect and self-actualization. Based on this hypothesis, we would expect to find a threshold point in the data, a level of income at which those basic needs are met and beyond which income provides little additional benefit in terms of happiness. In the case of Japan, if people already had most of their basic needs met at their 1958 income levels, then the rising standard of living across the 20th century would have done little to contribute to their happiness. Other research has shown, in fact, that income does matter more to happiness in the lower income brackets than in the higher income brackets, supporting the needs hypothesis. At the same time, other findings raise questions about this hypothesis. It is not clear, for example, why we see differences in reported happiness between the top two income brackets in a society. We would expect that any association between income and happiness would be limited to those living under or near the poverty line, but this is not the case.

Another explanation for the Easterlin paradox is that it is not just absolute income that matters for our happiness but also our income in relation to our aspirations, our past selves, and those around us (Bartram 2012). If, over time, our income rises but our aspirations, our desired standard of living, increase as well, then the income gains will not bring additional happiness. This is because the additional income has not narrowed the gap between our standard of living and our aspirational standard of living. In this way, although a rise in income may bring a short-term boost in our happiness, as our expectations increase once more, we are likely to adapt to our new income level and return to our previous happiness level. This ratcheting up of expectations with increases in income is referred to as the "hedonic treadmill" (Brickman and Campbell 1971), so named because the person has to keep walking, as if on a treadmill, just to keep his or her happiness from sinking.

Similarly, if the happiness we gain from income is based on how we compare ourselves to those around us, then our increased income will only bring greater happiness if those around us are also *not* gaining income. In the example of Japan, overall happiness in Japanese society may not have risen in the postwar period because, as Japan developed economically, not only did income rise but aspirations for a higher standard of living grew as well. Nearly everyone benefitted from economic development. Therefore, most people did not receive a happiness boost from their own rising income because their neighbors and friends and families were also experiencing similar income gains at the same time.

Here again, the sociological intuition reminds us that human beings are social creatures. Consciously or subconsciously, we are wired to make social comparisons. As Robert Merton (1968) explains, individuals choose reference groups that become the standard to evaluate themselves against. In the relationship between money and happiness, individuals are happy as long as they are outperforming their reference groups. On the other hand, increasing income does not necessarily bring greater happiness if we see those around us making similar gains. Worse yet, if individuals perform worse than their reference groups, they experience relative deprivation which is a gap, be it perceived or real, between what one has and what one should or could have. Relative deprivation can be a source of great strain and dissatisfaction. We will discuss relative deprivation in the context of post-communist societies in Chapter 8.

Other scholars have looked more carefully at the role of social comparison in influencing an individual's happiness. Firebaugh and Schroeder (2009) set out to test how social comparisons to neighbors matter in shaping our happiness. We might hypothesize that if we are happier when we are doing better than those around us, then, all else equal, we should be happier when we live in poor neighborhoods because we would compare more favorably to those around us than if we live in a rich neighborhood. Their findings, however, are a bit more complicated. They found that living in poorer neighborhoods was associated with lower happiness. Further, respondents were happier when they lived in richer neighborhoods in poorer counties. As the authors point out, there are special amenities in richer neighborhoods: well-maintained houses and yards, safe streets, and good schools. Residents in these neighborhoods benefit from these amenities and these benefits outweigh any detriment to happiness resulting from feeling relatively "disadvantaged" compared to your proximate neighbors. At the same time, having poorer distant neighbors (in the same county) allows individuals to see that they are relatively advantaged compared to those in the broader geographic vicinity.

Overall, there is some evidence that money buys happiness but only if we are looking within a particular society at a particular point in time. It is clear that increases in income do not necessarily bring with them an automatic increase in happiness. It is important to note that, as with other correlates of happiness, it is likely that greater income not only brings happiness but greater happiness may also bring greater income.

But it is not just those members of society with the highest social status that also enjoy the greatest happiness. Gender is a more complicated predictor of happiness. Men continue to enjoy higher social status in the United States. This is evidenced by a gendered pay gap (in 2013, women working full-time earned on average about 78% of what men earned),[1] by the lower proportion of women in management positions (the proportion of women in top management positions remains below 9%) and in government (women hold only 18.5% of congressional seats and are only 20% of U.S. senators),[2] as well as by the greater proportion of unpaid household labor performed by women (on average, women do 1.6 times the amount of unpaid housework as men; for married mothers, the ratio increases to 1.9) (Bianchi et al. 2012). We might expect that the advantages enjoyed by men translate into greater happiness. But most research finds either no difference by gender (Diener et al. 1999) or that women are happier (Bartram 2012). One interesting caveat, however, is that women are more likely to suffer from depression than men are (Diener et al. 1999). Some psychologists have argued that this is because women are socialized to have more extreme emotional lives than men—feeling both positive and negative emotions more strongly than men do.

Age is similarly complicated. We live in an age-stratified society in which different rewards, rights, and opportunities are afforded to people in different age groups (Riley 1987). Based on this, we might expect those at the top of the age stratification system (those in the young to middle adulthood stages) would be happier than those in the beginning and ending stages of life. Children have very constrained rights and those nearing the end of their life are socially devalued because of their perceived lack of economic contribution to society as well as their perceived physical and mental limitations. Despite this, using sophisticated statistical methods to untangle the unique effects of age and birth year on happiness, Yang (2008) found that happiness increases with age, even after controlling for other individual characteristics like income, health, marital status, and religious attendance. Interestingly, the effects of these other factors that are important for predicting happiness earlier in life seem to decline with age (George 2010).

Although income seems to make people happier at all ages, the effects of gender, race, and higher education on happiness disappear later in life. But we do not entirely know why this is the case. Cumulative disadvantage theory states that inequality within a cohort increases over time. Based on this, we would expect to see growing education, gender, and racial disparities with age. Yet we do not. It is possible that life changes so much in later life (because of our departure from the labor force, the death of spouses and loved ones) that the advantages enjoyed by the privileged members of society no longer matter as much in predicting happiness in the face of these major life changes. In addition, eligibility for social welfare policies like Medicare and Social Security may reduce some of the economic and health disparities among social groups present earlier in life and may, therefore, reduce some of the happiness disparities observed at earlier ages.

One final possibility is that happier people survive longer than unhappy people and so when we look at happiness in the population of older adults, we are observing only those individuals who were the happiest members of their birth cohort; those who were less happy over their lives have already died and left the population that we are studying. In other words, there may simply be less variation in happiness in the population of older adults compared to populations of younger people (Yang 2008). In order to test which of these explanations does the best job of explaining the decline in social disparities in happiness with age, we need longitudinal data following individuals as they age and recording fluctuations in their happiness with time.

SEEING THE INDIVIDUAL IN CONTEXT

This chapter has examined the characteristics of an individual that are associated with happiness. In the psychology literature, the primary focus of researchers studying happiness is in explaining how happiness varies for an individual over time or between individuals with different personal characteristics. But even here, in this focus on the individual, social context factors came creeping in. Our genes matter in interaction with the environment and social groups we live in, happiness is contagious within social networks, and neighborhoods can play a role in the social comparisons we make and ultimately in our happiness. This is because it is impossible for us to draw a clear line between the individual and the social, institutional, and historical context in which the individual lives. Studying happiness in the social context is the focus of the next chapter.

3

Happiness Is: Social Context

The sources of happiness can come internally, from within the individual, and they can also come externally from our social surroundings. People who live in peaceful societies lead happier lives than people who live in areas fraught with war and turmoil. High levels of unemployment and economic uncertainty can instill anxiety into people's lives and lower their happiness.

Our work is framed in the sociological tradition, which assumes that our behavior and our feelings are affected by the social context in which we live. People do not live in isolation. Rather, how we behave and how we feel are to a great extent determined by the people around us, and by larger social forces. The focus of the current chapter is on the social context, and how it relates to happiness.

Let us start by looking at happiness at the country level, as presented in Table 3.1. The happiness data reported here are aggregate-level data derived from the 2002 International Social Survey Programme (hereafter ISSP).

We collected macro-level economic and social indicators from various international sources, and examined how these indicators are correlated with aggregate happiness. This is not a comprehensive list, but rather a list of the commonly used indicators, in addition to some measures that are related to our research interests. Happiness scholars are always searching for better predictors of happiness, be it at the individual- or country level.

We briefly describe the macro-level measures of interest. Log gross domestic product (GDP) is the natural logarithm of GDP (World Bank 2007). The Gini index shows the extent of income inequality in the country (World Bank 2007), with larger numbers indicating greater inequality.[1] Scandinavian countries such as Sweden, Norway, and Denmark have low inequality, with Gini scores typically in the 0.25 range. Latin American countries

Table 3.1 Happiness by Country

	Happiness[a]	
	Mean	S.D.
Australia	5.38	(0.92)
Austria	5.55	(0.93)
Belgium	5.20	(0.90)
Brazil	5.42	(0.89)
Bulgaria[b]	4.58	(0.98)
Chile	5.54	(1.02)
Cyprus	5.29	(1.08)
Czech Republic	5.03	(0.99)
Denmark	5.34	(0.96)
Finland	5.24	(0.96)
France	5.25	(0.95)
Germany East	5.03	(0.91)
Germany West	5.16	(0.85)
Hungary	5.04	(1.11)
Israel	5.34	(1.10)
Latvia	4.85	(0.97)
Mexico	5.58	(1.06)
New Zealand	5.48	(0.96)
Norway	5.30	(0.92)
Philippines	5.41	(1.25)
Poland	4.97	(1.03)
Portugal	5.19	(1.06)
Russia	4.87	(1.14)
Slovak Republic	4.88	(1.05)
Spain	5.26	(0.89)
Sweden	5.24	(0.97)
Switzerland	5.52	(0.77)
Taiwan	5.19	(1.10)
UK	5.42	(1.00)
USA	5.52	(0.96)

NOTES:

[a] Happiness is a measure of aggregate happiness based on authors' own estimations using the 2002 International Social Survey Programme.

[b] Bulgaria was dropped from the empirical analysis in Chapters 5 and 6 due to missing information in some areas.

usually have high inequality, with Gini scores over 0.5. Public social expenditures (PSE) is the percentage share of GDP spent on welfare excluding education (OECD 2009). Tax revenue is shown as percentage of GDP (Index of Economic Freedom, Heritage Foundation 2002). Religious context is a proxy measure, which captures societal religiosity for all countries included in the ISSP dataset (see Chapter 5 for details of coding procedure). A high score on this measure indicates a stronger religious context with clearer moral guidelines regarding right and wrong. We also constructed a single measure of "traditional gender beliefs," using a battery of questions relating to marriage, family, and gender roles from the ISSP data. A higher score on this measure indicates a more traditional gender climate regarding the division of labor between men and women in such areas as working and parenting. For example, societies that strongly believe that women should stay at home and men should work would score highly on the traditional gender climate scale. Finally, post-communist countries are here classified as those countries that belong to the former Soviet bloc.

We present the correlations between these macro-level indicators and aggregate happiness in Table 3.2. The strengths of the association are illustrated by the asterisks, with more asterisks indicating stronger associations. As we can see, the association between macro-level indicators and aggregate happiness is not very strong for the most part. The table also shows associations in unexpected areas, as well as no associations in expected areas. We discuss highlights next.

Table 3.2 Correlations between Happiness and Macro-Level Indicators

	Correlation with happiness
GDP (logged)	0.09
Gini index of inequality	0.25
Public social expenditures (PSE)	0.03
Tax revenues (as % of GDP)	−0.20
Religious context	0.34[†]
Traditional gender beliefs (Men and women)	−0.11
Traditional gender beliefs (Men only)	0.04
Traditional gender beliefs (Women only)	−0.22
Post-communist countries	−0.83[***]

† $p < .10$, * $p < .05$, ** $p < .01$, *** $p < .001$.

NOTE: Shown are simple correlations between each indicator and happiness. Macro-level indicators are taken from various international statistics. See text for description of sources.

MACROECONOMIC INDICATORS

How does happiness measure up with macroeconomic performance? A good starting point for discussion is to look at macroeconomic indicators, such as national income and GDP as proxy measures of a country's economic progress and well-being.

As we can see from Table 3.2, the correlation between logged GDP and aggregate happiness is weak and not statistically significant. We confirm again that economic well-being and subjective well-being are not closely related across countries. Aggregate happiness does not vary greatly with national income per person, at least among the countries that were surveyed in the ISSP data.

Would the associations be stronger among a greater number of countries? We turn to Figure 3.1, which shows the relationship between gross national

Figure 3.1 Aggregate Happiness by Gross National Product (GNP) per Capita

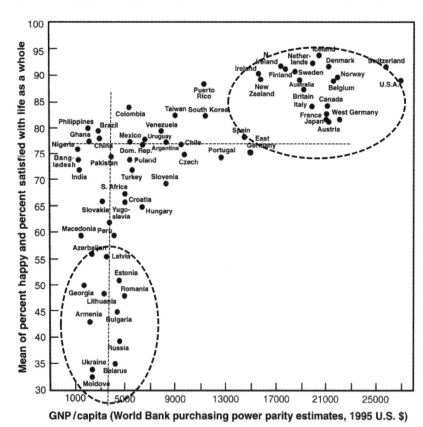

Note: Based on the World Values Survey data.

Source: Inglehart and Klingemann (2000).

product (GNP) per capita and aggregate happiness from 65 countries based on the World Values Survey (Inglehart and Klingemann 2000).

We observe a slightly positive association, as indicated by the moderately positive slope. More specifically, we see that the slope (which shows the improvement in happiness as national income changes) is greater among low-income countries, and flatter among high-income countries. In fact, if we look at only the high-income countries, clustered at the top right-end of the distribution, then the variation in happiness is quite small.

Another way to interpret this graph is to draw a horizontal line that cuts across countries—for example, from the Philippines to Austria. Such a line indicates that happiness is indistinguishable between a low-income country, such as the Philippines, and a high-income country, such as Austria. In other words, the horizontal line suggests that national income does *not* explain variations in happiness very well. Interestingly, a graph that plots life satisfaction (instead of happiness) against GNP per capita looks nearly identical, and was featured in the front page article of the *Financial Times* in 2004.[2] Alongside the graph was a photograph of a football fan from Ghana, to emphasize the point that Ghanians are among the happiest in the world (comparable to the United States in fact) despite the high poverty rate in their country.

We can also draw a vertical line around the GNP per capita $5,000 mark, which would cut across the happiness of Belarus and Russia, all the way up to Brazil and Columbia. This vertical line indicates that there is huge variation in happiness *within* a national income level. In other words, Belarus and Brazil are nearly identical in terms of national income, but worlds apart in terms of happiness. We thus arrive at the same conclusion, that national income is not a good predictor of happiness.

INEQUALITY

Inequality is a divisive issue. It can be viewed as a social ill depending on the way it is manifested—for example, if a tiny fraction of the superrich start to pull away from the middle and the poor. At the same time, inequality within reasonable range is desirable because it can facilitate social mobility, where the less advantaged have ample opportunities for upward mobility. Zero inequality means that everyone is rewarded exactly the same regardless of effort or achievement. Such a society is undesirable because there would be no incentive for anyone to work hard.

The relationship between inequality and happiness is tenuous. In the ISSP data, the correlation is weak and statistically insignificant (Table 3.2). Likewise, previous research has shown mixed results with empirical studies reporting only a weak correlation or no correlation at all. Guriev and

Zhuravskaya (2009) review the existing literature and explain that the relationship between inequality and happiness depends on the specific countries included in the sample.

Alesina et al. (2004) studied the relationship between inequality and happiness in Europe and the United States. Their key finding is that greater inequality is associated with lower happiness among Europeans but less so among Americans. Interestingly, Americans seem to be more accepting of inequality than are Europeans. The authors explain that these gaps may originate from ingrained differences in perceptions of inequality and social mobility between Americans and Europeans.

Americans believe that their society is mobile; the poor feel that they can move up and the rich fear falling behind. In Europe, a perception of a more immobile society makes the poor dislike inequality since they feel "stuck." Alesina et al. (2001) provide different evidence that this is indeed the case. For instance, according to the World Values Survey less than 30 percent of Americans believe that the poor are trapped in poverty while 60 percent of Europeans have this belief. Americans definitively believe that society is mobile and one can escape poverty with hard work. When asked about poverty, in fact about 60 percent of Americans believe that the poor are lazy while less than 30 percent of Europeans have the same beliefs. The same authors point out the large mismatch between these strong beliefs and available measures of actual mobility in Europe and the United States, but for our purposes what matters are individuals' beliefs.

In reality, Americans are more "stuck" in their social class than they think they are (see Box 3.1). However, in spite of the reality, Americans continue to believe in the American Dream, and that the United States is the land of abundant opportunity and fluid social mobility. It is the *perception* of mobility that keeps them kicking. Presumably for these reasons, greater inequality and lack of social mobility are not related with lower happiness in America.

In contrast, greater inequality and poverty are sources of unhappiness among Europeans. Poverty is not the result of individual laziness, but an outcome of greater social maladies.

Poverty and inequality can lower happiness through greater anxiety and social distrust. In their paper, "Why Inequality Makes Europeans Less Happy," Delhey and Dragolov (2014) examine data from 30 European countries using the European Quality of Life Survey from 2007. Among these countries, the correlation between income inequality and subjective well-being is −0.65 and highly significant. They further explore the relationship through structural equation modeling, and discover two key mediating variables—trust (or distrust) and status anxiety. People are less trustful in countries with greater income inequality. The lower trust in turn is associated with lower subjective well-being. Likewise, greater inequality is associated with greater status

Box 3.1 Social Mobility and the American Dream

The American Dream is the belief that individuals should have abundant opportunities for upward social mobility regardless of class position. One way to conceptualize social mobility is to map it out in a table consisting of the parents' social class (= origin) and the children's social class (= destination). In sociology, this table is known as the mobility table.

		Destination: Children's social class		
		Low	Middle	High
Origin:	Low			
Parents'	Middle			
social				
class	High			

There are statistical techniques to estimate the extent to which children move away from the parents' social class. To take an extreme example, suppose all children end up in the same class standing as their parents—that is, class origin and class destination are the same for everyone. This is the case of zero mobility, and we end up with a perfect correlation of 1.0. A high correlation thus implies less mobility (or high immobility) and greater social inheritance.

One way to estimate the extent of intergenerational class mobility is to convert class into income categories. According to a summary provided by Esping-Andersen (2007), the correlation between parents' and children's income was 0.46 in the United States, 0.30 in Germany, 0.20 in Canada, and 0.15 in Scandinavia. These results indicate that the United States is "exceptionally immobile." He surmises that "far from being in the vanguard, the United States is an equal-opportunity underachiever" (p. 23).

Empirical studies continue to document the lack of economic and social mobility in the United States (see, e.g., Aaberge et al. 2002). Indeed, the book *Class Matters* published by *The New York Times* in 2005 was dedicated to the momentous task of reporting how mobility is diminishing and social class is solidifying in America.

Alert readers may have come across satire, which pokes fun at this emerging trend. For example, the comedian George Carlin jokes: "That's why they call it the American Dream, because you have to be asleep to believe it." Noting that social mobility is far better in Finland than in the United States, the *Huffington Post* and other outlets reported, "If you want the American dream, go to Finland" (*Huffington Post*, December 14, 2013).

worries, which in turn decreases subjective well-being. For example, rising inequality following the transition to market economy instilled a sense of social injustice and unfairness in Bulgaria (Boyadjieva and Kabakchieva 2015), as we discuss in Chapter 8.

The differing views on inequality and mobility between the United States and Europe feed into larger differences in political ideologies. Americans and Europeans differ greatly in their views concerning the role of the state versus the market, a topic we turn to next.

THE STATE VERSUS THE MARKET: THE ROLE OF PUBLIC SOCIAL EXPENDITURES AND TAXES

Broadly speaking, there are two ways to think about equality: equality of outcomes and equality of opportunities. Societies that espouse equality of opportunities generally believe in the power of the market. Everyone should have an equal opportunity to compete for the ultimate prize. Unequal outcomes, which separate the winners from the losers, are but a consequence of free competition.

Societies that espouse equality of outcomes are more concerned about the outcome of the competition. Ensuring equal opportunities in the race is important, but generating huge inequalities as a result of it is socially and economically undesirable. Competition cannot be left to pure market forces. The government must become involved to ensure that inequality of outcomes does not go unchecked. Ideally, a society that maintains a reasonable balance of both mechanisms would be desirable, or as Paul Krugman describes it, "[A society] in which the hard-working, talented and/or lucky can get rich, but in which some of their wealth is taxed away to pay for a social safety net, because you could have been one of those who strikes out."[3]

That social safety net is social insurance. Paying taxes to provide social insurance is one way to ensure that people can be saved from ruin in the face of crisis. Everyone will be protected, but everyone must pay into the system. The idea thus contrasts greatly with the free market regime where only the ones that want to pay or the ones that can afford to pay insurance will be protected.

Redistribution, where resources are transferred between low- and high-risk groups, is achieved mainly through taxes and public social expenditures (PSE). The state collects revenue through taxes, and provides social insurance through PSE. Although taxes and public social expenditures are not equivalent, they are highly correlated as we can see in Figure 3.2 (the correlation coefficient is 0.78 and highly significant among the countries in the ISSP dataset).

In general, the high-PSE/high-tax countries are also the ones that provide extensive social insurance. The most generous of these include Sweden, Denmark, and Norway, which are commonly known as the Scandinavian welfare states or the social democratic welfare states (Esping-Andersen 1999) to reflect their geography and political ideology.

Are the people happier in countries where the government takes an active role in redistribution? Or are they happier in a more market-driven country

Figure 3.2 Public Social Expenditures (PSE) and Taxes

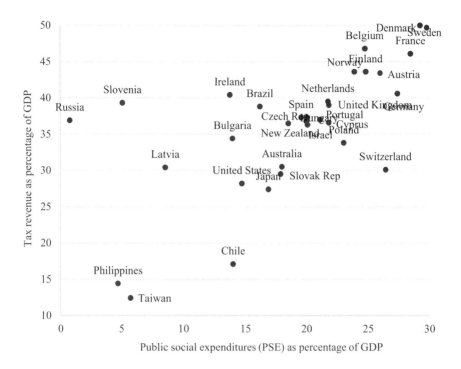

where the government takes a more hands-off approach? Relatedly, are people happier in high-tax countries compared to low-tax countries? If we use public social expenditures and tax revenues as a proxy for social insurance, then we can see to what extent these macro-level measures of state intervention are related to happiness.

As we can see from Table 3.2, the correlation between happiness and PSE and the correlation between happiness and tax revenues are weak and statistically insignificant, at least among the countries included in the ISSP data. The people in the social democratic welfare states—that is, the high-PSE and high-tax countries are no happier than the people in other regions—that is, the low-PSE and low-tax countries.

But such a conclusion can be misleading. A simple correlation between aggregate happiness and public social expenditures (or taxes) masks the underlying redistributive mechanisms of the social democratic welfare states. By definition, redistribution is a transfer of resources from low-risk to high-risk groups, with the aim of leveling out the uneven distribution of resources and wealth. Redistribution cannot be targeted at all demographic groups.

Our key hypothesis, which we shall explore in Chapter 6, is that the redistribution of resources is closely linked to the (re)distribution of happiness.

For example, Sweden is one of the most generous welfare states in the world, often heralded as the poster child of the Scandinavian welfare state. In Figure 3.2, Sweden occupies the upper right corner making it a high-PSE/ high-tax country. We often hear stories that Sweden is the happiest place to live, *for families with small children*. But is it the happiest place to live for *all* demographic groups? Indeed, Sweden is extremely generous to families with small children; they receive tax breaks and plenty of benefits such as free healthcare, extended maternity and paternity leave, and subsidized child-care. But Sweden is less generous to single people; they pay higher taxes and receive fewer benefits than families do. Given this redistribution of resources, is it possible that Sweden is not a happy place to live for single people? In Chapter 6, we explore in great depth how the redistributive mechanisms of the social democratic welfare states influence the happiness of the people.

RELIGIOUS CONTEXT

Is there a link between religion and happiness? Dating back to Emile Durkheim's (1897/1951) classic work on religion, there is widespread recognition in both theoretical and empirical research, which links religious involvement and well-being. According to Durkheim, religion provides social cohesion and social support; it is a means to integrate individuals into society, and to protect them from *anomie* (social disintegration). As we discussed in Chapter 2, studies have consistently uncovered the positive association between religion and life satisfaction at the micro-individual level (Ferriss 2002; Stark and Maier 2008). In particular, the support that can be offered by religious groups and social networks is understood to be a valuable source of social capital (Lim and Putnam 2010).

In one classic study titled "Religion, Disability, Depression, and the Timing of Death," Idler and Kasl (1992) found that religious involvement has significant protective effects against disability and depression. Most interestingly, the researchers discovered a systematic pattern regarding the timing of death following religious holidays. For example, for Christians, the timing of death is significantly lower in the 29 days preceding Christian holidays—for example, Easter and Christmas, compared to the 30 days following it. Their findings thus show great support for Durkheim's theory of religion as a social support system.

How does religion affect happiness at the societal level? Is it possible that the mechanisms that link religious involvement to well-being at the individual level also operate at the societal level? We examine the correlation between religious climate and aggregate happiness. To reiterate, a high score on the religious context measure indicates a stronger religious climate with clearer moral guidelines regarding right and wrong. We can see from

Table 3.2 that the correlation between happiness and religious context is positive and marginally significant; happiness is greater in societies with a stronger religious context.

And although we cannot speak to all religions, Inglehart and Klingemann (2000) point out that the historically Protestant societies tend to dominate the high end of the happiness distribution, as illustrated in Figure 3.3. This clustering of countries may be one reason that the correlation between Protestantism and happiness is positive in international comparisons. But we have to be careful with our interpretations because as we can see from Figure 3.3, the Protestant countries are also the most affluent countries. So it is not entirely clear if it is national income or Protestantism that is the source of happiness for these countries. The Protestant work ethic was compatible

Figure 3.3 Aggregate Happiness by Gross National Product (GNP) per Capita and Historical Heritage of Given Societies

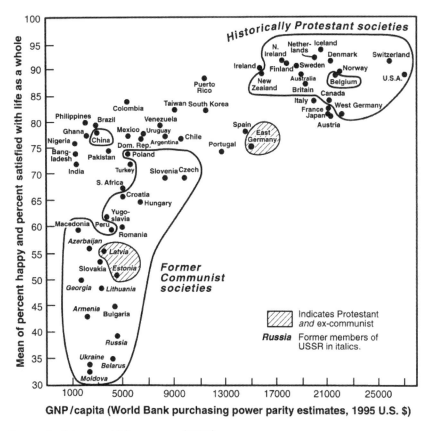

Source: Inglehart and Klingemann (2000).

with the spirit of market capitalism, as Max Weber (1976) described in his classic work. Protestant societies are also further advanced in economic development because of this early lead (Inglehart and Klingemann 2000).

But a fuller understanding of the relationship between religious context and happiness requires a closer examination of the various links between the macro and the micro. The effect of religion on happiness may not be uniform across all demographic groups. Rather, it may lift happiness for some, but lower it for others. Chapter 5 will explore in greater detail the linkages between religious context and individual-level happiness.

GENDER CLIMATE

Some societies are more gender equal than others. Many countries, especially in the developed world, have come a long way in advancing the socioeconomic status of women in the areas of education, labor force participation, wages, leadership roles, and so forth. But there still remains significant disparity in their economic standing across societies.

How do these variations in the gender climate affect people's subjective well-being? The correlation coefficient reported in Table 3.2 indicates no significant association between traditional gender beliefs and aggregate happiness.

But is it possible that the gender climate in the country affects men and women differently? In a society that espouses a traditional division of labor between the sexes, men are expected to work, and women are expected to take care of home and the family. Are men and women *both* happy with that arrangement? We have to look at the responses of men and women separately because one may benefit more than the other.

The correlation coefficients broken down by gender reported in Table 3.2 give us some insight. Although the coefficients are still not significant, we can see that the correlation is now much weaker for men at 0.04. In other words, the gender climate does not seem to have much effect, positive or negative, on men's happiness. On the other hand, the correlation becomes stronger and more negative for women at −0.22. On average, women are less happy if they live in a society that espouses a traditional division of labor between the sexes.

This is but a small glimpse of what we mean by the sociological analysis—the effect of the social context is not universal across demographic groups. Gender climate (which will be the focus of our discussion in Chapter 5), religious context, public social expenditures, and taxes are all macro-level factors that can influence the well-being of individuals. But they affect some people more and others less so.

POST-COMMUNIST COUNTRIES

Take a look at the clustering of countries on the low-end of happiness in Figure 3.3. Note the conspicuous pattern—Moldova, Belarus, Ukraine, Russia, Armenia and Bulgaria. These are the former communist countries, or the transition economies that transitioned from centrally planned economies to market economies in the post-Soviet era. Research has consistently shown that the transition economies are among the *un*happiest countries in the world (Guriev and Zhuravskaya 2009). Table 3.2 confirms this position. The category for "post-communist countries" has by far the strongest negative correlation: Happiness in the post-communist countries is significantly lower than the happiness in other countries.

In recent years, the sources of unhappiness in post-communist countries have attracted attention from happiness scholars, and we are just starting to learn more. The main reason appears to be that the transition to market capitalism did not deliver on the people's promises. While expectations were high for market reform, poor economic performance, unfulfilled promises, widespread corruption, deteriorating safety nets, and greater inequality dashed people's hopes for a better society, leading to diminished aspirations and a sense of powerlessness. We will share the findings from the recent literature, as well as provide our own explanations in Chapter 8.

POSITIVITY AND LIFE SATISFACTION: IS IT CULTURE?

As we have discussed throughout this chapter, economic and social indicators are not strong predictors of happiness at the country level. For example, Colombia ranks among the poorest countries in the world, has high levels of violence, and yet, ranks high on the worldwide happiness scale. On the other hand, Japan is among the richest and safest countries in the world, but ranks low in happiness. Why do some countries achieve higher happiness in spite of low economic performance, and vice versa?

A group of psychologists collected happiness and life satisfaction data from 41 countries to try to better understand the variation in happiness across countries (Diener et al. 2000). They constructed a composite index of "positivity" to measure how people evaluate their satisfaction and outlook in life. The index aimed to identify the extent to which individual respondents "inflate" certain responses in their life domain. For example, if we ask college students about their satisfaction in education, there will be one broad (or global) question about their overall satisfaction, followed by narrow and specific questions about their professors, textbooks, and lectures. Empirically,

Figure 3.4 Differences in Positivity across Countries

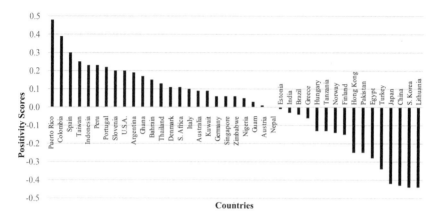

Source: Diener et al. 2000.

positivity is estimated as the discrepancy between the global and the specific, more specifically, the degree to which global is inflated over the specific.

Their results revealed substantial variation in positivity disposition. Two Latin American countries, Puerto Rico and Colombia, ranked highest in positivity. At the low end of the positivity scale was Lithuania, followed by South Korea, China, and Japan (see Figure 3.4). The researchers discovered a strong correlation between positivity scores and life satisfaction across countries. In fact, this correlation was equally strong, if not stronger than the correlation between objective measures (such as income) and life satisfaction.

How do we explain the variation in positivity across countries? Why do people in Latin America have such a positive disposition and outlook in life compared to the people in Asian countries? Is it the sunny beaches, frozen drinks, laidback lifestyle, late-night dinners with friends and family? Is it "culture"? As social scientists, we shy away from cultural explanations because culture is one of those elusive concepts that are hard to define and even harder to measure empirically. But we can conclude that people who have a positive disposition are happier in life. Positivity is a powerful predictor of happiness across countries.

SEEING HAPPINESS IN CONTEXT

We have now reviewed the key predictors of happiness at the individual level in Chapter 2, and at the societal level in the current chapter. In the sociological mind, the two are not separate but complementary ways to think about the sources of happiness. The individual characteristics are in many ways contingent on the context in which the person is living.

As we discussed in Chapter 1 (see Figure 1.2), we believe that this attention to the interplay of individual and context is what makes a sociological approach to happiness so compelling. The attention to what Mills called "the intersection of history and biography" gives us the best understanding of the complexity of factors that shape happiness. It is this interaction of individual and society that we turn to in Chapters 4, 5, and 6.

4

Marriage and Happiness in the United States and Japan

In the next three chapters, we take a sociological perspective in analyzing happiness as situated in a particular social and institutional context. This means that we will investigate how the social norms, employment opportunities, gender roles, and government policies in a country influence who is happy and who is not. This chapter looks at a particular type of happiness—marital happiness—in just two countries so that we can explore the role of norms and social beliefs in-depth before widening the lens of our investigation to look at general happiness in more than 25 countries in Chapters 5 and 6.

We start by examining marital happiness in the United States and Japan. In Chapter 2, we discussed how marriage overall makes us happier. Quite a bit of research has been devoted to examining what makes people happy in marriage, and why married people report higher levels of happiness than do their single peers (see Glenn 1990; Hicks and Platt 1970; Spanier and Lewis 1980). Because marriage and happiness are so closely linked and the exact nature of the relationship between marriage and happiness is a subject of debate, we will devote the next two chapters to the exploration of marriage and happiness. First, in this chapter, we ask what makes people more or less happy in marriage and does this vary across countries? Then, in the next chapter, we examine what factors make married people happier than their cohabiting and single peers and we tackle the question of whether or not it is marriage itself that makes people happier or if it is instead something about the social norms and beliefs in a society that celebrate and support marriage and make married people happier.

Why do we look at the United States and Japan? In Chapter 5, we expand our analyses to include a broader range of countries, but to start with, we focus on the United States and Japan, two countries with very different norms surrounding gender and marriage, to illustrate just how important social context is in shaping happiness in marriage. We make the case that what makes married people happy in one country does not necessarily have the same effect in another. In doing so, we challenge some theories of marital happiness that lack an attention to social context.

WHAT MAKES PEOPLE HAPPY (AND UNHAPPY) IN MARRIAGE?

Happiness in marriage is based on a number of factors: How long we have been married, whether or not we have children, and the socioeconomic status, and financial standing of the family, among other things. Included in the economic characteristics of the family are whether or not both spouses are working, what type of job they are working in, and how much money each spouse makes on their own and combined. Economists have focused on these economic characteristics of the family in theorizing which marriages are happy and which ones are not, which marriages will fail and which will succeed. In our analysis of marital happiness, we will focus on these theories about the economic characteristics of the family and their relationship to marital happiness.

One economic theory of marital happiness and stability is the specialization model. Becker (1991) as well as Parsons (1942) argued that interdependence and efficiency are created in a marriage when one spouse works outside the home and the other cares for the home. When each spouse specializes in one domain, they can spend their time learning skills in that domain and become more productive than if they divided their attentions across work and family tasks. For example, when a woman is a domestic specialist, she can devote all of her time and energy to learning how to cook healthy gourmet meals, how to rear her children with the latest childrearing methods, and how to be a supportive spouse for her husband. She will become very efficient at producing well-fed children and a spouse who is productive at his job. When both spouses work outside the home, this decreases the efficiency of the household unit and has the potential to cause competition, rather than cooperation, between spouses. Based on this logic, it can be argued that the benefits of marriage, the reason to get married and stay married, lie in this kind of specialized division of household labor.

Along similar lines, the independence hypothesis specifically predicts that when women work in greater numbers outside the home, rates of marital disruption will increase (see, e.g., Cherlin 1992; Preston and Richards 1975). To the extent that people get divorced because of marital unhappiness, we can infer from this that women's increased labor force participation would result in lower levels of marital happiness or would allow women in already unhappy marriages to seek divorce. It should be noted that the independence hypothesis should actually be called the "wife's" independence hypothesis (Ono 1998); it speaks specifically to the effect of the wife's economic resources, but is less clear on the effect of the husband's resources on marital happiness. Both the specialization model and the independence hypothesis are particularly important to our analysis because, in Japan, falling marriage rates have been partially attributed by scholars to women's increasing "independence" from men (Raymo and Iwasawa 2005). In other words, women's employment has been blamed for declining marriage rates.

But other theories have different predictions regarding the effect of women's employment on marital stability and happiness. It is possible that women's employment and earnings do not necessarily have a negative effect on marital happiness, and may even boost marital happiness. For example, the "revised independence hypothesis" states that an improvement in family income from any source will have a positive effect on marital happiness because it improves the family's overall quality of life and stability (Cherlin 1979; Oppenheimer 1997). However, when the income boost comes from a wife's earnings, there is not only this positive income effect on marital happiness but also an independence effect that may decrease marital stability as predicted by Becker (1991). In other words, the overall effect of a boost in family income from the wife's earnings on marital happiness is ambiguous.

The role homophily perspective (Simpson and England 1981) claims that marital happiness will be highest when men and women share similar roles in society and in the home. According to this perspective, spouses are able to communicate more effectively and serve as companions for one another when they share the breadwinning role in the family. Similarly, the equity perspective (Mueller et al. 1979) asserts that spouses are happiest when household tasks are divided equitably. Although the role homophily perspective focuses primarily on the benefits of a shared worldview and companionship derived from occupying similar roles and the equity perspective focuses on the benefits of sharing household responsibilities fairly, both point to similar roles for husband and wife as leading to greater marital happiness. In this way, there may be some marital happiness gained from sharing similar roles and similar responsibilities with your spouse. If spouses are occupying entirely different spheres of activity, it is feasible that this could lead to a decline in marital happiness.

The final theory that speaks specifically to the relationship between the economic characteristics of spouses and marital happiness is the bargaining model (England and Farkas 1986; Presser 1994; Sorensen and McLanahan 1987; South and Spitze 1994). According to this perspective, individuals gain bargaining power in a marriage from economic resources. In other words, individuals use their earnings and their status derived from their education and their job in negotiating with their spouse to get out of doing unpleasant household tasks, such as changing dirty diapers or washing the floors. Or, individuals may use their bargaining power to get to make important decisions for the family like where they will live and what type of car they will drive. Complete specialization (which assumes that one spouse is specialized in the household, and therefore, earns no income) creates an extreme form of dependency where one spouse has no bargaining power over the other. The more bargaining power held by an individual, the more work he or she can get his or her spouse to do, and the happier they will be.

Of course, the economic characteristics of the family are not the only factors that determine how happy people are in their marriage. But we will discuss those other factors (e.g., age, gender, and children) in more detail in Chapter 5. For now, we will focus on how these economic characteristics matter in different cultural contexts.

If we look at the results of previous studies to see which of the theories of marital happiness and stability are supported, the findings are mixed. The results of these analyses vary depending on the measure of family economic characteristics used. Several scholars looking at the effects of wives' employment on marital happiness or stability have found no relationship (Locksley 1980; Schoen et al. 2002; Spitze 1988; White and Rogers 2000). If, however, we look at the effects of wives' earnings on marital happiness and stability, the results are more mixed. Some scholars found that when women earn more, this leads to a more equal sharing of household tasks and also greater stability (Sayer and Bianchi 2000), while others found that when wives earn a greater proportion of the household income, the risk of divorce increases (Rogers 2004; Brines and Joyner 1999). Rogers and DeBoer (2001), on the other hand, found that increases in women's income are associated with greater marital happiness for women. Overall, the evidence regarding the effects of women's employment and earnings on marital happiness is mixed. We think that part of the reason that previous findings have been mixed is that differences in social and cultural context have not been directly considered. In the current analysis, it is our goal to explore how social and institutional contexts shape the effect of economic characteristics on marital happiness.

A COMPARATIVE PERSPECTIVE: THE UNITED STATES AND JAPAN

One limitation of previous research on marital happiness is that the role of social context in shaping what makes married people happy is generally unspecified. This also means that it is unclear whether results from the United States can be generalized to other cultural contexts. Some past research has examined marital happiness in different cultural contexts, but none of these studies specifically looked at what makes people happy in marriage in one country versus another. Westley (1998) compared levels of marital satisfaction in the United States and Japan, finding that respondents in the United States report higher levels of marital satisfaction than respondents in Japan. Stack and Eshleman (1998) analyzed the relationship between marital status and happiness in 17 countries (including the United States and Japan), finding that the effect of marital status on happiness was similar in the United States and Japan. Ono and Raymo (2006) examined the consequences of changes in marital satisfaction for women's market and household work hours in Japan. Yamaguchi (2006) studied the relationship between work-family balance and marital satisfaction among women in Japan. None of these studies speak to the correlates of marital happiness in a comparative framework, however, and this is the aim of our analysis.

For our comparative study of marital happiness we chose to focus on the United States and Japan. These two countries differ in their norms governing family and work life, making them ideal cases to examine the effects of context (e.g., social norms, laws, and policies) on marital happiness. First, the meaning of marriage is different in the United States and Japan. While the relationship between the husband and the wife in Japan has been described as being "like air" (Iwao 1993) in that it is vital for survival but its presence is not felt, Americans look to their spouses to fulfill emotional and companionship needs. Furthermore, dependency is a taken-for-granted aspect of married life in Japan, whereas, in the United States, dependency is often looked down upon as a form of weakness. For these reasons, Western theories of marital happiness are unlikely to apply in the same way in Japan.

The norms surrounding women's workforce participation and role in the family are also very different in these two countries. Gender inequality is greater in Japan than in the United States by almost any measure (e.g., employment, wages, and educational attainment), and Japan has lower divorce rates. Mean age at first marriage is also considerably higher in Japan (Raymo and Iwasawa 2005) and marriage rates are lower. This creates a different context for marriage and work in the United States and Japan. This means that the economic characteristics of the family are likely to have different implications for marital happiness in these two countries.

In Japan, identities as a wife and mother are central to cultural conceptions of adult femininity. Ueno (2001, p. 215) cautions, however, that "'Japanese femininity' is a modern construct, and not at all traditional." In the aftermath of World War II, the Japanese government emphasized women's role as mothers despite the new constitutional guarantee of gender equality and women's increased work experience outside the home in the war industries. Women returned to the home as housewives in the postwar period when Japan was experiencing rapid economic growth. According to Ochiai

(1997, p. 35), "In the postwar period, the state of being a housewife became so strongly normative that it was practically synonymous with womanhood." From 1950 on, women's labor force participation rate has fluctuated between 46 and 50 percent.[1]

Japanese wives occupy special positions of power in the household because of their husbands' disinterest in household management and, more specifically, their control of the family budget (Hayashi 1990; Iwao 1993; Lebra 1984; White 2002). In most households, the husband hands over his paycheck to his wife and, in turn, receives a set spending allowance (Lebra 1984). Kimura (2001) reports that in 61 percent of households, the husband transfers his entire salary to the wife. According to the prime minister's 1995 annual survey, over 80 percent of Japanese respondents considered household finances and shopping to be women's work (White 2002). Who controls the family's budget is an important difference between the United States and Japan. According to Iwao (1993, p. 86), "Although the battle for economic independence for women in the United States has been overt and often bitter, Japanese women have exercised great authority in this realm for a long time." In the United States, money management practices in the family may differ across social groups, but control of the household budget has not historically been a source of power for women.

In addition to social norms supporting a gendered division of labor, employment policies in Japan work to discourage women from full-time labor force participation. Spouses benefit from tax deductions as long as their annual income is less than 1.3 million yen (Ministry of Finance 2000). Since wives are typically secondary earners in the household, the tax system discourages married women from seeking full-time employment.[2] Female workers are expected to quit their jobs after marriage or childbirth because most firms operate under a seniority system that rewards workers according to their tenure. This expectation results in a vicious cycle where women are hired into noncareer track (or secondary) positions consisting of menial, dead-end jobs.

These norms and economic incentives that support a specialized division of labor (with men working outside the home and women caring for the family) are reflected in survey statistics that consistently show that Japanese women are more likely to support this kind of gendered division of labor than are women in Western societies. For example, survey results from the Tokyo Metropolitan Government (1994) highlight these gender differences between the United States and Japan. Women in Japan were significantly more likely to agree with the statement: "The husband should be the breadwinner, and the wife should stay at home" (56% in Japan versus 24% in the United States). They were also more likely to agree that marriage is the ultimate form of happiness for women (79% in Japan versus 29% in the United States). At the same time, Japanese women's beliefs about the gendered division of labor are considerably more egalitarian than Japanese men's. Some have suggested that this gap between men and women may explain why women have increasingly postponed or even foregone marriage in the recent past (Sugihara and Katsurada 2002).

If we look at studies that document how men and women spend their time, we see further evidence of specialized roles for men and women in Japan. According to OECD statistics released in 2014, Japanese men spent 62 minutes a day on housework while Japanese women spent 300 minutes a day.[3] It is no surprise that with all of the household responsibilities Japanese women are shouldering that they find it challenging to work outside the home. Perhaps for all of these reasons, Japanese women's status is derived more from their husband's status than their own work status (Ogasawara 1998). This means that women's social position is not based as much on their own achievements as on the achievements of their husbands.

In the United States, despite the myth of the 1950s family as the traditional family form, the reality is that the 1950s housewife was somewhat of a historical anomaly (Coontz 1992) sparked by increasing faith in U.S. institutions (Cherlin 1992) and a high standard of living vis-à-vis the previous generation (Easterlin 1987). This meant that middle-class white women in particular stayed at home in greater numbers than in the generations following or even preceding them. For women in working class racial and ethnic minority families, this specialization in the household in the 1950s did not occur. According to the U.S. Census Bureau, women's labor force participation rate increased from 30 percent in 1950 to 61 percent in 2000. Although a smaller proportion of U.S. women than Japanese women were in the labor force in 1950, it is clear that over the second half of the 20th century, women in the United States increased their labor force participation much more dramatically. Today, women in the United States are considerably more likely to be in the labor force than their Japanese counterparts.

Another important difference between the United States and Japan is in the household division of labor, or how men and women divide up all the work that is done in families. Although there is certainly a gender imbalance in the United States, with women taking on more of the routine, inflexible household work—preparing meals, caring for children, doing laundry—this imbalance is not as extreme as in Japan. In their analysis of NSFH data, Bianchi et al. (2000) estimated that in 1995, women in the United States were doing 1.8 times more housework than men, compared to six times more in 1965.[4] In other words, the gender gap in the performance of household tasks has been closing over the past half century. Women in the United States are more hesitant than their Japanese counterparts to embrace dependence on their husbands both financially and in terms of status because of the relatively higher divorce rate and also the American desire for independence and self-reliance. In a social context in which divorce is so common, it is risky to put all of your eggs in your husband's basket.

From all of this past research and theories of marital happiness, we created hypotheses for our analysis of marital happiness in the United States and Japan. Based on the differences in work and family in the United States and Japan that we discussed, we expect to find significant differences in what makes married people happy in these two countries. We predict that while working could have a positive or negative effect on marital happiness for women in the United States depending on the theory (specialization versus role homophily or bargaining), it is likely to have a negative effect for women in Japan because of the norms of appropriate roles for women in Japan as well as the more limited opportunities for Japanese women to find and keep good jobs with promotion opportunities. Similarly, while there are different predictions regarding the effect of spouse's income on U.S. women's marital happiness depending on the theory, we can predict that Japanese women's marital happiness should increase when their spouses earn more since Japanese women's status is largely a reflection of their husband's status. When their husbands earn more, Japanese women enjoy greater status and also, we argue, greater marital happiness. We also expect that Japanese women should express greater marital happiness when they are economically dependent on their husbands. But we expect that U.S. women will be less happy in their marriages when they are economically dependent on their husbands. As for the men, we expect men in both countries to express greater marital happiness when they earn more and, in Japan in particular, lower levels of marital happiness when their wives earn more.

AN ANALYSIS OF MARITAL HAPPINESS IN THE UNITED STATES AND JAPAN

The data we analyze in this comparison of just two countries is different from the data we use in subsequent chapters. For this analysis, we used data from the General Social Survey administered in the United States and Japan. The Japanese General Social Survey (hereafter JGSS) is the Japanese version of the U.S. General Social Survey (hereafter GSS).[5] Both the GSS and JGSS include a wide range of survey questions that are directly comparable. For our analysis, we use the survey years 2000, 2002, and 2004 for the GSS; and 2000, 2001, 2002, and 2003 for the JGSS.

We were interested in analyzing what individual characteristics were associated with higher (and lower) levels of marital happiness in these two countries. Our measure of marital happiness is a question asking the respondent: Taking things all together, how would you describe your marriage? In the GSS, marital happiness is recorded in three categories ranging from 1 = not too happy to 3 = very happy. In the JGSS, it is coded in five categories.[6]

We used ordered logistic regression to predict an individual's marital happiness on the basis of their other measured characteristics. More specifically, we estimated the effects of the individual's age, education, employment status, their spouse's employment status, whether or not they have children, their health, and their income on their reported marital happiness. Because the predicted effects of family economic characteristics on marital happiness are hypothesized to be very different for men and women, we estimated separate models by gender. We also estimate models on specific subsamples—just those respondents who are working and finally, respondents who are working and also have a working spouse. These subsample analyses allow us to test the predictions of the different theories of marital happiness.

One concern in doing this type of analysis is the fact that we are studying only marital happiness among currently married people. This means that people who were so unhappy in their marriage that they separated or divorced will be excluded in the analysis. We did some statistical tests to see if this significantly biases our results and we found that it did not.

Our findings from this analysis show that most of the predictors of marital happiness discussed in the literature matter in both the United States and Japan but in different, and sometimes surprising, ways. We provide a summary table of our main findings in Table 4.1. Interested readers may see the results

Table 4.1 Summary Table Showing Predictors of Marital Happiness in the United States and Japan

	United States		Japan	
	Men	Women	Men	Women
Respondent is working				(−)
Spouse is working	(−)			(+)
Presence of children		(−−)	(−)	(−−)
Health	(+)	(+)	(+)	(+)
Income categories				
(1) Respondent's income		(+)	(+)	
(2) Spouse's income				(+)
(3) Household income			(+)	(+)
(4) % contribution to household income	(−)			

Table was compiled from results reported in Lee and Ono (2008). See Tables A.1 to A.3 in the Appendix for full description.

(+) shows positive effect, (−) shows negative effect, (−−) shows strong negative effect, and blank cells indicate no effect on the outcome. Each income category shows results from separate regressions.

of our regression analyses reported in the Appendix. Our research underscores the importance of how marital happiness is affected by the institutional context and the normative environment. In other words, some factors associated with marital happiness in a particular group of people in a particular context are associated with unhappiness for other groups in other contexts. Social contexts matters and must be taken into consideration when studying what makes people happy in marriage.

To begin, one important difference we found between the United States and Japan is the level of marital happiness for men and women. In the United States, men and women are equally happy in marriage, but in Japan this is not the case. In Japan, women are systematically less happy in marriage than are men.

As expected, children are related to lower levels of marital happiness for women in both the United States and Japan. (Children are related to lower marital happiness for men in Japan also, but the effect is stronger—i.e., more negative, for women). This is consistent with the role strain or restriction of freedom explanation for declining marital happiness in parenthood (Twenge et al. 2003) because the negative effect is largely limited to women. It seems possible that women in both countries may bear the primary burden of caring for children, with their husbands showing little change in their marital happiness with the presence of children. In addition, health is significantly, positively associated with marital happiness for both women and men in the United States and Japan.

Economic Characteristics, Marital Happiness, and Social Context

In the United States, the marital happiness of women is less tied to their husbands' income than is Japanese women's marital happiness. Women in the United States report higher levels of marital happiness when they are earning money themselves. Whether or not a woman is economically dependent on her husband has no effect on her reported marital happiness.

Surprisingly, in the case of the United States, we discovered that on average, men are unhappy if their wives are working as shown by the negative effect of "spouse is working" in Table 4.1. But also note the negative effect of "percentage contribution to the household income." This means that men are less happy if they have to increase their contribution to the household income. Since we assume here that the wife's income is the inverse of the husband's income, it also means that he is happier if the wife increases her contribution to the household income. In other words, men are happy as long as they are married to wives who earn a high income, and contribute a *lot of money* to the household income. The question remains, however, how much is a lot of money? In percentage terms, we estimate that wives would have to contribute at least 70 percent to the household income. In other words, if the pooled income of husband and wife was $100,000, the wife would have to bring home at least $70,000 to satisfy her husband.

We can see what this looks like in Figure 4.1 (see Appendix for further details of the estimation procedure). The vertical axis shows the line $\Delta U = 0$, which corresponds to the level of men's happiness in marriage if their wives are not working. The upward sloping line shows how wives' contribution to the household income affects men's happiness in marriage. The region with the minus sign is the "unhappy" zone and the region with the plus sign is the "happy" zone.

For men, the path to optimizing their happiness in marriage is shown by the thick dotted lines in Figure 4.1. The triangular region from 0 to 70 percent is below the line $\Delta U = 0$. In this region the husbands are unhappy because their wives are working, but not contributing enough to the household income. In other word, in this zone the men would be happier if their wives were *not* working. In contrast, the region from 70 to 100 percent lies above the line $\Delta U = 0$. This is the happy zone. In order to compensate for the disutility of being married to working wives, the husbands would require at least a 70 percent contribution to the household finances from their wives.

In sociological terms, our findings reveal a case of competing values, and the disconnect between the global and the local. At the greater societal level, Americans by and large would uphold the ideals of gender equality, and support, for example, issues relating to equal opportunities and eliminating the

Figure 4.1 The Relationship between Wife's Contribution to Household Income and Men's Happiness in Marriage in the United States

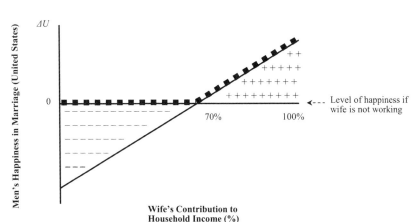

Note: Reprinted from Lee and Ono (2008).

gender-wage gap. But at the micro-individual level, not everyone may *act* on these ideals. Our study has revealed that although we may live in a society that espouses gender equality, married men maintain values that are not consistent with these ideals.

Of course, we are analyzing data from one point-in-time and so we do not know with certainty in which direction causality runs. It is also possible that in happier marriages, women feel freer to either be economically dependent on their husbands or to reject pressures to follow traditional gender norms that dictate women should earn less than their husbands. The findings for women show some support for the bargaining model since women with more resources have greater power to leave the marriage, and therefore, have greater bargaining power. Men seem to embrace a specialization model in which they are either the sole breadwinner or the financially dependent spouse.

In Japan, economic characteristics of the family are related to marital happiness in expected ways for the most part. Overall, Japanese women's marital happiness closely follows the predictions of a specialization model. As we hypothesized, we find that women are happier in marriage if their husbands are working, but they are not working themselves (Table 4.1). Happiness is not related to their own income, but to their husband's income and their overall household income. These findings are consistent with the view that Japanese women's status is "reflected"; it is based on their husband's status rather than on their own work status (Ogasawara 1998). Men are happier in marriage when their own income is higher or when the household income is higher. The men's role in the household thus appears to be consistent with the male breadwinner model. He is happy when he can see himself supporting the household financially. It does not seem to make a difference whether or not their wives work, or even whether or not they are economically dependent on their wives. Our findings support the hypothesis that because of gender norms and workplace constraints on women's employment in Japan, men's marital happiness is more strongly related to their own income while women's is tied to their husband's income.

These findings are surprising because the correlates of marital happiness are similar for Japanese men and for U.S. women. For both Japanese men and the U.S. women, when they earn more money themselves, they are happier in their marriages. And neither their spouse's income nor being economically dependent on their spouse is related to the marital happiness of either of these groups. The potential explanations for these findings differ for the two groups, however. A specialization model for Japanese men and a bargaining model for U.S. women provide the best fit to the data. A role homophily model does not seem to be supported for U.S. women since neither husband's work status nor his income is significantly associated with working women's marital happiness.

U.S. men and Japanese women also share some similarities. U.S. men express greater marital happiness, overall, when their wives are not working. Japanese women, on average, would be happier in marriage if their husbands were working but they were not working themselves. We interpret Japanese women's responses as consistent with a specialization model in which women specialize in the domestic sphere and men in the market.

U.S. men, however, are polarized, with some men expressing greater marital happiness when they are the sole breadwinner and others reporting greater marital happiness while economically dependent on their wives. This finding is consistent with previous research in the United States that found the lowest levels of marital stability in marriages in which both partners make equal economic contributions (e.g., Rogers 2004). Research by Buss and colleagues (2001) further supports our results. They found that over the past half century, men have increased the importance they place on finding a mate with good financial prospects while, at the same time, decreasing the importance they place on finding a mate who is a good cook. Perhaps the economic foundation for a stable marriage is changing in the United States along with increasing female labor force participation rates over the past 50 years and the declining popularity of the traditional division of labor.

DISCUSSION

Differences in the correlates of marital happiness for Japanese and U.S. women are likely attributable to the different norms, employment structures, and family structures in these two countries. U.S. women live in a context in which divorce is common (making dependency on one's spouse a risky strategy) and in which full-time employment is normative for women. Japanese women, however, face a lower risk of divorce than their peers in the United States and live in a climate less supportive of women's full-time employment (both in terms of economic and social sanctions) and of an egalitarian division of household labor. We argue that these differences in norms and in workplace opportunities for women underlie the different predictors of marital happiness in the United States and Japan.

It is possible that the differences observed between women in Japan and women in the United States could also be partially determined by the different arrangements for managing household money in the two countries. In Japan, where the wife controls the husband's earnings, greater earnings by the husband translate into greater economic power for the wife. Her own earnings, however, are often considered only for the purchase of extras and luxuries, and therefore, not as important in shaping the family's standard of living (Iwao 1993). In the United States, on the other hand, where women typically do not exercise the same control over their husbands' paychecks, husband's income is less important to a woman's marital happiness vis-à-vis her own earnings.

On the whole, while Japanese men and women seem to embrace marriages based on specialization, in the United States, there are noticeable disparities in men and women's perceptions of a good marriage. Our analyses show that U.S. women want to earn high incomes and contribute to the family financially while men are polarized with some men wanting their wives to take financial responsibility for the family and others preferring to maintain the sole breadwinner role. Perhaps this polarization among U.S. men is evidence of cultural lag, with some men holding onto a model of marriage that may not be efficient or practical in today's society. Social change is uneven and different groups within a society may change at different rates. Over time, we expect to see a reduction in this polarization among men as men's beliefs about marriage "catch up" with women's.

These comparative insights bring us closer to an understanding of the cross-cultural correlates of marital happiness. In the following chapters, we will expand this cross-national comparison of happiness to further our understanding of what it is about a particular social context that matters for happiness in different contexts. We can begin to see how social norms about gender, societal religious beliefs, and public social spending and taxation are associated with the happiness of different social groups in these countries.

* * *

The empirical work presented in this chapter is based on our previous research, which we published in more technical form: see Lee and Ono 2008.

5

A Happy Couple

We are surrounded by cultural messages telling us that marriage is the path to happiness. Benjamin Franklin said: "The happy state of matrimony is, undoubtedly, the surest and most lasting foundation of comfort and love." It is said that the key to happiness lies in finding your perfect companion, settling down, and starting a family. Literature and films are filled with stories of people who resolve their struggle and live happily ever after following marriage to their true love. Disney films like *Cinderella* and *Snow White*, Shakespearean comedies like *A Midsummer Night Dream*, Victorian literature like *Sense and Sensibility* all rely on marriage as a symbol of resolving past troubles, of creating new happy beginnings. In the *New York Times* bestselling book *The Happiness Project*, Gretchen Rubin devotes an entire month of her year-long project to increase her happiness to working on her marriage. It is no wonder that so many of us assume that getting married will increase our happiness, and that staying single, or even just living with someone long term without plans of marriage, is a recipe for unhappiness.

But to what extent is this idea supported by social science research? If there is a relationship between being married and being happy, is this because there is something intrinsic to marriage that creates happiness or is it something about the social groups and society that we live in that makes it easier to be happy as a married person? Some social scientists have made the argument that marriage itself makes people happier. Linda Waite and Maggie Gallagher (2000) argued this point in their book *The Case for Marriage*. They insist that there is no substitute for marriage: "When love seeks permanence, a safe home for children who long for both parents, when men and women look for someone they can count on, there are no substitutes. The word for what we want is *marriage*" (Waite and Gallagher 2000, p. 203). They argue that marriage as an institution provides emotional, health, and well-being benefits not provided by cohabitation. Married people live longer, have better sex, and save more money than the non-married.

But what is it exactly about marriage that provides all of these benefits? Waite and Gallagher argue that there are a host of reasons for the differences observed between married and cohabiting or single people. Married people take better care of themselves because they have a spouse relying on them. They have better sex because they are committed to each other. They earn more money because they are more productive. They are happier because they have someone who has promised to take care of them and also because they enjoy a level of social support not experienced by cohabiters and singles. They explain: "The commitment married people make to each other is reinforced and supported not only by their own private efforts and emotions, but by the wider community—by the expectations and support of friends, families, bosses, and colleagues who share basic notions about how married people behave" (p. 77).

Based on their research, Waite and Gallagher argue that we need to do more as a society to support marriage. This means not only providing special privileges and protections to married couples, but also excluding cohabiting couples from these rights and privileges. They argue: "Extending marriage benefits to cohabiting men and women who have refused to marry sends a message social scientists now know to be dangerously false—that cohabitation is the functional equivalent of marriage. Cohabitation is not just like marriage" (p. 201). If we want what is best for couples and their children, they argue, then we need to promote marriage: to encourage singles and cohabiters to marry and discourage married couples from divorcing (except in those cases where marriage is actually harmful because of domestic violence for example).

Waite and Gallagher (2000) are not the only ones to have tackled this question of the benefits of marriage versus cohabitation for an individual's happiness. Many scholars in sociology, psychology, and economics have pointed to the happiness boost enjoyed by married people. The explanations given for "the marriage premium" are varied. Some say cohabiters have a weaker bond than married people and that is why they don't enjoy the same benefits from their relationships (Popenoe and Whitehead 2002; Waite and Gallagher 2000). Cohabiters are perhaps not as committed to each other, promising to share only the rent and not their lives with each other. Because of the lower level of commitment, cohabiting partners may not receive the health and well-being benefits of knowing they have a partner on whom they can rely, in good times and bad.

Others point to the social and financial support received from spouses as protecting an individual's well-being (Stack and Eshleman 1998). Married couples are one another's financial safety nets and emotional support systems. This support received from a spouse, some say, makes married people feel happier and more secure in a way that cohabitation does not.

But what if it is not marriage per se that makes people happier, but the social and institutional support given to married people (but not to others) that makes them happier? Then does it make sense to spend public dollars encouraging couples to tie the knot? Maybe cohabiters report less happiness because cohabitation is not as accepted as a family form in our society and so, as a result, cohabiters do not enjoy the same kind of social and institutional support that married people do (Diener et al. 2000). Maybe instead of promoting marriage, we could alternatively increase the happiness of cohabiters by encouraging social acceptance and institutional support for couples choosing to co-reside without marriage. We have laws and rituals and social norms protecting the sanctity of marriage. Our friends and families stand with us when we take our marriage vows and vow themselves to do their best to uphold the marital union. The same rituals, laws, and social norms do not necessarily apply to cohabitational unions. In many social circles, being a live-in romantic partner does not afford the same status and respect as being a spouse. It may not earn you a seat at the family holiday dinner, you may not receive the same kind of support and consideration from your partner's family when you face difficult times, and so, as a result, you may be somewhat less happy than someone enjoying the rights and privileges associated with marriage.

Other scholars are skeptical that there really is something about marriage itself that causes people to become happier (see, e.g., Soons and Kalmijn 2009). Instead, they argue, we see an association between marriage and happiness because happier people are more likely to get, and stay, married than unhappier people. Even if those happy people had never found the right person to settle down with, they still would be happier than their generally unhappy counterparts; this is referred to as a "selection effect." Not everyone has equal odds of getting married and it's generally happy people who have the best chances of getting married and maintaining their sunny disposition. In other words, if we were to account for the fact that a select group of people choose to get married, the apparent benefits of marriage would be reduced greatly. Waite and Gallagher do not rule out the selection effect of marriage, but cite longitudinal research showing that when people get married, their mental health improved. This research design is superior to an analysis comparing married and unmarried individuals at one point in time because it is instead comparing a married individual to their pre-married self and assessing to what extent their happiness changed after they married. Because people actually reported that they were happier after they married, Waite and Gallagher conclude the relationship between marriage and happiness is causal;

something about marriage itself (and not cohabitation) *causes* people's happiness to increase. Overall, most research has favored explanations for the benefits of marriage that focus on marriage as causing people to become happier (Kim and McKenry 2002; Stack and Eshleman 1998) rather than on selection effects alone.

However, just because there is evidence in the United States that marriage may improve the health, wealth, and happiness of individuals, does not necessarily mean that there is something intrinsic to marriage per se that causes these observed benefits across time and place. Is it possible that many of the benefits observed are attributable to the special status we afford marriage in the United States? Andrew Cherlin (2010) has argued that Americans place a higher value on marriage than citizens of many other countries. If this is the case, it is possible that perhaps the benefits enjoyed by married couples in the United States compared to their cohabiting counterparts might not be present in other countries where cohabiters and married people are treated equally. In other countries, cohabitation is replacing marriage as the normative family form and so we might expect to find important differences in the experiences of the married and the cohabiting in these countries compared to the United States. In order to evaluate this possibility, we must look at global data on marriage, cohabitation, and happiness.

A GLOBAL PERSPECTIVE

Cohabitation before, or as an alternative to marriage, is quite common in some countries while almost nonexistent in others. According to Heuveline and Timberlake (2004), in Italy, only 9.4 percent of women experience unmarried cohabitation. This contrasts with France where about 83 percent of adult women cohabit at some point. From these statistics, we can see that there is considerable variation across countries in the rates of nonmarital cohabitation. Different countries vary in the extent to which cohabitation is institutionalized. In Europe, for example, France and the Netherlands treat cohabitation much like marriage in the law while Germany and Switzerland treat marriage and cohabitation as distinct under the law, reserving special privileges for married couples (Perelli-Harris and Gassen 2012). Similarly, we might expect that the experience of cohabiters in a country like Sweden or the Netherlands, where cohabiting is so common, might be quite different than the experience of cohabiters in countries like Italy, where marriage is still the normative pathway for adults in committed romantic relationships. Heuveline and Timberlake (2004) classified countries based on the role cohabitation plays in family formation. While cohabitation is "marginal" in Italy and Spain, it serves as a "prelude to marriage" in Belgium and Switzerland. In Canada and France, cohabitation is seen as an "alternative to marriage" and it is "indistinguishable from marriage" in Sweden. Although the United States does not fit neatly into their classification system (perhaps because of the heterogeneity in the population of cohabiters), they make the case that cohabitation is seen as an alternative to being single in the United States, because cohabitating unions are typically brief and do not end in marriage. Perhaps previous research findings based on data collected in the United States describe the benefits of marriage versus cohabitation in the United States but do not apply as directly to other countries.

Some researchers have looked at cross-national comparisons in their happiness studies (Stack and Eshleman 1998; Diener et al. 2000; Soons and Kalmijn 2009). Much of this research has confirmed a happiness benefit for married people around the world compared to their cohabiting counterparts. Even after accounting for the financial satisfaction and health benefits of marriage that are believed to account for much of the happiness premium associated with marriage, some researchers have found a happiness boost among married people around the world. But not all research has found support for this claim. Research specifically looking at marital status and happiness in Europe, for example, found that we must consider the social context for cohabitation in studying the happiness of married and cohabiting individuals. In countries where cohabitation is prevalent and in which cohabiting couples receive social support, the happiness gap between married and cohabiting individuals disappears or is even reversed (Soons and Kalmijn 2009). This suggests that maybe there is some evidence to support the idea that it is not just the marriage vow that makes people happier but something about the level of support—be it private or social, formal or informal—for married and cohabiting couples in a society that shapes the happiness of these groups.

But even after looking at these studies of happiness globally, some questions still remain. For example, is it only attitudes toward cohabitation that matter in shaping the relative happiness of married and cohabiting persons? How do other societal characteristics influence happiness, and the happiness of men versus women, and cohabiters versus married persons in particular? This is where our cross-national analysis of happiness steps in.

In our study we are interested in looking at not just how the benefits of marriage are different across countries, but what it is about those countries that matters in shaping the happiness of these two groups. We focus on two societal factors in particular: societal religiosity and gender norms. Religion and marriage are closely related, because most religious denominations uphold the institution of marriage. Societies with strong religious beliefs are likely to be less supportive of partnerships formed outside of marriage. The social support provided to married couples and the stigma of cohabitation in conservative religious climates may in turn increase the happiness gap between married and cohabiting individuals. Similarly, we expect societal gender beliefs to also impact the happiness of married and cohabiting people. Because rising gender egalitarianism is associated with a trend toward non-traditional family forms and tolerance of nonmarital cohabitation in particular, we predict that there is a smaller happiness gap by marital status in more egalitarian countries. This contrasts with societies with more traditional gender beliefs in which the appropriate roles for men and women are separate and clearly defined. In these societies, there is a sharper distinction between marriage and cohabitation and, we predict, a larger happiness gap associated with marital status. By analyzing the happiness of married and cohabiting individuals in countries with different levels of gender egalitarianism and religiosity, we are able to investigate to what extent the happiness premium associated with marriage is intrinsic to marriage and universal, and to what extent it is a product of the social context and therefore variable cross-nationally.

OUR DATA AND ANALYSIS

In our analyses of happiness in 27 different countries reported in this chapter and in Chapter 6, we analyze data from the 2002 International Social Survey Program's (ISSP) Family and Changing Gender Roles module. These data allow us to examine happiness in countries in different geographic regions and stages of economic development. The survey asked respondents to answer questions about their beliefs and attitudes related to family, their roles inside and outside the home, and their happiness.

We use multilevel regression models to analyze our data so that we could group together individuals living in the same country and analyze how characteristics of the society (religious climate, gender climate, and GDP in this chapter; public social expenditures and taxes in Chapter 6) are related to the happiness of different social groups (e.g., social classes or marital statuses) in each country. Multilevel regression models allow us to account for the fact that people living in the same country are likely to be more similar than people living in different countries. Using multilevel models, we can partition out how much of the variation in reports of happiness is found between individuals and how much is found between countries. We can allow for the effects of our predictors of happiness to vary across countries, rather than assuming that all predictor variables have the same fixed value in each country. Interested readers may read the Appendix for a fuller description of the multilevel-modeling approach.

To measure happiness in our research, we use a survey question that asked people: "If you were to consider your life in general, how happy or unhappy would you say you are, on the whole?" Responses could range from

1 (*completely unhappy*) to 7 (*completely happy*). Although in-depth interview data would provide us with an individual's rationale for how they rate their happiness, survey measures like the one we used are particularly useful for comparing the overall happiness of groups living in different social contexts. This measure allows us to compute the average happiness score of married, cohabiting, and single people in the countries we studied and make comparisons across these groups.

Our analysis differs from the research conducted by psychologists in that we are less interested in the individual-level determinants of happiness, such as personality traits and mental patterns. We are more interested in explaining the happiness of different groups of people (married and cohabiting individuals) as a product of the social context in which those individuals are living. In describing the sociological method, Mills said: "The sociological imagination enables us to grasp history and biography and the relations between the two within society. That is its task and its promise." This is what we set out to do: To understand how the happiness of individuals is intimately related to the laws, norms, and traditions of the society in which that individual lives.

Marriage and Happiness Cross-Nationally

Before we turn to a discussion of what we found about the relationship between marriage and happiness in different societies, first we will summarize what other individual characteristics are associated with happiness in the 27 countries we analyzed. We found that some characteristics of individuals are associated with happiness in all of the countries we studied. On average, married people are happier than non-married persons. Married persons are happier than cohabiting persons, who are in turn happier than single persons (which in this case includes divorced, separated, and widowed respondents). But as we will show, the difference in the happiness of married and cohabiting people is bigger in some countries and smaller, or even nonexistent, in others.

People with stronger religious beliefs, who earn more money, and who have more education (a college degree or more) are also happier overall. Men, but not women, are happier when employed full-time. We suspect this probably is because of societal expectations that men should act as the breadwinners in their families. Men who are not fulfilling this masculine role are likely to be less happy. We decided to explore this possibility by looking to see if full-time employment mattered differently for men in countries with different societal gender beliefs. As we expected, in societies with more traditional gender beliefs, men's happiness is much more closely tied to their employment status. In countries with the most egalitarian gender beliefs, on the other hand, men with and without full-time employment are equally happy. Women are less happy when they have children but men's happiness is not impacted by children. This is also not surprising to us and is consistent with our discussion in Chapter 4 regarding children and marital happiness in the United States and Japan. Around the world women carry most of the responsibility of childcare and so it makes sense that children would more directly impact their happiness than that of their less-involved spouses.

We also found a U-shaped relationship between happiness and age, which suggests that we start off happy in young adulthood, our happiness decreases through midlife, and picks up again later in life. However, as we discussed in Chapter 2, because we are only analyzing one year (or one cross-section) of survey data, we cannot clearly distinguish whether happiness changes in this way as we age or if it is instead the case that people born at different points in history have different levels of happiness.

This analysis of the characteristics of an individual that make him or her happy is only part of the story of happiness. We suspected that the difference in the happiness reported by married, cohabiting, and single people would be different across countries. A simple comparison of the average reported happiness of married and cohabiting people confirmed our intuition. We found that the happiness gap, or the difference in average happiness between married and cohabiting people, varied quite a bit across countries. Keeping in mind that happiness is measured on a 7 point scale, we found that cohabiting people reported slightly higher happiness than married people in countries such as Austria (0.17 happier) and Belgium (0.16 happier), but reported considerably lower levels of happiness than married people in countries such as Taiwan and Mexico (0.4 points lower). Table 5.1 lists the average happiness score (out of 7) for single, cohabiting, and married people in each of the countries we studied.

Based on this simple descriptive finding, we started to hypothesize what it is about different societies that leads to variations in the happiness gap. We reasoned that perhaps societies with more traditional gender norms and with stronger religious beliefs would reward couples choosing to marry and sanction those living together without marrying. In the second part of our study, we tested these hypotheses for the cross-national variation in the happiness gap that we observed.

To understand who is happy and who is not from a sociological perspective, we needed to consider the characteristics of the individual, the characteristics of the society, and the interplay between these individual and societal traits. We looked more closely at how both individual beliefs about gender and societal gender beliefs are related to an individual's happiness. We measured an individual's gender beliefs based on his or her level of agreement with six statements: (1) A working mother cannot establish just as warm and secure a relationship with her children as a mother who does not work; (2) A preschool-age child is likely to suffer if his or her mother works; (3) All

Table 5.1 Descriptive Statistics by Country

Country	GDP Per Capita	Religious Climate	Gender Climate	Happiness by Marital Status		
				Single	Cohabiting	Married
Australia	42,279	0.10	−0.10	5.09	5.34	5.45
Austria	46,019	0.18	0.09	5.54	5.88	5.71
Belgium	43,430	−0.50	0.01	5.22	5.43	5.27
Brazil	8,114	1.51	0.74	5.39	5.24	5.55
Chile	9,645	1.28	0.59	5.47	5.55	5.65
Czech Republic	18,139	−1.71	0.00	5.12	5.15	5.14
Denmark	55,992	−0.92	−0.63	5.28	5.51	5.45
Finland	44,491	0.14	−0.25	4.86	5.41	5.35
France	41,051	−0.88	−0.22	5.08	5.34	5.42
Germany East	40,873	−1.15	−0.71	5.15	5.34	5.26
Germany West	40,873	−1.15	−0.18	4.92	5.05	5.17
Hungary	12,868	−0.56	0.38	5.03	5.20	5.28
Latvia	11,616	−0.17	0.16	4.86	4.71	5.03
Mexico	8,000	1.71	0.50	5.57	5.20	5.63
Netherlands	47,917	−0.83	−0.15	5.22	5.36	5.41
New Zealand	29,000	0.01	−0.07	5.40	5.57	5.57
Norway	79,089	−0.58	−0.45	5.25	5.41	5.41
Philippines	1,745	2.00	0.16	5.27	4.57	5.48
Poland	11,273	1.45	0.07	4.86	5.29	5.15
Portugal	21,414	0.94	0.35	5.15	5.12	5.39
Russia	8,676	−0.36	0.27	4.88	5.09	5.12
Slovakia	16,176	0.48	0.18	4.90	4.68	5.02
Spain	31,774	−0.40	−0.03	5.28	5.29	5.37
Sweden	43,654	0.11	−0.51	5.15	5.33	5.37
Switzerland	63,629	−1.18	0.06	5.43	5.55	5.67
Taiwan	16,400	−0.08	−0.05	5.19	4.86	5.24
UK	35,165	0.31	−0.20	5.21	5.50	5.60
USA	46,436	1.50	−0.24	5.46	5.53	5.70

NOTE: GDP = gross domestic product. Single persons include divorced, separated, and widowed persons. Happiness data are country averages aggregated from the 2002 ISSP data.

in all, family life suffers when the woman has a full-time job; (4) A job is all right, but what most women really want are a home and children; (5) Being a housewife is just as fulfilling as working for pay; (6) Having a job is not the best way for a woman to be an independent person.

We first discovered that individuals who agreed more strongly with these statements, in other words, those with traditional gender beliefs, reported lower happiness overall.

But another pattern emerges at the societal level. Different societies also have different average beliefs about gender. Table 5.1 reports the average score for the gender belief measure we created in each country we studied. In some countries, most citizens would agree with the aforementioned statements about gender while in other countries, most citizens would disagree. We found that these societal beliefs affected the happiness of men and women differently. For men in particular, societal beliefs about gender mattered to happiness; men who lived in a country with more traditional gender beliefs were happier than men in more egalitarian countries. We think this is because men benefit from living in more traditional societies; they are more likely to enjoy a higher status in the family, and they are less likely to be expected to pitch in around the house. In more egalitarian societies, men more often share decision-making with their spouses and are also expected to contribute to what is often unpleasant and undervalued household labor. We think that it is for all of these reasons that men in particular report greater happiness in the countries with more traditional beliefs about gender.

When we change our analyses to look at how societal gender beliefs influence the happiness of married versus cohabiting men and women, we find that they matter only for women. When we look at men by themselves, we find that married men are happier than cohabiting men around the globe, regardless of the society's gender beliefs. In fact, married women living in societies with traditional beliefs about gender had nearly twice the odds of attaining happiness as cohabiting women in those countries. It is among women that we find no measurable happiness gap between married and cohabiting individuals in societies with the most egalitarian beliefs about gender. Also for women, being single is associated with lower levels of happiness, regardless of societal gender beliefs.

Why is the happiness of women more closely related to their marital status in countries with traditional gender beliefs but not men? There are two ways of making sense of these findings. One explanation is that women are more constrained by social norms and social conventions than are men, and these social constraints lower their happiness. Women living in very traditional societies are perhaps more harshly judged by their families and neighbors when living with a man outside of marriage. Men may not receive the same social pressure and may not be judged as harshly as women in these situations. Or, alternatively, men may not be as sensitive to these informal social pressures and may, therefore, be in some ways insulated from the negative social judgment of their living situation. The other possible explanation is that married women in more traditional societies receive greater social support and social status than their cohabiting peers, and this translates into greater happiness. In more gender egalitarian societies, married women may not receive as many special benefits or as much extra support from their families and neighbors compared to their cohabiting counterparts. In these egalitarian societies, married and cohabiting women may be treated fairly similarly. In other words, it is the benefits associated with marriage in more traditional societies that explain the happiness gap between married and cohabiting women, rather than the stigma associated with cohabitation in these societies. Again, we argue that men either receive fewer of these benefits associated with marriage or are in general less sensitive to the social benefits and social support awarded to married couples in societies with more traditional beliefs about gender.

Figure 5.1 provides a graphic representation of our findings. Along the x-axis is the level of traditional views toward gender and gender roles in a country, where the scale ranges from low (= egalitarian or progressive) to high (= traditional). Along the y-axis is the predicted odds of happiness; this means we are plotting the odds that a particular group will report greater

Figure 5.1 Predicted Happiness for Married and Cohabiting Women as a Function of Gender Context

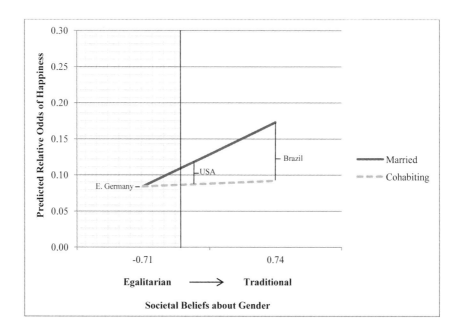

happiness. The solid line in the figure shows how the predicted odds of happiness for married people change as we move from societies with more egalitarian gender beliefs to societies with more traditional beliefs. Similarly, the dotted line shows how the predicted odds of happiness for cohabiting people change as we move toward societies with more traditional beliefs.

What we learn from this figure is that the happiness gap between married and cohabiting people is much greater in societies with traditional gender beliefs than in societies with more egalitarian gender beliefs. In fact, in those societies with societal gender beliefs scores falling in the cross-hatch area of the graph, there is no statistical difference between the happiness of married and cohabiting individuals.

We also investigated the implications of societal religious beliefs for the happiness of married and cohabiting people. To create our measure of societal religious beliefs, we used 12 measures of religion in a society. The 12 measures were taken from the 2003 U.S. State Department's International Religious Freedom Reports as compiled and archived by the Association of Religion Data Archives. We combined these individual factors to create a single measure of societal religiosity.[1] The individual indicators used to construct this measure include the percentage of people in a country who: (1) belong to a religious denomination, (2) self-identify as a religious person, (3) attend religious services at least once a month, (4) believe in God, (5) believe in heaven, (6) believe in hell, (7) believe in life after death, (8) believe that there are clear guidelines on good and evil, (9) find comfort and strength from religion, (10) consider religion important, (11) consider that God is important in their life, and (12) are confident in religious organizations. A country with a higher score on this measure has a stronger religious context with clearer moral guidelines regarding right and wrong. Table 5.1 reports the societal religious beliefs score for each country we studied.

Once more, we find a relationship between societal beliefs and individual happiness. While we find a measurable difference in the happiness of married and cohabiting individuals in the countries with the strongest religious beliefs (e.g., Mexico, the Philippines, and the United States), we find no happiness gap between these groups in the most secular societies (e.g., the Czech Republic and Germany). Again we find that single people are less happy than married or cohabiting individuals but that the size of the happiness gap is different in countries that are more or less religious. Again, to really explore these findings, we conducted separate analyses for women and men.

Once more, it is women whose happiness is shaped by the religious beliefs in the society in which they live. We again find no measurable difference in the happiness of married and cohabiting women in the most secular countries, but find that married women in the most religious societies have more than twice the odds of attaining happiness as a cohabiting woman in those societies. Single women are less happy than cohabiting or married women around the globe, regardless of societal religious beliefs. We also find some differences in the happiness gap between married and cohabiting men in different countries. The happiness gap for men is somewhat greater in societies with strong religious beliefs compared to societies with weaker religious beliefs.

Once more, we have evidence that women's happiness is more closely connected to their marital status in societies with more traditional or conservative beliefs than is men's. We think the explanation of the findings for societal religious beliefs mirrors those for societal gender beliefs. Women are either more sensitive to, or are judged more intensely by, the religious beliefs in a society. Because sex outside of marriage is denounced by many religions, it makes sense that the stigma attached to nonmarital cohabitation and the benefits associated with legal marriage would be greater in the most religious societies. In more secular societies, sex outside of marriage does not violate moral guidelines in the same way and cohabiting couples may not face the same stigma and social pressure in these societies with weaker religious beliefs. While men may be given some leeway in violating societal religious beliefs, women may be expected to comply more closely with religious doctrine and may have their virtue called into question when violating societal religious norms by choosing to form a nonmarital household.

Like Figure 5.1, Figure 5.2 provides a graphic representation of our findings. As in the previous figure, along the y-axis is the predicted relative odds

Figure 5.2 Predicted Happiness for Married and Cohabiting Women as a Function of Religious Context

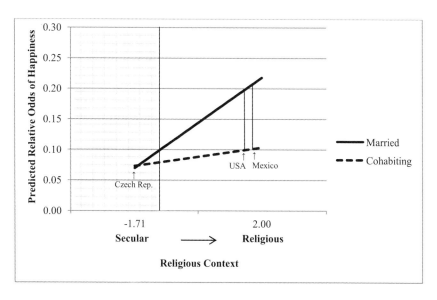

of happiness. In this figure, societal religiosity is along the x-axis, moving from less religious societies to more religious ones. Again, the solid line shows how the predicted odds of greater happiness for married people change as we move from more secular to more religious societies and the dotted line shows how the predicted odds of greater happiness for cohabiting people change as we move from more secular to more religious societies. Countries that fall in the cross-hatch area of the graph (the most secular societies in the sample) show no statistically significant difference in happiness between married and cohabiting people while the largest happiness gap between these groups is found in the most religious societies.

MAKING SENSE OF MARRIAGE AND HAPPINESS IN CONTEXT

What do the findings from our cross-national analysis tell us about the links between marriage and happiness? By comparing the happiness of married and cohabiting individuals in different countries, we were able to show that it is not something entirely intrinsic to marriage that is responsible for the happiness boost associated with marriage. Because we found that this marriage premium exists only in societies with more traditional gender beliefs and stronger religious beliefs, this suggests it is something about the meaning attached to marriage in these societies that results in the greater happiness of married people. These findings suggest that it is the social support provided to married couples or, conversely, the social stigma attached to cohabitation in these more gender traditional and religious societies that may ultimately be responsible for the greater happiness expressed by married people. If instead it was something intrinsic to marriage, something about the level of commitment entailed or the greater security enjoyed in marriage, that was responsible for the marital happiness gap, then we would have expected married people to express greater happiness in every country and regardless of social context. But this is not what we found.

We also find some crucial asymmetries between the sexes. Most importantly, when we analyzed the data separately for men and women, we found that women's happiness is more sensitive to the social context than is men's. Societal beliefs and the religious climate affect the happiness gap between married and cohabiting persons for women, but not for men. Men are happier when married in almost every country, regardless of the social-institutional context. This may be because men and women have such different experiences in, and benefit in such different ways from, marriage. A rich sociological literature has investigated "His" marriage and "Her" marriage, finding that many of the benefits of marriage are enjoyed exclusively by men (Bernard 1972).

Women, on the other hand, benefit less in marriage. Women are the ones, in most countries of the world, who are expected to perform the majority of the unpaid and devalued family labor. This work is necessary for our society to function—we need well-raised children and productive workers who have meals to eat and clean clothes to wear, for example—but because this domestic labor does not have an economic value to it and because the primary and most obvious beneficiaries of this labor are children, it is undervalued in most societies. When women marry, and agree to specialize in this unpaid domestic labor, they are receiving the benefits of the financial security offered by the breadwinner (assuming the marriage remains intact), but they are taking on an enormous burden of domestic labor with little societal reward. For these reasons, we can see why marriage might always make men happier (if they are reaping the rewards of increased productivity, improved health, and emotional support) while the benefits of marriage for women may depend more on the social context. In those contexts in which cohabitation is a socially accepted and generally gender egalitarian alternative to marriage, it makes sense that women might be equally happy in marriage and in cohabitation. In the societies with more traditional gender beliefs and stronger religious beliefs, on the other hand, it makes sense that the stigma associated with cohabitation, or the social support provided to married couples, has the potential to outweigh the benefits of greater egalitarianism in cohabitation relative to marriage.

To return to the question posed at the beginning of the chapter, does happiness increase with marriage, the answer is: It depends. It depends on the type of society you live in as well as whether you are a man or a woman. For men, the answer that comes from our analysis is that yes, marriage is associated with greater happiness, *universally*. But for women, the answer is much more nuanced. We cannot understand what marriage means to the happiness of women without thinking about the social context the woman is living in. Because marriage and cohabitation have such different meanings in different societies, the benefits of marriage vis-à-vis cohabitation are also quite different across countries. We suspect that if we had direct measures of the level of social support and of social stigma experienced by married and cohabiting women in these different countries, this would account for most of the difference in the reported happiness of these two groups. For these reasons, we would argue that it is not something intrinsic to marriage that necessarily makes people happier but rather something about the meaning of marriage in particular social contexts that has consequences for happiness. Therefore, we would argue that public dollars spent promoting marriage could be better spent elsewhere. This is because couples do not necessarily need to be married to be happy; they just need the social support given to married people.

WHERE DO WE GO FROM HERE?

There is still a lot of work left to be done before we can fully understand the relationship between marriage and happiness around the world. Our study has important limitations based on the data we had available to analyze. We think that the benefits of being able to compare the happiness of married and cohabiting people around the world outweigh these limitations but they are important to discuss so that they can be addressed in the future.

Earlier in the chapter, we discussed the potential pitfalls of research on marriage and happiness associated with selection effects. In other words, there is the possibility that it is not marriage or cohabitation that matters per se in understanding happiness but rather the *type of people* who choose to marry or cohabit that really matters for happiness. If healthier, more optimistic, more financially secure, more highly educated people choose to marry rather than cohabit, it may be these individual characteristics, rather than marriage per se, that is associated with greater happiness. In other words, even if these people never married, they would still be happier than those in the cohabiting group because of their sunny dispositions and higher social status. In a cross-national analysis, there is the additional complication that if these individual characteristics are more strongly associated with someone's likelihood of marrying in one country versus another country, this could further introduce bias into our analysis.

How can we address this potential selection effect problem? First, it is important to point out that previous research has rejected the notion that the benefits of marriage are entirely due to selection effects. Instead, married people are happier than non-married people probably because marriage makes them happier and because they have individual characteristics that make them more likely to marry and to be happy. We addressed selection effects in our analysis in the way many previous researchers have also done. We include as many measures of individual characteristics understood to be associated with both likelihood of marriage and likelihood of happiness as possible in order to control for them in our analysis. In other words, we remove their effects from the analysis of the relationship between marriage and happiness. More specifically, we control for an individual's age, employment status, education, whether or not they have children, their religious beliefs, and their household income. It is likely that all of these factors affect an individual's chances of getting married and of finding happiness so by including them in our analyses, we are partially addressing the issue of selection effects.

There are several things that future researchers should do to try to reduce the impact of selection effects in their research and get to the heart of the relationship between marriage and happiness. First, there are still other factors that we did not have measures of in our analysis that likely affect both an individual's chances of getting married and his or her chances of finding happiness. An individual's mental health and individual disposition likely influence his or her happiness. Although these factors are unlikely to influence our analysis of the relative happiness of married and cohabiting individuals (unless of course, cohabiting people are more likely than their married peers to suffer from depression or to maintain a more pessimistic outlook), they are important predictors of an individual's happiness and should be studied in future research. An individual's marital history may also be important to include in future analyses. If we are interested in studying the happiness boost enjoyed by married people, then we should consider the possibility that second or third marriages may have different implications for happiness than first marriages. This becomes particularly important to consider in cross-national studies like ours in which different countries have different rates of divorce and remarriage. While the population of married people may be almost entirely made up of individuals in their first marriage in a society with low divorce rates, in a society with higher divorce rates a greater proportion of the married respondents may be in their second or even third marriage. To really understand the effect of marriage on happiness, future research should account for marital history to see if perhaps a marriage premium exists around the world, but only for first marriages.

Future research should also investigate the relationship between health and happiness. We know that how healthy you are is strongly associated with how happy you are. We did not have good measures of an individual's physical health in our dataset, and so we could not investigate the extent to which the differences we found between married and cohabiting people could be related to health. If healthier people are both more likely to get married and stay married and are more likely to be happy, then this is something that future researchers should include in their analyses. In general, data collected over time from individuals about their health, happiness, and marital status could address many of the shortcomings of analyses based on cross-sectional data. This kind of longitudinal (or panel) data from countries around the world would allow researchers to start making claims about what causes what: Does marriage lead to happiness or is it in fact the other way around? Only longitudinal data can shed light on this question.

What we can say from our analysis is that, when we look at marriage and happiness in different countries, marriage in and of itself does not cause people to become happier around the globe. Instead, marriage has different meanings and benefits associated with it in different countries. For this reason, while married people are clearly happier than cohabiters in some countries, in other countries cohabiting with someone outside of marriage can make you just as happy as tying the knot.

* * *

The empirical work presented in this chapter is based on our previous research, which we published in more technical form: see Lee and Ono 2012.

6

The (Re)Distribution of Happiness

In 2009, the OECD announced that the happiest country in the world was Denmark, followed by Finland, the Netherlands, and Sweden. The United States was ranked 13th among the countries surveyed. The media's reaction to this announcement was decidedly predictable. Since the high-taxed countries of Scandinavia occupied the top of the happiness rankings, a number of media outlets jumped to the conclusion that "the happiest people on earth are heavily taxed," thereby alluding to the positive correlation (and maybe even causation) between taxes and happiness.[1] This was not the first time that Western European countries outranked the United States in happiness. Ronald Inglehart's (2004) study of subjective well-being of 82 societies using the World Values Survey showed similar results. The message seemed abundantly clear. Taxes are not the source of evil but a source of happiness. Big government is not the problem but the solution.

These findings did not bode well with some conservative scholars in the United States, who perceived them as a threat to their libertarian ideals.[2] How could high taxes and big government prevail over limited government and free markets? How could socialism prevail over capitalism? Scholars who espouse American exceptionalism even argued that any study that places the United States below the Scandinavian welfare states must be fundamentally flawed. They went on to discredit happiness science, arguing that it was not a science at all but an unreliable field of inquiry that has been corroded by ideological bias. Happiness science, they warned, has been taken over by free-thinking liberals who want to advocate big government as a path toward higher quality of life. Suddenly, happiness science was thrust into the spotlight of an ideological conflict between the left and the right.

Do higher taxes and big government bring happiness to their citizens? As we have already shown in Chapter 3, the correlation between taxes and happiness across countries is not very strong. But cross-country comparisons at the aggregate level are misleading because the answer is actually not so simple. Taxes are used to redistribute money and wealth within a country. Resources are transferred from low-risk to high-risk persons in the form of social insurance. The transfer may benefit the high-risk persons whose happiness and well-being may otherwise be diminished by uncertainty and exposure to market risk. At the same time, the transfer of resources may lower the happiness of low-risk persons because they may not need the insurance at all, and/or because they have more to lose than to gain from redistribution.

In this chapter, we argue that taxes and transfers may lift happiness for some, but lower it for others. Aggregate happiness provides just one measure of happiness for the entire country. Such a measure can overlook the variation in happiness across demographic groups within a country. Figuring out which groups gain and which lose out requires unpacking the redistributive mechanisms of the welfare states.

THE MARKET VERSUS THE STATE

The extent to which the state and the market provide for the welfare of citizens has been the subject of great debate in political economy and in public policy. Even Albert Einstein joined the debate in 1949, and expressed his views advocating for a movement toward socialism and away from capitalism as the path toward higher quality of life (see Box 6.1). Esping-Andersen's (1999) work on the "Varieties of Welfare Capitalism" is a notable example of how modern capitalist societies can be categorized according to their contrasting positions regarding the roles of the state and the market. As happiness becomes vital in defining the nation's health and well-being, there is renewed interest in studying the association between happiness and the role of the state. While the goal of any society is to improve the welfare of its citizens, there is greater disagreement regarding how this can be achieved. Would individuals be happier if the state played an active role? Or should the pursuit of happiness be left to individual choice and market forces?

Against this backdrop, the concept of happiness becomes a pawn in the debates between competing ideologies, with political and economic systems pitted against each other. Indeed there is now a growing body of research that examines the "political economy of happiness" which examines the relationship between happiness and political ideology (see, e.g., Bjørnskov et al. 2007; Radcliff 2001, 2013; Rothstein 2010; Veenhoven 2000). However, aside from the politics, international comparisons using rigorous analytical methods remain few.

Box 6.1 Albert Einstein—Physicist, Socialist, and Sociologist

Albert Einstein was most famous for his work in theoretical physics. But he was also outspoken in his views against capitalism. In 1949, *Monthly Review*, an independent socialist magazine, asked Albert Einstein for a contribution to their inaugural issue. Einstein accepted, and contributed an article entitled, "Why Socialism?" (Einstein 1949) in which he laid out his criticism of the capitalist society.

The article is written from a deeply sociological perspective, and emphasizes the dependence and embeddedness of the individual within society. For example:

"Man is, at one and the same time, a solitary being and a social being" (p. 10).
"It is evident, therefore, that the dependence of the individual upon society is a fact of nature which cannot be abolished—just as in the case of ants and bees" (p. 11).

Einstein argues that capitalism results in excessive competition that pits individuals against each other and weakens social relationships. Indeed, individuals come to view their dependence on society not as an asset but as a weakness. The competitive drive results in extreme concentration of wealth, extreme poverty, and social deterioration. Einstein writes that "[t]he economic anarchy of capitalist society as it exists today is, in my opinion, the real source of evil" (p. 12). He advocates for the establishment of a socialist economy as a path toward prosperity and recovery.

We examine the sources of happiness in an international context. Our research is grounded in methodology and not ideology. We argue that happiness is best understood as an individual-level outcome that is simultaneously shaped by larger social forces. At the macro-level, we are mainly interested in studying how the countries' welfare expenditures and taxes affect the happiness of their citizens.

Is happiness greater in the social democratic welfare states? The pursuit for the "optimal level" of state or market intervention may be quantitatively and qualitatively difficult to assess. State intervention and welfare outcomes are both empirically vague notions that require more precise specifications. We focus on particular measures, mainly public social expenditures and tax revenue as share of gross domestic product (GDP), as proxy measures of state intervention, and happiness as the specific measure of welfare outcome. The "happiness equation" would then have aggregate happiness as the outcome and macro-level indicators as the predictors.

But this formulation by itself has a strictly macro-level orientation. Indeed, one of the methodological shortcomings of earlier studies that examine welfare capitalism and its outcomes is that they have been limited to the macro-level (Esping-Andersen 1999). Underlying this macro formulation is the assumption that *all* persons, regardless of socioeconomic status or demographics, are made better off (or worse off) in the social democratic welfare states. This line of inquiry may be empirically interesting to the study of political economy. But as our discussion of contextual effect models suggests (see Figure 1.2 in Chapter 1), sociologists are keener on probing the macro-micro link (Coleman 1990). We ask: *How do macro-level forces affect micro-level outcomes? How does the social-institutional context influence the happiness of individuals?*

Our second question explores this interaction effect, specifically by asking: Who gains and who loses *within* the social democratic welfare states? The operations of the social democratic welfare states must be considered in conjunction with *both* distinguishable features—universalism and redistribution. The social democratic welfare states provide a universal safety net with comprehensive coverage of social risks. These countries achieve egalitarianism through the massive redistribution of income, and the transfer of resources from low-risk to high-risk groups. If happiness follows this path, then we may in fact observe a similar pattern whereby happiness is redistributed from the privileged to the less privileged. The beneficiaries of the social democratic welfare states gain at the cost of the benefactor.

At the micro-level, we focus especially on the institutions of family and marriage. According to Esping-Andersen (1999), social policy is the "public management of social risk" (p. 36). Under this framework, the family is a social institution that is exposed to higher risk, at least in comparison to nonfamily units, notably single persons. Accordingly, the social democratic welfare states maintain a strong pro-family ideology, where considerable resources are allocated to improve the welfare and well-being of families. These countries also allow for flexible family forms whereby cohabiting persons receive similar (if not identical) benefits as do married persons. Our focus on family and marriage thus allows us to better isolate the association between state intervention and happiness. We take advantage of hierarchically structured data with individuals nested within countries. We apply a multilevel modeling approach to reveal how macro-level forces affect the micro-level foundations of society.

HAPPINESS IN SOCIAL CONTEXT

The state can take a direct role in improving social welfare, through greater involvement and direct subsidies in the everyday lives of their citizens. Our analytical framework begins with the idea that countries can be mapped along a continuum of state's involvement in providing social welfare. The measure of our central interest is the public social expenditure (PSE), here defined as welfare expenditures as a percentage share of GDP, excluding education. We use PSE as a proxy measure that captures the extent of government's role in providing for the welfare of its citizens.[3] Our framework is a modification of Esping-Andersen's (1990; 1999) welfare regime typology. While Esping-Andersen outlines welfare systems according to the role of the market, state, and family, we are primarily concerned with the distinction between market versus the state.

On one end of the continuum lies the market-based economies characterized by low PSE and low involvement by the state. These countries maintain "a political commitment to minimize the state, to individualize risks, and to promote market solutions" (Esping-Andersen 1999, p. 75). On the other end of this spectrum lies welfare capitalism characterized by high PSE and extensive involvement of the state. The extreme manifestation of this welfare state model is the social democratic welfare state. Denmark, Norway, and Sweden are the notable countries that fall in this category. This Scandinavian Welfare Model is first and foremost identified by "unusually heavy social spending, benefits and services of high standards, and a high degree of government intervention" (Esping-Andersen and Korpi 1987, p. 42). It is also distinguished by its universalism and comprehensive provision of welfare services and transfers (Kangas and Palme 1993, p. 3).

Welfare provision by the state is a form of social insurance, because it provides a safety net that ensures a basic standard of living for their citizens, and protects their citizens from unforeseen events or social risk in general. The welfare states can be seen as "rational responses to market failures" (Lindbeck 2004, p. 63). In essence, the state has made "a powerful commitment to collective social responsibility for the optimal welfare of citizens" (Esping-Andersen and Korpi 1987, p. 53). This commitment involves such measures as government subsidized healthcare, generous and far-reaching family policies, and extensive care for the elderly. All citizens, regardless of income or background, are entitled to these social benefits.

The social welfare programs help to reduce poverty, and the overall level of economic and social inequality (Kenworthy 1999; Korpi and Palme 1998; Lindbeck 1997). For example, OECD (2008) data shows that the tax and transfer systems reduced income inequality by 45 percent in Sweden, Belgium, and Denmark, compared to 17 percent in the United States, and less than 8 percent in South Korea (see Figure 6.1). This reduction in inequality creates the potential for greater social solidarity (Esping-Andersen 1990; Kenworthy 2004). When social welfare benefits are more universal, there is less stigma attached to receiving them, compared to market-based economies where social welfare is targeted primarily for the poor.

Figure 6.1 Percentage Reduction in Inequality before and after Taxes and Transfers in OECD Countries

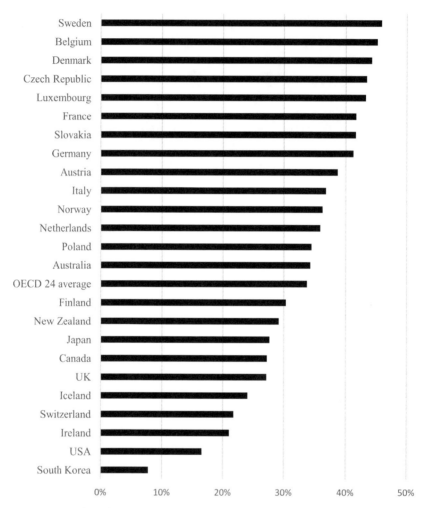

Source: OECD (2008).

The arrangement in the social democratic welfare states, therefore, contrasts greatly to that observed in other countries where the market plays a greater role in providing for benefits and services. In the market-based regimes, social insurance is replaced by private insurance, and many of the publicly provided services such as healthcare and childcare are replaced by market mechanisms (Esping-Andersen and Korpi 1987). The market-based system generates a more stratified society consisting of those who can afford such services versus those who cannot.

The other feature of the social democratic welfare states is massive resource redistribution. The state collects revenue through a combination of progressive income taxes, where the rich are taxed at higher rates compared to the poor, flat consumption taxes, flat social security taxes, and heavy taxation on addiction goods, such as alcohol and tobacco (Lindert 2004; Steinmo 1989). Tax revenue is then returned in the form of social programs that are intended to benefit those who paid into the system. Ultimately, however, "there is a definitive redistributive element to all social spending" (Lindert 2004, p. 6). Indeed, the degree of redistribution in the welfare states is far greater than the one that is in place in the United States. For example, Alesina et al. (2004) elaborate on the contrasting role of government in redistribution between the United States and Europe:

> Most governments redistribute income, using both direct and indirect means. Even though this role of the public sector has increased vastly in the last few decades in all industrial countries, European governments are more heavily involved with redistribution than that of the United States. European fiscal systems are more progressive than in the United States and the welfare state is more generous in Europe, where the share of government in the economy is substantially larger than in the United States. For instance, in 2000 the share of total government spending (excluding interest payments) over GDP was about 30% in the US, versus 45% in Continental Europe. (Alesina et al. 2004; 2010)

As we showed in Figure 6.1, reduction in inequality after transfers is greatest in the Scandinavian welfare states. The consequence of such extreme measures is a compressed income distribution. Figure 6.2 shows the Gini coefficients among the OECD countries, where the low scores show low income inequality and high scores show greater income inequality. We can see from Figure 6.2 that income inequality in the Scandinavian countries is lower in comparison to the other OECD countries.

The redistribution of resources has the objective of reducing inequality and social risk in the cross-section *and* across the life span, where the latter is often termed the *cradle to grave* arrangement of the welfare state (Jonsson and Collins 2001; Lindbeck 2004):[4]

> A notable feature of this structure is the way in which it acts to redistribute resources across life-course stages. An important legitimating feature of welfare state spending in Sweden has been its tendency to collect taxes from citizens in their productive years, only to return the money in the form of universal benefits tied to significant life events, in the form of child allowances, unemployment benefits, heavily subsidized

Figure 6.2 Gini Coefficients in OECD Countries

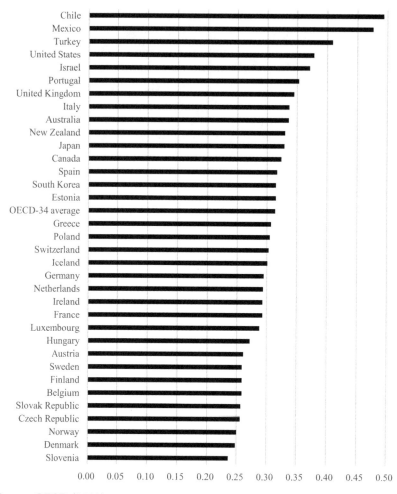

Source: OECD (2011).

healthcare, daycare, schooling and pensions. The implication for the life-course is not only that cross-sectional inequality is reduced, but also that the amplitudes of life-course cycles. . . are attenuated. (Jonsson and Collins 2001, p. xiv)

We want to emphasize here that even within the social democratic welfare state, *some persons benefit more than do others.* To the extent that redistribution disturbs the social relations of the status quo, the process itself can create an alternative system of stratification (Esping-Andersen 1990). Some types of social insurance benefit all citizens, but others are targeted specifically for families with small children. This pro-family policy is based on the view that families are exposed to greater social risk than are single persons. For example, a single person may only be concerned with his or her own job and health. But a parent in a family of four must ensure that he or she is protected against the risk of illness, job loss, and poverty not only for himself or herself but also for the spouse and two children.

As we discussed in Chapter 5, nonmarital cohabitation is now institutionalized in many European countries; it is considered to be a socially acceptable family form (Märtinson 2007; Soons and Kalmijn 2009). The benefits of the welfare state extend to cohabiting couples in the same manner as to married couples. These policies are the states' responses toward more inclusion, tolerance, and acceptance toward diverse family forms. The state does not discriminate between married persons and cohabiting persons in deciding the eligibility of social benefits, and in the level of their benefits. The inclusion of cohabiters in social benefits is both the consequence and the driving force for greater social acceptance of cohabitation as a legally recognized alternative to marriage.

Universal welfare can be sustained only through high taxes. Indeed the citizens of the Scandinavian welfare states benefit from the most generous level of social insurance, but they also pay the highest taxes in the world in terms of both average and marginal taxes (OECD 2009). The rich are taxed heavily to subsidize the poor. Hence, while the benefits of the welfare states are many, so are the costs associated with this system. The effect of the welfare provision on happiness must be evaluated in light of its costs and benefits.

Social democratic welfare states encourage family formation through nondiscriminatory treatment of cohabitation, and their strong commitment to families with small children. But all policies have their blind spots and unintended consequences. If the welfare states discriminate, they do so against single people. The pro-family bias leads to a less generous treatment of single persons. In terms of costs, single people on average pay *higher* personal income tax and contributions to Social Security (as a percentage of gross wage earnings) than do married persons (OECD 2009).[5] While single persons do benefit from some forms of social insurance such as sick leave, unemployment, healthcare, and old age assistance, they obviously do not qualify for the benefits that are targeted for families with children.

Hence, in this regard, the social democratic welfare state is partial to families, but single persons bear the costs of the pro-family policy. Conceptually, redistribution may transfer resources away from single persons in favor of families with small children. From the viewpoint of costs, benefits, and incentives, the social democratic welfare states' pro-family policy is one that encourages their citizens to have children. In the case of Norway, Kravdal

(2008) argues that the generous childbearing benefits and flexible family forms, such as cohabitation, are two key reasons why fertility in Norway remains high. Similarly, in Swedish families where the father took parental leave after birth of the first child, the couple was more likely to go on to have additional children (Olah 2003). Pro-family policies can provide incentives to have children.

HAPPINESS AT THE INDIVIDUAL LEVEL

Much of the previous research on happiness has focused on the demographic and socioeconomic characteristics associated with greater happiness. Scholars have argued that general well-being reflects a composite of satisfaction in different life domains such as work, family, and housing (Campbell et al. 1976). There is an overall positive association between income and happiness within countries (Blanchflower and Oswald 2004; Clark and Oswald 1996; Easterlin 2001; Schyns 2002). Past research has explored variations in happiness over the life span (Rodgers 1982). Recent work in this area finds that there is an overall increase in happiness with age (Yang 2008) and that family, income, and health become increasingly important in explaining happiness with age (Margolis and Myrskylä 2013). Overall, women report greater life happiness than do men (e.g., Aldous and Ganey 1999).

As we discussed in the previous chapter, an extensive literature documents the relationship between marriage and general happiness (see, e.g., Nock 1995; Waite and Gallagher 2000), and confirms first and foremost the positive effects of marriage relative to being single. Married individuals are also found to be happier than cohabiters (Stack and Eshleman 1998; Waite and Gallagher 2000), although the happiness gap between married and cohabiting individuals varies depending on the social context, such as the religious and gender climate, as we demonstrated in Chapter 5.

Although the relationship between children and well-being varies depending on the timing of childbirth, the age of the child, social class, parent gender, and marital status among other factors (Umberson et al. 2010), the overall consensus is that parents of minor co-resident children report poorer life satisfaction than childless persons (McLanahan and Adams 1987). Working mothers in particular experience lower levels of well-being associated with parenting because of their greater involvement in childcare, compared to fathers (Nomaguchi et al. 2005).

What has been given less attention in the literature, however, is the role played by the social-institutional context in shaping the happiness of individuals and families.[6] Such an approach is particularly important when we examine happiness across a wide spectrum of countries. Individuals and families are embedded in a specific cultural, economic, and social context that defines the parameters of their well-being. A more precise understanding of happiness requires that happiness be studied in the specific macro-institutional context in which individuals are situated.

MACRO-MICRO INTERACTION

The debate over welfare states and happiness is hardly new. While some scholars contend that happiness is greater in the welfare states (Pacek and Radcliff 2008; Radcliff 2001), others argue that there is no link (Veenhoven 2000). These contrasting views stem in part from differences in data collection and the methodologies employed.

We argue that aggregate measures of happiness at the country-level in and by themselves are not informative from a social policy perspective. Aggregate rankings of happiness assume that all demographic groups report the same level of happiness and thus fail to capture the mechanisms that relate contextual-level effects to happiness at the individual-level.[7]

For example, consider the case of happiness among families with small children. In the United States, institutional support to help with parenting is limited. Simon (2008) explains:

In America we lack institutional supports that would help ease the social and economic burdens—and subsequent stressfulness and emotional disadvantages—associated with parenthood. Instituting better tax credits, developing more and better day care and after school options, as well as offering flexible work schedules for employed mothers and fathers would go far toward alleviating some of the stress for parents raising children. (pp. 44–45)

In contrast, owing to the most generous social insurance system in the world, the Swedes benefit from the extensive menu of services that are available for parents with small children. In comparison to their U.S. counterparts, the "penalty" (Budig and England 2001) of taking time off to raise children in Sweden is thus significantly offset by the direct and indirect subsidies offered by the state. The institutional support provided by the social democratic welfare states may compensate for the burden of parenting and ease the stress associated with parenting, which may lead to greater happiness for families living in these countries.

The effects of public social expenditures on happiness may not be symmetrical between men and women. Cross-national research has shown how macro-level forces can affect the happiness of men and women in different ways. As we discussed in Chapter 5, societal factors such as traditional gender beliefs can lead to a happiness gap between men and women. Bjørnskov et al.'s (2007) more nuanced empirical analysis of government size on life satisfaction shows that women benefit more in countries with greater government consumption compared to men in these countries.

To the extent that women of all countries take on a disproportionate share of raising children, women may benefit more from pro-family policies of the social democratic welfare states than do men. As Esping-Andersen (1999) explains, "The Nordic welfare state remains the only ones where social policy is explicitly designed to maximize women's economic independence" (p. 45). The institutionalization of cohabitation in the European countries can also be viewed as a movement toward greater female autonomy in these countries (Märtinson 2007). Unsurprisingly, the Scandinavian welfare states consistently top the list of "best countries to raise kids." For example, a 2015 study of 179 countries (Save the Children 2015) found that the well-being of mothers was highest in the Scandinavian countries of Norway, Finland, Iceland, Denmark, and Sweden, on the basis of maternal health, children's well-being, women's educational status, economic status, and political status (the United States ranked 33rd in the survey).

In sum, we expect to find a pattern of "happiness redistribution" in the social democratic welfare states that mirrors the pattern of resource redistribution in these countries. Happiness is redistributed from low-risk to high-risk persons, and from privileged to less privileged persons. We examine these redistributive effects in the areas of family, marriage, and income.

Hypotheses

We use public social expenditures (PSE) as a proxy measure for the degree of state intervention in social welfare. PSE distinguishes the market-based economies (our benchmark) from the social democratic welfare states. We use multilevel models and specify macro-micro interactions with PSE and individual-level covariates to capture the extent to which state intervention affects individual happiness.

Our first research question is: *Is happiness greater in the welfare states?* We expect that aggregate happiness does not vary by level of public social expenditures. Our second question is: *Who gains and who loses* within *the welfare states?* We hypothesize here that public social expenditures will be associated with the redistribution of happiness *within* countries. This redistribution will create an alternate form of "happiness inequality" with different winners and losers within the high PSE countries.

In line with the social democratic welfare states' pro-family ideology, we expect redistribution to be strongest among the institutions of family and marriage. We expect cohabiters and parents to be relatively happier in high-PSE countries compared to their counterparts in low-PSE countries.

Income redistribution in the social democratic welfare states is achieved through taxation, and by transferring money from high-income earners to low-income earners. We expect happiness redistribution in the social democratic welfare states to occur in the same direction as income redistribution. Mirroring the largely compressed distribution of income in these countries, we expect the happiness gap between the rich and the poor to be smaller in the social democratic welfare states.

Analysis

For this analysis, we use the same data that we introduced in Chapter 5, the International Social Survey Program's ([ISSP] 2002) Family and Changing Gender Roles dataset. We use the same measure of happiness (measured on a scale of 1 to 7), but our measures of the country-level characteristics are different. In this analysis, we are particularly interested in the implications of state social welfare spending for happiness. We look at the percentage of the country's GDP that is spent on social welfare, excluding expenses related to education. This variable, PSE, is our measure of social welfare spending in a country. We also look at tax revenue in a country as a percentage of GDP. Finally, we have a variable that indicates whether or not the country is a post-communist country. We include this indicator because in earlier analyses (and as we discussed in Chapter 3), we found that post-communist countries reported the lowest average happiness levels in our sample.

We summarize our main findings here. Interested readers can view the actual estimation results presented in Tables A.6 to A.8 in the Appendix.

Findings

We begin by taking on our first research question: *Is happiness greater in the social democratic welfare states?* The answer is no. Our statistical models show that public social expenditures and happiness are not correlated. This is consistent with what we discussed in Chapter 3 based on simple correlations (see Table 3.1). So aggregate happiness does *not* vary by the size of the welfare state, at least among the sample of countries included in the ISSP. Table 6.1 reports aggregate levels of happiness, public social expenditures, and tax revenue as a proportion of the GDP. No clear pattern can be found across countries.

But we did discover one pattern across countries that was consistent in all statistical models. Happiness is significantly lower in the post-communist countries, such as Czech Republic, Latvia, Poland, and Slovak Republic. This unhappy finding has actually been reported in other statistical studies. We felt it deserves a separate treatment, and we will revisit the topic in greater detail in Chapter 8.

Table 6.1 Descriptive Statistics by Country

	Public Social Expenditures (PSE) as % of GDP[a]	Tax Revenue as % of GDP[b]	Happiness[c]	
			Mean	S.D.
Australia	17.3	30.5	5.38	(0.92)
Austria	26.0	43.4	5.55	(0.93)
Belgium	24.7	46.8	5.20	(0.90)
Brazil	16.2	38.8	5.42	(0.89)
Chile	11.2	17.1	5.54	(1.02)
Cyprus	21.8	36.6	5.29	(1.08)
Czech Republic	19.5	36.3	5.03	(0.99)
Denmark	29.2	50.0	5.34	(0.96)
Finland	24.2	43.6	5.24	(0.96)
France	28.5	46.1	5.25	(0.95)
Germany East	27.4	40.6	5.03	(0.91)
Germany West	27.4	40.6	5.16	(0.85)
Hungary	20.1	37.3	5.04	(1.11)
Israel	20.0	36.8	5.34	(1.10)
Latvia	8.6	30.4	4.85	(0.97)
Mexico	4.3	9.7	5.58	(1.06)
New Zealand	18.1	36.5	5.48	(0.96)
Norway	21.3	43.6	5.30	(0.92)
Philippines	4.7	14.4	5.41	(1.25)
Poland	20.5	33.8	4.97	(1.03)
Portugal	18.9	37.0	5.19	(1.06)
Russia	10.0	36.9	4.87	(1.14)
Slovak Republic	15.7	29.5	4.88	(1.05)
Spain	19.6	37.3	5.26	(0.89)
Sweden	29.8	49.7	5.24	(0.97)
Switzerland	17.5	30.1	5.52	(0.77)
Taiwan	5.7	12.4	5.19	(1.10)
UK	21.8	39.0	5.42	(1.00)
USA	14.5	28.2	5.52	(0.96)

[a] *Source:* OECD, various years.
[b] *Source:* Index of Economic Freedom, Heritage Foundation 2002.
[c] The data are country averages aggregated from the 2002 ISSP data.

Now we turn to our second research question: *Who gains and who loses in the social democratic welfare state?* We address this question by looking at the happiness of those demographic groups that are specifically targeted by social insurance. We first examine the hypothesis that cohabiters and parents with small children will be happier in countries with high PSE. We discuss our findings in the order of marriage and family, followed by a separate analysis of men and women. In our discussions, a *low-PSE country* refers to a country with the minimum level of PSE, and a *high-PSE country* refers to a country with the maximum level of PSE. In all models, college education and income are positive and significant. We also find that happiness is U-shaped as a function of age: Happiness is high among younger persons, declines among middle-aged persons, then recovers again among older persons. We do not know, however, if these age differences reflect changes in happiness associated with aging or cohort differences in happiness.

First, women and men are equally happy. On the whole, their happiness does not vary by the size of the welfare state. But this finding requires further elaboration because the happiness of women and men depends largely on the presence of family. We will explore the interactions between gender, family, and PSE in separate analysis next.

Second, married persons report greater happiness than do unmarried persons. This gap in happiness by marital status is greater in the high-PSE countries. In these countries, our statistical models predict that the happiness for married people is more than three times higher compared to non-married, non-cohabiting individuals. But in low-PSE countries, the same odds ratio drops to about two.[8]

Third (and consistent with our findings from Chapter 5), cohabiters report lower happiness than do married persons. But the gap between the two disappears in the high-PSE countries, specifically in countries where PSE is greater than 26.2 (e.g., Denmark and Sweden). This finding suggests that the happiness of cohabiting persons reaches parity with that of married persons in the high-PSE countries presumably because, as we discussed previously, cohabitation is widely accepted and receives greater institutional support in the high-PSE countries.

Fourth, having children under 18 in the home (hereafter children) is not correlated with happiness overall in this model. The relationship between children and happiness will be examined in greater detail in the next analysis, which separates the sample into men and women.

And finally, we find that on average, single persons are more likely to report lower happiness than are married persons. More interestingly, the negative effect of being single is even stronger, that is, even more negative in high-PSE countries. This is essentially the opposite of what we observe for married and cohabiting persons discussed earlier. The policies of the social democratic welfare states are explicit family-support policies with the goal of improving the welfare of married and cohabiting persons. The welfare states achieve their goal, but at the cost of lowering the happiness of single persons.

The Happiness Gap between Men and Women

If women are more likely to take on a disproportionate share of family responsibilities, then women, and particularly those with children, may benefit more than do men under the pro-family policies of the social democratic welfare states. We study the sample of men and women separately to get a clearer picture.

Marriage and cohabitation are associated with higher odds of greater happiness, especially among the higher-PSE countries. For both sexes, the benefits of marriage and cohabitation are greater in the high-PSE countries. Full-time employment is associated with higher happiness for men, but it does nothing to improve happiness for women.

The relationship between having children and happiness exposes the gender asymmetries of parenthood commonly discussed in the literature; mainly that the burden of raising children falls disproportionately on women (see Chapters 4 and 5). The direct effect of children is negative for women. But this effect is not statistically significant for men, meaning that children do nothing to influence men's happiness—positive or negative.

To further elaborate on the effect of children on women, the default is that the presence of small children in the home is associated with *lower* happiness for women—that is, there is a disutility associated with small children. However, women in the social democratic welfare states receive extensive institutional support to help families with children. The positive gain in happiness (from the institutional support) is large enough to compensate for the *disutility* of having small children in high-PSE countries. Empirically, we find that the happiness gap for women with and without children disappears in the high-PSE countries.

More interestingly, this offsetting effect is even stronger for cohabiting women (relative to married women). Earlier we reported that cohabiting persons are much happier in high-PSE countries. It makes sense that high level of institutional support for cohabitation makes the high PSE countries even more attractive and hospitable for cohabiting women with small children. We illustrate this relationship in Figure 6.3 that shows predicted happiness for the case of cohabiting women with and without children. Predicted happiness is much higher in the high-PSE countries for both groups of women, but the slopes are not the same. In high-PSE countries, specifically among countries with PSE greater than 21, the happiness gap between cohabiting women with and without kids becomes statistically indistinguishable. In

Figure 6.3 Predicted Happiness for Cohabiting Women as a Function of Public Social Expenditures (PSE)

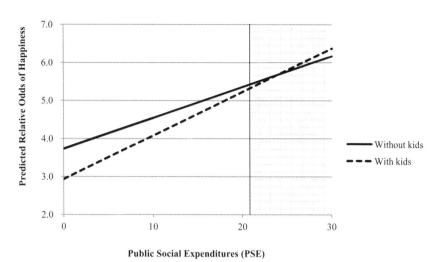

Public Social Expenditures (PSE)

Note: The cross-hatched area of the graph indicates a nonsignificant happiness gap.

other words, for cohabiting women, small children as a source of unhappiness disappears in the high-PSE countries.

Income and Happiness

Our results thus far show that higher income is associated with greater happiness. But does this positive association vary across countries with respect to tax revenues and welfare spending at the country level? We next examine our hypothesis that the happiness gap between rich and poor will be smaller in the social democratic welfare states.

Most countries employ progressive taxation, with high-income earners facing higher marginal tax rates than do low-income earners. Marginal tax rates are generally higher in the Scandinavian welfare states (OECD 2009), as previously discussed. The redistribution mechanism, where money income is transferred from the rich to the poor, has an equalizing effect where the after-tax income is compressed across income levels. If money and happiness are closely linked, then the happiness gained from money income may be smaller in high-PSE/high-taxed countries, because the income distribution will be more compressed in these countries. In other words, if the distribution of happiness mirrors the distribution of money income, then it should be more compressed in the high-PSE countries compared to the low PSE countries.

We can illustrate how happiness changes with income as we move from low- to high-PSE countries (see Figure 6.4). In this three-dimensional illustration, the

Figure 6.4 Happiness as a Function of Income and Public Social Expenditures (PSE)

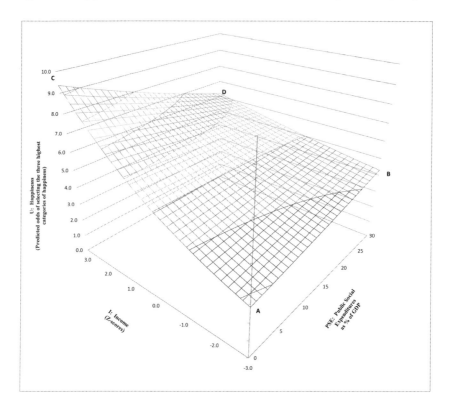

vertical axis is predicted happiness (U), or more specifically, the predicted log odds of belonging to one of the three highest categories of happiness. One horizontal axis is income (I) expressed in Z-scores (a standardized measure of how many standard deviations a value is above or below the mean), and the other axis is PSE. For reference, we indicate the four corners of the graph. Point A is the lowest income group in the lowest PSE country; at the other extreme is point D, which is the highest income group in the highest PSE country. AC and BD are the happiness curves with respect to income. These curves show how happiness changes as income grows. AC is the happiness curve for the low-PSE country. BD is the happiness curve for the high-PSE country. AB and CD capture how happiness changes as PSE increases from low to high.

First, money has a much bigger effect on happiness in the low-PSE countries than in the high-PSE countries. From Figure 6.4, we can see that the slope of AC is steeper than the slope of BD. Higher income is associated with higher happiness in all countries, but this association is much stronger in the low-PSE countries.

Second, the effect of PSE on happiness is positive for the poor, but negative for the rich. Poor people are happier if they live in high-PSE countries than in low-PSE countries. In contrast, rich people are happier if they live in low-PSE countries than in high-PSE countries. As an illustrative example, we can say that a rich person in Mexico (low-tax/low-PSE country) is a lot happier than a rich person in Sweden (high-tax/high-PSE country). In sum, the happiest person is the rich person in a low-PSE country and the unhappiest person is the poor person in a low-PSE country.

Does money buy happiness? Our answer is yes, but with qualifications. Overall, we observe a gain in happiness associated with a gain in money income across all countries in our sample. But this gain is not uniform across countries. Specifically, people in the low-tax/low-PSE countries stand to benefit most from higher incomes when it comes to happiness. In contrast, people in the high-tax/high-PSE countries derive little happiness from money income.

Figure 6.4 informs us visually of the intervening role of the social safety net in the social democratic welfare states. If the market-based regime was the "natural state" of society, we can see how redistribution (vis-à-vis public social expenditures) alters the shape of the happiness curves as one moves in the direction of the social democratic welfare states. True to the definition of social insurance, these societies ensure that all persons are protected from social risk. The people at the bottom of the income distribution gain the most from this generous safety net. We can thus surmise that the social democratic welfare state is a society that prioritizes eliminating misery for the poor, rather than maximizing happiness for the rich.

Our findings are largely consistent with our hypothesis: Happiness redistribution in the social democratic welfare states mirrors income redistribution in these countries. The redistributive mechanism of "spreading the wealth around" among the social democratic welfare states diminishes the gain in happiness from money income, which equalizes people's happiness regardless of their income levels. Clearly, we see that the distribution of happiness is compressed much like income in these countries. There is a smaller happiness gap between the rich and the poor, suggesting a more egalitarian society with less economic and social inequality.

The fact that poor persons are happier in high-PSE countries (than in low-PSE countries) suggests that the social welfare programs not only improve the economic well-being of the poor and protect them from poverty, but they also improve their subjective well-being. Further, the fact that rich persons are less happy in the high-PSE countries may indicate that the poor achieve greater happiness *at the cost of rich persons* in these countries.[9]

Summary and Discussion

What makes people happy or unhappy? We offer a classic sociological explanation: *It depends on whom you ask, and it depends on where you live.* The social democratic welfare state does not produce greater happiness for the whole, but makes some people happier and others less so. Studying happiness in the social democratic welfare states requires unpacking the various interactions between the macro and the micro. Aggregate happiness does not vary by the size of the welfare state. Public social expenditures do not raise happiness for all citizens. Rather, our multilevel analysis clearly shows that social insurance improves the life conditions in the demographic groups it targets specifically, but leaves others worse off.

When the world happiness rankings showed that the Scandinavian welfare states are the happiest countries in the world, it quickly became part of the left-leaning agenda with the right joining the ideological battle. Given the association between taxes and happiness, one may conclude that high taxes and big government lead to greater happiness. But this is not exactly true. High taxes and big government can provide a source of happiness for some, but not for the whole population.

Our key contribution is in the discovery that the redistribution of happiness in the social democratic welfare states mirrors the redistribution of resources and income in these countries. The transfer of resources from low-risk to high-risk individuals in the social democratic welfare states is associated with a leveling effect on happiness in these countries. It is a pro-family policy that is associated with greater happiness for women with small children and cohabiting persons. The redistribution of income reduces the happiness gap between the rich and the poor: The happiness of the poor is lifted, and the happiness of the rich is lowered. Our findings are thus consistent with the ideological foundations of the social democratic welfare states. By providing a generous safety net against social risk, the welfare states have made the "pursuit of happiness" more accessible for high-risk groups. It is a society that places greater importance on reducing misery for the poor rather than increasing happiness for the rich.

Aside from the obvious disutility associated with high taxes, our analysis has also uncovered some areas where the social democratic welfare state may be associated with *lower* happiness. High taxes and high expenditures on social welfare do not make everyone happy across the board. The beneficiaries of the social democratic welfare states achieve happiness at the cost of the benefactor. By attempting to rectify inequality through redistribution mechanisms, the social democratic welfare state generates an alternate form of "happiness inequality" in which winners and losers are defined by marital status, presence of children, and income. While the system looks after the welfare of families, it is less generous in its treatment of unmarried and single persons. On average, single people face a higher tax burden than do married persons, but they gain the least in return. Indeed, the tax system implicitly encourages union formation, be it marriage or cohabitation, and even more, to have children. This taxation and incentive structure are attributed to one of the leading causes for the recovery of fertility in Sweden and Norway during the 1990s. Interestingly, the tax and incentive system among the Scandinavian welfare states resembles the taxation scheme that was legislated by Emperor Augustus in ancient Rome to encourage family formation (see Box 6.2).

Methodologically, we have demonstrated the strengths of multilevel modeling as an effective strategy for examining happiness across countries by uncovering the mechanisms that shape macro- and micro-level variations in happiness. We first showed that aggregate happiness is lower in the

---

Box 6.2 Taxation and Family Formation—Lessons from the Roman Empire

Taxing single people to subsidize families is hardly new. In ancient Rome, Emperor Augustus legislated lex Julia et Papia that was a taxation scheme designed to encourage family formation by penalizing unmarried people. Alarmed by immorality, degradation of marriage, and the declining fertility that ensued, Augustus addressed the senate about the importance of preserving marriage and family values: "We must plan for our lasting preservation rather than for our temporary pleasure" (Berkowitz 2012, p. 111). The law offered incentives for marriage and procreation, and penalized single persons, childless couples, and those who strayed from their marriage by imposing heavier taxes.

It should be noted that single persons in the United States may also feel that taxes favor married persons with children. In a "Letter to the Editor" section of the New York Times in 2013, one writer discusses "lifestyle discrimination," or the idea that taxes implicitly discriminate against single persons. He expresses his frustrations at the current taxation scheme:

It is difficult, however, to celebrate anything that treats me like a second-class citizen. Because I am a single renter with no children, the 1040 is a reminder that I am a loser in the federal government's game of "lifestyle discrimination."

Since I do not benefit from married tax rates, multiple dependency exemptions, child tax credits or housing-related deductions, my effective tax rate is often 10 percentage points higher than that of most of my married friends with identical incomes.

While I am happy that my friends have achieved the American dream, I do not agree that it is my duty to subsidize their lifestyles, particularly in the cases of single-earner families making low six-figure incomes.

Source: "Lifestyle and Taxes: Writers Discuss Incentives to Marry, Procreate and Buy a Home." The New York Times, April 13, 2013.

post-communist countries. But aside from this there are few country-level factors that are associated with happiness. At the individual level, we find that characteristics such as income (Blanchflower and Oswald 2004), the presence of children (Umberson et al. 2010), and marital status (Nock 1995; Waite and Gallagher 2000) are important correlates of happiness. Cross-national variation in happiness is best explained not by looking at country- or individual-level factors alone, but by probing their interactions. This conclusion would have been overlooked had we employed methods that do not account for the interplay of macro- and micro-factors. The significant associations found in the macro-micro interactions underscore the importance of considering the social and institutional context in which respondents live.

By considering public social expenditures, we gain insight into how the policies of the social democratic welfare state differentially impact individuals and families. Most importantly, our work has shown that happiness is socially embedded in a larger cultural and institutional framework. Understanding what makes people happy requires a deeper analysis of the social mechanisms that link individual actors to their social-institutional environments.

* * *

The empirical work presented in this chapter is based on our previous research, which we published in more technical form: see Ono and Lee 2013.

7

An Unhappy Person

We have examined what makes people happy. We now have a good grasp of both individual-level and societal-level factors that are related to happiness and how the interaction of individual and society matters in determining happiness.

In this chapter, we turn the discussion to the topic of unhappiness. What events or characteristics are most strongly associated with unhappiness? And should we try to eliminate those factors from our lives? Should the ultimate goal be a happy life—or is there a downside to prioritizing happiness above all else?

THE SOURCES OF UNHAPPINESS

Children

As we discussed in Chapter 2, we know that children do not make us happier and that, in many cases, they are even a source of unhappiness. Although parenthood may have some positive effects on happiness because of the meaning children can add to our lives and the social connections they foster with those around us, these positive effects are overshadowed by the anxiety and even anger our children at times inspire in us, not to mention the disrupted sleep, strained relationships with our romantic partners, and financial strains of parenthood (Nelson et al. 2014).

We are brought up to think that marriage and family are the sources of happiness. Unfortunately, our research and the research conducted by countless others tell us overwhelmingly that marriage is a big plus, but children are a minus. Studies dating as far back as the 1950s (e.g., LeMasters 1957) have documented this negative association, and continue to do so today. There was some optimism in 2009, when the *Journal of Happiness Studies* published results to the contrary. The media reacted with great enthusiasm at the release of the new findings, with some outlets erroneously suggesting causality, that raising children improves happiness.[1] The excitement was short-lived, however, as the findings were later retracted because of coding error.

Why is parenting a drag on our happiness? Why is there a disjuncture between our expectations about parenthood and the reality? Perhaps parenting is something that is overly romanticized. Perhaps our cultural understandings of the joy associated with dedicating our time and energy to the rearing of small children are unrealistic and the reality of daily life with a small child is much more mundane and tiring. Perhaps the stress of worrying about your child's behavioral problems, the financial strain of trying to pay for extracurricular activities and new clothes, all the while saving for college, outweigh the perks. Perhaps the second shift of cooking, cleaning, washing clothes, shuttling children from activity to activity crowds out the time spent enjoying children.

Alice Rossi (1968) argued that the transition to parenthood is more disruptive than other life transitions because we have so little preparation for it; we do not really know what we are getting ourselves into when we make the leap into parenthood. Similarly, LeMasters (1957) viewed parenthood as a crisis:

> If the family is conceptualized as a small social system, would it not follow that the *adding* of a new member to the system could force a reorganization of the system as drastic (or nearly so) as does the *removal* of a member? (p. 352)

LeMasters likens the birth of a first child to a crisis that disrupts the precarious equilibrium of the family. He then documents the extensive adjustments that parents need to make in order to accommodate the new family member.

Disruptions in the status quo can be many. First, there are the psychological adjustments. Children can be a major source of worry and stress for parents. Raising children requires a minutia of administration, coordination, and logistics that are usually perceived as negative experiences. Powdthavee (2009) explains:

> It is . . . much more likely that we as parents will end up spending a large chunk of our time attending to the very core process of child care such as "Am I going to be able to pick up David from his school in time?" or "How do I stop Sarah from crying?" Most of these negative

experiences are a lot less salient than the positive experiences we have with our kids, which is probably why we tend not to think about them when prompted with a question of whether or not children bring us happiness. Nevertheless, it is these small but more frequent negative experiences, rather than the less frequent but meaningful experiences, that take up most of our attention in a day. It should therefore come to no surprise to us that these negative experiences that come with parenthood will show up much more often in our subjective experiences, including happiness and life satisfaction, than activities that are, although rewarding, relatively rare. (p. 309)

As we considered in Chapter 2, we may relish our moments of sheer bliss with our children, such as going on a bike ride or enjoying a beautiful classical music concert. But such joyful events are often overshadowed by the daily mundane routines of parenting, so the overall effect on our happiness may be a net negative.

Another shock to the status quo from having children is the financial costs and time constraints. Raising kids can be very expensive, especially if one lives in an advanced economy. Historically, we are witnessing a "quantity-quality tradeoff of children" (Becker 1991). Children have transitioned from being producers—that is, helping out in the household production—to being consumers. Parents have fewer children than they used to because producing "high-quality" children (generally viewed as highly educated children) requires major investments in time, money, and other resources.

Sociologists have documented the ratcheting up of expectations of good parenting across the 20th century in the United States. As the returns to higher education have increased and the middle class continues to shrink, parents have become anxious about preparing their children to compete for the good jobs that remain. Annette Lareau (2003) refers to the middle class parenting style of intensive investment in children—shuttling them to soccer practice and piano lessons, engaging their critical thinking skills and preparing them for college admissions—as "concerted cultivation." It makes sense that, in the context of these intense parenting expectations and pressures, raising children may increase our anxiety and decrease our happiness. In fact, some researchers have found just that—parents who practice this intensive form of parenting also report greater stress and depression as well as less happiness (Rizzo et al. 2013).

But just like with everything else, the relationship between children and unhappiness depends on a lot of things. First, it depends how old the children are. In the case of happiness in marriage in Japan, for example, our own research found that the negative effect of children on happiness is U-shaped with respect to the age of the youngest child, as we see in Figure 7.1.[2]

Figure 7.1 Marital Happiness and Age of Youngest Child in Japan

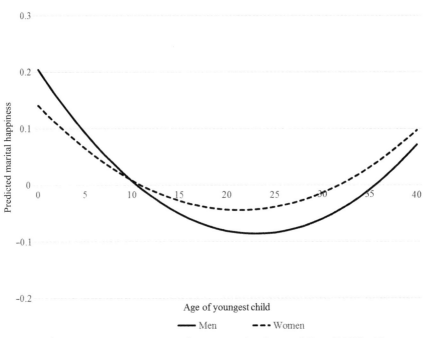

Age of youngest child

——— Men   - - - Women

Note: Authors' own estimations using data reported in Lee and Ono (2008). Happiness measures are standardized to have a mean of zero. Vertical axis shows +/– deviations from the mean.

According to this graph, the happiness of parents drops as soon as the child is born, and recovers as the child becomes older. Interestingly, the low point of happiness occurs when the children are in their 20s—that is, around the age when they start leaving for college. Perhaps it is then that the parents feel relieved from the responsibilities of parenting, and their happiness recovers accordingly.

Researchers examining the link between child age and parental happiness in other cultural contexts have found different trajectories of change. While some find that marital happiness declines with the birth of the first child (McLanahan and Adams 1987; Twenge et al. 2003) others find that overall happiness increases in the years around the birth of a first child but then decreases to levels reported before children were born (Myrskylä and Margolis 2014; Pollmann-Schult 2014).

Why are there these differences in findings across studies? Some of the difference may be attributable to whether the researcher is looking at marital happiness or general happiness, although these are often closely related. More likely, much of the difference may be due to the type of data being analyzed. While some research has analyzed longitudinal data (and in particular the changes in happiness that occur when a child is born), others have relied on cross-sectional data to analyze the association between child age and happiness. When cross-sectional data are analyzed, what appears to be a relationship between age and happiness may actually be one between birth cohort and happiness. The use of cross-sectional data to examine age-related changes in happiness has been widely criticized by life course scholars who argue that such analyses not only fail to distinguish between changes associated with parents' age, children's age, and marital duration, but also fail to distinguish changes that occur for an individual as they age (age effects) from differences across groups of people born in different cohorts (cohort effects) (VanLaningham et al. 2001). For example, some research has found differences across cohorts in marital satisfaction, with more recent cohorts showing greater marital dissatisfaction with parenthood. This means that some of the apparent increase in marital satisfaction with the child's age may actually be attributable to the higher levels of marital satisfaction in older cohort groups.

Second, as we discussed in the earlier chapters, the relationship between children and happiness depends on your gender. Across the countries that we studied, the negative effect of children is greater for mothers than for fathers. Sociologists have pointed out how the increasingly intensive demands of parenting have fallen disproportionately on women (Hays 1996). It is not just the childcare burden that women are disproportionately shouldering; when couples have children, the gendered division of labor becomes much more unequal overall (Yavorsky et al. 2015). It is not all that surprising then that women's happiness is more negatively impacted by children than is men's.

Third, it depends on whether or not you are married and working. Married parents are happier than single parents, probably because they have more support in shouldering the costs of parenthood. Parents in male breadwinner households are happier than dual-career couples because they do not face the same kind of role strain that dual-career households do in trying to balance the demands of the workplace (with expectations of complete devotion to the firm) and the demands of the family (with expectations of intensive parenting). However, this is true only in families in which the stay-at-home parent wants to be at home and feels his or her investment of time in the home is worthwhile. For those stay-at-home parents who would rather be working, we see higher rates of depression and unhappiness (Nelson et al. 2014).

Fourth, it depends on where you live. As we discussed in Chapter 6, the negative effect of children on mothers disappears in the social democratic welfare states. The Scandinavian countries offer extensive benefits to families with small children. The generous support in turn compensates for the disutility of having children and elevates the happiness of mothers and reduces the happiness gap between single and married parents (Nelson et al. 2014).

Divorce, Separation, and Widowhood

If marriage brings happiness, then the opposite is also true. Divorce, separation, and widowhood are sources of great unhappiness. When we look at how happiness varies across marital status, we see these three groups at the bottom of the happiness scale, followed by single persons, cohabiting persons, then married persons. An interesting study by two economists even put a dollar figure on these unfortunate events (Blanchflower and Oswald 2004). The authors estimate that a lasting marriage is worth $100,000 per annum. In other words, a widowed or separated person would have to receive $100,000 per year to compensate for their grief or disutility.

What about the *change* in happiness resulting from a break in marriage? Certainly, not all marriages are happy, and some may ponder the question: Is it better to stay in an unhappy marriage than to get divorced? A 2012 study from the UK, which looked at change in happiness levels before and after life events among 10,000 individuals, showed that happiness levels do increase after divorce (Clark and Georgellis 2013). Here again, the authors discover gender asymmetries. The improvement in women's happiness from divorce was greater compared to their male counterparts. As one author explains in a press release, it may be that "women who enter into an unhappy marriage feel much more liberated after divorce than their male counterparts."[3]

Nonemployment

Having a job may be a great source of economic well-being, but it is also a large component of subjective well-being. While not all persons may be happy in their jobs, studies have consistently shown that people are happier to *have* a job than not to have one.[4] The negative effect of job loss on happiness can be substantial. In the case of men in the United States, Blanchflower and Oswald (2004) estimate that "compensating" men for unemployment would require a rise in income of $60,000 per annum—less than the $100,000 price tag of a broken marriage, but still sizeable.

Unemployment can have devastating effects and aftershocks that are not isolated to job loss. In terms of wages and income, unemployment can leave "scarring effects" (Arulampalam 2001; Gangl 2006) where workers experience a sizeable drop in wages that lingers for many years following unemployment spells. According to Gangl (2006), the scarring effect and its accompanying wage loss can be explained by "stigma effects of unemployment, loss of workers' firm-specific human capital, human capital depreciation through intensified economic restructuring, and constraints on worker search behavior" (p. 988).

Studies have shown that the change in happiness associated with unemployment moves in the same direction as does wage loss. After people experience bouts of unemployment, their happiness drops and over time it gradually increases again. But the level of happiness they return to is lower than their pre-unemployment baseline level. Even after finding work again, there is evidence that people do not fully regain their former level of happiness (Eichhorn 2013). This suggests that unemployment has a deep and persisting effect on an individual's happiness. But like the other factors associated with unhappiness, this effect varies across people and social contexts.

And the effects of nonemployment on unhappiness vary depending on economic, social, and cultural characteristics. This means that when we look across countries (or across time for a single country), we expect to find differences in the relationship between nonemployment and happiness. As we discussed in Chapter 4, the negative effect of not working for men and women may vary across countries, because of different gender roles and expectations. Our findings suggest that in societies with more traditional gender beliefs, men's happiness is much more closely tied to their employment status, perhaps because they are subject to stronger expectations. So men without jobs may feel that they are not fulfilling their expectations. The insecurity and anxiety may lower their happiness. The expectation to work and keep the household running may be weaker for women, so their happiness is not affected by their employment status. In countries with the most egalitarian gender beliefs, on the other hand, men with and without full-time employment are equally happy.

Cultural models of behavior can take a long time to change. These gender asymmetries may be evidence of a cultural lag, with some men (and some women) holding onto a model of marriage from the past. As these cultural models of the appropriate roles for men and women in the family change slowly over time, we would expect to see the implications of nonemployment for men and women's happiness to become more similar.

Economic conditions and beliefs about work may also moderate the impact of not working on happiness. We might expect, for example, that in societies or regions where working is highly valued, where all able-bodied adults are expected to be in the labor force, that nonemployment will have a more devastating effect on happiness. There is some evidence that high unemployment rates buffer the effect of not working on unhappiness, but this effect depends on the level of aggregation at which unemployment is measured (county, state, national) and also whether or not other characteristics of the individual are accounted for as well (Eichhorn 2013). In countries with a higher female labor force participation rate, which may serve as an indicator of how pervasive norms of employment are in a country, the effects of unemployment are more severe. If we look at more direct measures of cultural attitudes about work, in countries where respondents more strongly endorse the importance of work in attitudinal measures, unemployment has a more negative effect on happiness.

We might even expect to find differences within a society in the expectation to work, and therefore, the consequences of not working on happiness. We would expect that in older age groups where it is socially acceptable to not be working (because you have already paid your dues or because of the physical limitations associated with old age), the effects of not working on happiness would be less negative or even positive. Particularly if there is a cultural expectation that retirement should be a time of rest and relaxation after a long career, continued employment could feasibly be associated with unhappiness.

Poor Health and Disability

Our health has a powerful effect on our happiness, more powerful, for example, than income. Poor health, and in particular chronic pain and anxiety, is associated with long-lasting unhappiness. Like income, the relationship between health and happiness (or unhappiness) is complex: Although less healthy members of a given society are more unhappy than healthier members, no such relationship is found looking cross-nationally (Graham 2008). Also, similar to income, the causal arrow between health and happiness runs in both directions. Yes, poor health leads to lower happiness but lower levels of happiness may also lead to poor health. One notable difference from income, though, is the relationship between the health of those around you and your own happiness. While having relatively wealthier people around you is associated with lower happiness, having healthier people around you is actually associated with better health and greater happiness (Graham et al. 2011). In this way, social comparison seems to operate in a different way when we are talking about health compared to wealth. Having healthy people around us may inspire us to adopt healthy behaviors like an active lifestyle and healthy eating.

Research on health and unhappiness suggests that while some health shocks cause only short-term dips in our happiness, other life events are so momentous that we never really recover from them. We have theories that predict that most people have a baseline level of happiness that we may fluctuate around but that we always return to. According to these theories, this return to baseline can be expected following both extremely positive events, like winning the lottery, and extremely negative events, like an accident that results in spinal cord injury.[5] A classic study of our ability to adapt to changing life circumstances looked at these two groups in particular (Brickman et al. 1978). The researchers hypothesized that both lottery winners and accident victims would eventually return to their prior baseline happiness levels for two reasons. One, they expected that after a major positive or negative event, our evaluation of other, everyday events would be changed. In the case of the accident victims, the unhappiness experienced in relation to the accident would be mitigated by the increased pleasure they would experience in every-day events like reading or eating breakfast. Similarly, the lotto winners would experience relatively less pleasure in these mundane events, because they would pale in comparison to the great joy felt at winning the lotto. Second, the authors argued that over time, people get used to the effects of the major event. The pain of the accident erodes over time and the thrill of winning the lotto dissipates as well. For both of these reasons, the authors hypothesized that, over time, people who experienced major life events would return to their previous baseline happiness levels. For a real-life story of someone who not only experienced a return to baseline happiness after winning the lotto but actually a dramatic downward trajectory, see Box 7.1.

But the accident victims did not quite follow the researchers' expectations. They did not take more pleasure in those everyday events and they rated themselves as less happy overall than people in the control group. Other researchers have reached similar conclusions about happiness following dis-ability: Adaptation to disability is not inevitable and disability is associated with lower levels of happiness overall, even several years after the onset of the

---

Box 7.1 Lotto Winnings Do Not Necessarily Buy Happiness

Winning the lotto is not necessarily the ticket to a life of happiness. Happiness researchers argue that over time, individuals who win the lottery will return to their baseline happiness level as new experiences pale in comparison to the joy they felt at winning the big jackpot. One West Virginia man is an extreme ex-ample of how winning the lottery does not necessarily bring happiness. In fact, for Jack Whittaker, winning the lottery was like a curse. Not only did he return to his baseline happiness after winning the $314.9 million Powerball jackpot in 2002, his life took a sharp downward turn after collecting the winnings. According to a *Businessweek* article on the lotto winner, he began drinking, lost his driver's license, and started frequenting strip-clubs, eventually driving away his wife and many friends (Samuels 2012). His granddaughter became addicted to prescription drugs and eventually died of an accidental overdose. Looking back, Whittaker says life was easier before winning the lottery. In his case, money certainly did not buy happiness.

Samuels, David. 2012. "Lottery Winner Jack Whittaker's Losing Ticket." *Businessweek*, December 13. Accessed on June 24, 2015, at: www .businessweek.com/articles/2012-12-13/lottery-winner-jack-whittakers-losing-ticket.

disability (Freedman et al. 2012; Lucas 2007). Anxiety and chronic pain similarly seem to sentence the sufferer with longer-term unhappiness. Compared to other physical impairments, individuals suffering from anxiety or chronic pain seem to have even greater difficulty adapting to their health problems. Oswald and Powdthavee (2008) found a rate of hedonic adaptation to disability between 30 and 50 percent; those suffering from chronic disease and chronic pain had even greater difficulty adapting. Scholars think this may be due to the greater uncertainty surrounding chronic pain and anxiety. Someone with a physical impairment may learn over time what to expect in his or her daily life and may even adjust his or her standard of comparison to others who face similar challenges. Anxiety and chronic pain are more pernicious in that you do not necessarily know when they will strike and this uncertainty may lead to a more persistent unhappiness.

Of course there is likely to be variation in the impact of health on (un)happiness depending on the social context. For example, poorer health in a country with overall poorer health outcomes and limited longevity may be associated with greater happiness than better health in a country with overall better health outcomes and longer lifespans. For example, a higher percentage of Kenyans are happy with their health than are Americans (Graham 2008). Similarly, norms and social stigma may influence the impact of health on (un)happiness. In the United States, obesity is much more strongly related to unhappiness in social groups where obesity is relatively less common—for example, in white-collar professions. In social groups where there is less stigma associated with obesity, there is also less unhappiness attached to it.

SHOULD HAPPINESS BE THE GOAL?

With this understanding of what makes people unhappy, there is an impulse to create policies, programs, interventions to stamp out unhappiness. If we know what makes people unhappy, should we not try to eliminate those conditions from our society? But is this possible or even desirable? Should our goal be to maximize happiness at all times and in all circumstances? Or is there a downside to the relentless pursuit of happiness?

Although happiness is something we all desire, there are perhaps limits to how much happiness is a good thing. Gruber and colleagues (2011) point out that we should consider the downside to too much happiness, pointing out that extreme levels of positive emotion are a marker of emotional dysfunction in clinical populations. Too much happiness may signal a disconnect between the individual and social reality. While it is reasonable to be overwhelmed with joy at the birth of a child or when landing the job of your dreams, a similar outpouring of positive emotion may be inappropriate when eating breakfast or when experiencing the loss of a loved one. The person who does not show appropriate negative emotions in the face of significant life challenges like divorce, serious illness, and death may not receive the same social support as someone who expresses grief and sadness. This is both because others may find the lack of negative emotion off-putting and also because the individual may seem less in need of support. If forming social connections is one of the keys to happiness and a lack of any negative emotion (or an over-abundance of positive emotion at inappropriate times) jeopardizes an individual's ability to form close social relationships, then this lack of negative emotion may have important consequences for the individual's long-term well-being.

A singular focus on happiness and positive thinking may also end up making individuals blame themselves for their own failures and may ultimately lead to lower happiness. According to Gruber and colleagues (2011), the more people strive for happiness, the lonelier they feel and the more likely they will become disappointed with how they feel. Similarly, if people adopt the belief that optimism and positive thinking are the key to success and upward mobility, then they will fail to see the structural constraints of social class, race, ethnicity, and gender in limiting their upward mobility and will focus on their own failure to maintain a happy disposition as being responsible for their lack of success.

Writer Barbara Ehrenreich explores this dark side of happiness and positive thinking in her 2009 book *Bright-Sided: How Positive Thinking Is Undermining America*. Ehrenreich documents how this uniquely American fixation on positive thinking is reinforced in medical communities (e.g., maintaining a positive outlook is the key to beating cancer), corporate culture (e.g., visualization will attract success and wealth), and evangelical religion (e.g., faith and positivity will keep you in God's good favor). The risk of this singular attention to happiness, optimism, and positivity is that it blames the victims for their troubles and it discourages critical thinking.

If positivity is all it takes to ensure your future success and well-being then those who face hardships such as unemployment, marital trouble, even natural disasters must have attracted their ill-fortune through their negativity. Similarly, if a positive outlook is essential to patients' recovery from disease, then it becomes the patients' obligation to push out any sadness or anger over their poor health and to maintain a constant happy disposition. If they fail to do so, then they are responsible for their poor health or failure to achieve remission. In this way, an excessive focus on positivity may drive people to have overly individualistic (and at times almost magical) explanations for social, economic, and health inequality. Instead of focusing on economic redistribution or universal healthcare as structural solutions to these forms of inequality, the positive thinker can blame individuals for their negativity as being ultimately responsible for their poor outcomes. Similarly, by relying on positive thinking, assuming that the best-case scenario will inevitably follow, we may miss real threats to our security. Ehrenreich argues that positive thinking may have been responsible for the financial meltdown in 2008. Instead, she argues we should value critical thinking and a more realistic understanding of the world around us, not one colored by the "cult of positivity."

Overall, this leads us to argue that maximizing happiness, and a singular pursuit of happiness above all else, is misguided. Just because we know what factors are associated with happiness and which are associated with unhappiness, this does not mean that (1) everyone is equally capable of achieving happiness and (2) that happiness alone should be our utopian goal. Instead, the argument we have crafted in this book is that happiness must be understood in context. There are inequalities that exist in our ability to achieve happiness, inequalities that are based on our race, ethnicity, gender, marital status, and social class in particular. In contexts where there are more egalitarian beliefs and attitudes, where different family types are accepted equally, some of these inequalities are lessened. In contexts where there are more progressive social spending programs, where resources are redistributed to working families and those living in poverty, some of these inequalities are lessened.

As we argue in this chapter, the change in happiness resulting from life events, whether it be in a positive or negative direction, is often short lived. As Kahneman and Krueger (2006) explain, "Life events, such as marriage and bereavement, have substantial short-run effects on happiness and life satisfaction, but these effects are mainly temporary" (p. 14). This is another reason to argue, as we did earlier, that a singular pursuit of happiness is inadvisable. The strategy of pursuing marriage for the sake of increasing happiness, for example, would be seriously misguided.

We advocate for policies that reduce economic and social disparities, targeting the structural factors underlying much of the unhappiness we have described in this chapter. Overall, the social policies we discussed in Chapter 6, as well as the more egalitarian social norms and beliefs discussed in Chapter 5, are the most promising avenues for reducing both economic and happiness disparities.

8

Unhappiness in Post-Communist Societies

What was it like to grow up under communism? At least for those of us in the Western world, the answer is that we don't really know. We don't know because information was limited during the Cold War. These were the days before the Internet, and the little information we learned about life in communist countries came from the selective and calculated information that was released from these countries. The arts and entertainment industry pitched in from the West but the images coming from fiction and film were ominous and far from rosy. In spite of the abundance of books and films that stoked our fears for the Cold War (e.g., *Fail Safe*, *Dr. Strangelove*, *War Games*, and the *Hunt for Red October*), we knew very little about the everyday lives of ordinary citizens under communism. Much was left to our imagination, and so we assumed the worst, or worse in comparison to Western democracies.

Partly, the Cold War may have been a necessary evil because the world needed a common enemy. The constant and imminent threat of war kept the Western Bloc united, and politics focused toward outsmarting the external enemy. Bad news coming from the communist countries was good, because it masked our own problems and made the West look better. Based on the logic "The enemy of my enemy is my friend," the world as we knew it was divided in two as communist countries like Russia and China became united in their opposition against the Western countries. It was naturally easier to keep the enemy as an evil dark force where citizens were not free and life was miserable. Centralized planning, rationing of food and supplies, the government as the vigilant "big brother" and controller of information, people working in factories like mindless drones. . . These were the stereotypes of life under communism. In the West, we simply *assumed* that people were unhappy there, and that they wanted to escape the iron grip of communism. The occasional news of citizens who risked their lives by climbing the Wall to escape from the East to the West only confirmed our preconceptions. People wanted to move from East to West to escape the tyranny of oppression, and not the other way around, although some filmmakers poked fun at this polarized view (see Box 8.1). The transition from communism to capitalism must be a transition to happiness. Why would we think otherwise?

Not much has been written, and even less has been empirically studied about happiness under the communist regime. From what little we know, it appears that life under communism was not a happy life indeed. In a rare study, Inglehart and Klingemann (2000) report happiness data from the World Values Survey in Russia in 1981. The results (see Figure 8.1) show that Russia in 1981 was in fact one of the unhappiest places in the world.

Ironically, promoting happiness played a big part in Soviet propaganda. Among the grand titles that Joseph Stalin carried was "Gardener of Human Happiness." Communist-era propaganda posters feature Stalin casting a vote

---

Box 8.1 Cold War Humor through Film

Letter to Brezhnev (1985) is a romantic comedy film produced during the height of the Cold War. It is a story about Teresa and Elaine, who are two working class women in Liverpool, England. The two women work in a meatpacking factory, and see no future in their lives. Elaine falls in love with a Russian sailor who happens to be visiting Liverpool. She knows little about life in Russia, but aspires to move there because she believes that anything is better than her mundane life in Liverpool. Teresa is just as miserable working in the meat factory, but she chooses to stay in England because it is the only life she knows.

Elaine faces fierce opposition from friends, family, and others who try to convince her that she is about to make a very bad decision. A newspaper reporter tells her that "most people want to get out of Russia, not get in." The foreign ministry official explains that she must "give up everything." The following conversation with a reporter highlights the stylized view of communism during the Cold War and Elaine's unorthodox and rebellious attitude.

REPORTER: Surely it must make you feel a bit strange. . . going to a country with food shortages and lack of freedom.
ELAINE: Have you been there?
REPORTER: No, I haven't been there.
ELAINE: Then how do you know about food shortages and lack of freedom? You just take a walk. . . around here and you'll soon see food shortages. . . . Going to live in Russia can't be any worse than living here. So why are you trying to discourage me from escaping?

Figure 8.1 Collapse of Communism and Decline of Subjective Well-Being in Russia

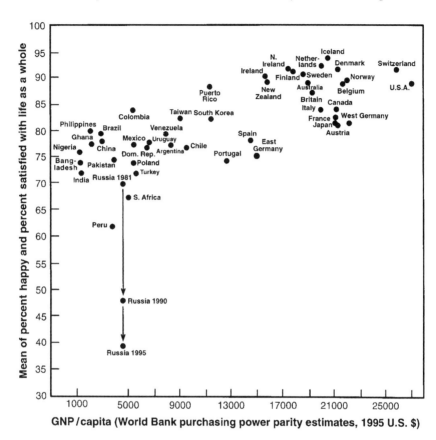

GNP / capita (World Bank purchasing power parity estimates, 1995 U.S. $)

"for the people's happiness." Just like under capitalism, where the pursuit of happiness was hailed as one of our fundamental rights in Western societies, happiness appears to have been an important part of the communist agenda during the Soviet era.

In recent years, happiness data are being collected and analyzed among the post-communist countries. As we observed in Chapters 3 and 6, we are now learning that one of the greatest sources of unhappiness at the country-level is whether one lives in a post-communist society or not. Looking back at Figure 3.3 from Chapter 3, we can see a systematic pattern where these countries of the former Soviet blocs are clustered in the lower left corner—that is, low national income and low happiness. There is now overwhelming evidence that these so-called transition economies that transitioned from centrally planned economy to market economy rank among the unhappiest countries in the world.

But what is most shocking is that happiness declined even more after the transition. Happiness was already low under communism. However (at least in our Western minds) we were hopeful that the end of the Cold War would bring greater happiness to the former-communist countries. One would assume that the transition from communism to capitalism, from controlled economy to market economy, and from tyranny and oppression to democracy and freedom would make people happier. But, in fact, the end of the Cold War had the opposite effect. Inglehart and Klingemann (2000) report happiness data for two transition economies—Hungary and Russia—before the transition (around 1981) and after. In both countries, happiness dropped dramatically to an even lower level after the transition. The case of Russia is illustrated in Figure 8.1. We can see that happiness in 1981 was the high point for Russia, although it was already low relative to other countries even then. But happiness plummeted to unforeseen levels in 1990 immediately following the collapse of the Soviet Union, and even more so in 1995. According to Inglehart et al. (2013), Russia recorded "the world's lowest level of subjective well-being, in fact, the lowest levels ever recorded" (p. 4). Similarly, Easterlin (2010) examined life satisfaction data from 13 Eastern European countries and showed a consistent pattern of decline among all 13 countries immediately following the transition, specifically around the years 1990 to 1994.[1] In some countries, life satisfaction bounced back after 1994, resulting in a V-shaped recovery.

Why are the people in post-communist societies so unhappy? Why does the transition from communism to capitalism lower people's happiness, and not the other way around? This chapter explores these questions in great depth. We first discuss the sources of unhappiness among the post-communist countries. We then examine unhappiness in two particular countries—Bulgaria, because it is consistently ranked among the unhappiest countries in the world, and China, because empirical data are finally becoming available and we are just beginning to get a glimpse of the state of well-being in this country of 1.4 billion people.[2]

SOURCES OF UNHAPPINESS

Unhappiness in post-communist countries comes from many sources. First, the transition from centrally planned economy to market economy did not improve people's lives. Rather, the transition left these countries worse off, with many still struggling to recover to pre-transition levels. Easterlin (2010) explains the economic facts of the transition process:

> Most notable was an abrupt and massive economic collapse, with measured GDP falling to levels of around 50 to 85 percent of the 1989 level, usually in a few years or less. Subsequently GDP recovered somewhat,

though rarely by 1999 to the initial level. A visiting economist from Mars, confronted only with these GDP data, might well conclude that an economic disaster on the scale of the Great Depression had befallen some 400 million of the world's population. (p. 83)

As economic conditions worsened, so did the job market. Easterlin explains that the 13 countries experienced a "sharp deterioration in employment conditions . . . with most countries experiencing double digit declines (in employment rates)" (p. 92). Considering that these countries operated at virtually full employment under communism, the deteriorating labor market conditions had a sizeable negative impact on happiness.

The poor performance of the transition economies has left dark impressions on the people. Citing a large-scale survey of 28,000 individuals in 28 transition countries, Guriev and Zhuravskaya (2009) report that half of the respondents in these countries believe that the transition has not brought any gains at all. According to a 2009 Pew Research Center survey, the majority of those surveyed in Russia, Ukraine, Lithuania, Slovakia, Bulgaria, and Hungary felt that they were better off economically under communism. In a study of six transition countries—Bulgaria, Hungary, Poland, Romania, Russia, and Slovakia—Czismady (2003) explains that "[w]ithout exception, interviewees in all countries remembered that they had a better life in 1988 than in 2000" (p. 5).

There is also the widespread misconception that people lived miserably under communism. Many Westerners have a strong conviction that these countries were liberated from the iron grip of communism and substandard level of living. The path toward democracy and free market capitalism must be a path toward happiness and prosperity. But for the people in transition economies, the reality was quite different. Many claim that they lived well and were in fact happier back then, as illustrated in Figure 8.1 in the case of Russia, before and after the transition. Under communism, people were fully "insured" under a comprehensive safety net, and people were guaranteed employment, education, and healthcare. One writer explains in the case of Hungary: "Communist Hungary, far from being hell on earth, was in fact, a rather fun place to live."[3] Another blogger reminisces the past, and explains that the people lived better then:[4]

> The dismantling of socialism has, in a word, been a catastrophe, a great swindle that has not only delivered none of what it promised, but has wreaked irreparable harm. . . . Numberless voices in Russia, Romania, East Germany and elsewhere lament what has been stolen from them—and from humanity as a whole: "We lived better under communism. We had jobs. We had security."

Unsurprisingly, the decline in satisfaction following the transition is most acute in the life domains where support was assured prior to the transition

(Easterlin 2010). For example, citing the former German Democratic Republic as an example, Easterlin explains that the largest drop in satisfaction was in the domains of childcare, work, and health. In contrast, gains in satisfaction were reported in material consumption, such as goods availability and dwelling. These findings are thus consistent with our main message from Chapter 6, which underscores the important link between social safety nets and happiness. Removing the safety net that people took for granted prior to the transition has significantly lowered people's subjective well-being and perceived quality of life.

Naturally, nostalgia and the longing for the communist past are felt more acutely among the older generation—that is, the people who grew up under communism. Iyengar (2010) explains:

> A remarkable 97 percent of East Germans reported being dissatisfied with German democracy and more than 90 percent believed socialism was a good idea in principle, one that had just been poorly implemented in the past. This longing for the Communist era is so widespread that there's a German word for it: *Ostalgie*, a portmanteau of *Ost* (east) and *Nostalgie* (nostalgia). How is it possible that Berliners went from that wild celebration of November 1989 to wanting to return to the very system they had longed to dismantle? (p. 62)

Consequently, we observe a considerable happiness gap between the old and the young in the transition economies (see Figure 8.2). Recall from Chapter 2 that happiness is typically U-shaped with respect to age. This is indeed the case among the *non*-transition countries shown in Figure 8.2. Happiness is high among young people, sinks to a low among middle-aged people, then recovers again among older people. This U-shaped curve does not exist in transition countries. Happiness declines with age, period. Data from Eurostat released in March 2015 also confirm this general trend in post-communist countries, especially in Bulgaria, where older people report happiness levels substantially lower than younger people.[5] This may be attributable to declining happiness with chronological age or to cohort differences: The older generation predominantly believes that life was better under communism. Market capitalism did not improve their quality of life, but made it worse.

Second, there is a deep sense of injustice and powerlessness among the citizens. People had high expectations that the transition toward the market economy would bring about a meritocratic society where there would be ample opportunities for advancement based on effort and achievement. The transition and its accompanying market reforms fell greatly short of people's expectations, and optimism was replaced by hopelessness. In the case of Hungary, Bukodi and Goldthorpe (2010) demonstrate that the transition from state socialism to market capitalism was not accompanied by meritocracy.

Figure 8.2 Age and Life Satisfaction in Transition Countries and Nontransition Countries with per Capita Income Comparable to Transition Countries

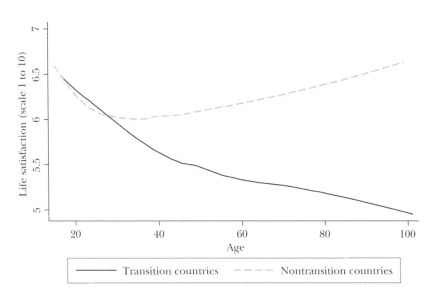

Note: The lines depict the results of nonparametric, locally weighted regressions with bandwidth = 0.8.
Source: Reprinted from Guriev and Zhuravskaya (2009).

In a sociological sense, blocked opportunities and unfulfilled expectations are sources of anomie that can lead to great frustration and dissatisfaction. After the transition, the people experienced "relative deprivation" (Merton 1968)—that is, a large gap emerged between what could have been achieved in contrast to what actually transpired. Summarizing the results from the aforementioned survey of six transition countries, Czismady (2003) explains that people report having experienced less relative deprivation and poverty under communism, in this case, 1988 compared to 2000.

Hopes of well-functioning markets were displaced by widespread corruption and organized crime following the transition. Romania, Bulgaria, Croatia, Slovakia, Czech Republic, Latvia, and other transition countries consistently rank among the most corrupt countries in the European Union according to Transparency International. The transition countries also rank low in the "trust index."[6] Overall, the transition has left these countries with a deep sense of injustice and unfairness. People feel powerless as they perceive that nothing can be done to overcome these market failures.

Third, many people of the post-communist countries experienced depreciation or devaluation of the skills that they had acquired prior to the transition (Guriev and Zhuravskaya 2009). In economic terms, people invest in their human capital expecting to collect the benefits through higher lifetime

earnings. Unfortunately, many who were educated under the command economy accumulated skills that became irrelevant, hence valueless, for the market economy. Consequently, many people lost their jobs and were forced to
reallocate and to adapt to the new labor market dynamics. For example, an
economics professor who had dedicated his life to studying Marxist ideology
in Romania will find no demand for his knowledge and skills, and he will be
forced to find work elsewhere.[7] Undoubtedly, the loss of purpose feeds into
the anomie of post-communism.

Guriev and Zhuravskaya (2009) find some empirical support for the
hypothesis that lower satisfaction following the transition is linked to human
capital depreciation. Specifically, they show that life satisfaction is higher
among people who were still enrolled in school when the transition started,
compared to the people who had graduated just before the transition. They
offer the following interpretation:

> A person who graduated just before transition and had secured a nice
> job is unhappy after the transition as this job is likely to be discontinued
> or paid less. A person who graduates right after the transition makes an
> informed career choice and therefore is happier. This explanation is
> very similar to the human capital depreciation story. (p. 165)

UNHAPPINESS IN BULGARIA

As we can see from Table 3.1 in Chapter 3, Bulgaria has the misfortune
of recording the lowest happiness level among the countries included in
the 2002 ISSP data. (Bulgaria had to be dropped in our empirical analyses
in Chapters 5 and 6 because of missing data in some crucial areas.) Other
sources also confirm this low standing; Bulgaria was ranked the unhappiest
country in the European Union according to the 2015 Eurostat survey.[8]

Like in other former communist countries, people had great expectations
toward the transition to capitalism in Bulgaria. Achieving membership status in
the European Union in 2007 was viewed as significant progress toward market
reform, and fueled people's expectations even higher. Sadly, these expectations
were largely unfulfilled, leaving a void and an overall feeling of betrayal and
hopelessness. The plunge from being the poster-child under communism to the
worst performing country in the EU (on the basis of GDP per capita in 2014)
left its citizens with an identity crisis and a sense of inferiority accompanied by
nostalgia and longing for the communist past. Rising inequality between the
rich and the poor did not nurture a hard work ethic (as may have been the case
in the United States [see Chapter 3]), but instilled a sense of social injustice and
unfairness among the people (Boyadjieva and Kabakchieva 2015).

> For a large part of Bulgarian society, the functional usefulness of inequal-
> ity remains doubtful. Inequalities do not mobilize the creative potential

and resources of individuals and social groups. Rather, they mainly seem to create a sense of injustice and abnormality, and as such constitute a threat to social integration. (p.632)

These demoralizing conditions have not only lowered the happiness and well-being of its citizens, but have also led to a massive population shrinkage in Bulgaria. Feeling powerless and seeing little hope in the nation's future, it was "no surprise that most people preferred 'exit' over 'voice,' choosing to leave in search of a better future abroad, rather than stay and fight for change" (Boyadjieva and Kabakchieva 2015, p. 633). Poverty and disconnected social networks prevented civil protest and social movements because the people were unable to collectively mobilize resources.

Consequently, Bulgaria now suffers from a serious brain drain of its skill base. As Figure 8.3 shows, Bulgaria's population grew at a steady pace in the postwar period, reaching a peak of 9 million persons in 1988. Since then, the country has experienced an enormous out-migration. Compounded by mortality rates that exceed fertility rates, the country has now shrunk to 7.2 million persons (in 2014), a loss of nearly 2 million people since 1988.

Since market wages were significantly lower in Bulgaria, workers fled the country in search of higher wages elsewhere.[9] Most were younger workers

Figure 8.3 Population Change in Bulgaria

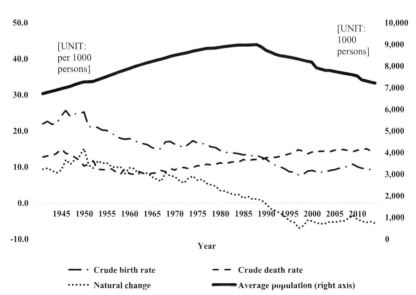

Source: United Nations.

between the ages of 25 and 50. This mass exodus of the younger generation has severely hurt Bulgaria's efforts to rebuild its economy. Although the
country is in dire need of young talent to move the country forward, many
have emigrated because, as one newspaper explained, "It is now easier to go
to Germany than to make Bulgaria function like Germany."[10]

More recently, there are signs of rebellion as young people have taken to
the streets to voice their frustrations. In 2013, students at Sofia University
launched an Occupy Movement to protest their frustrations and demanded
action from their government (see Box 8.2). Cleaning up the government,
implementing market reforms, and regaining people's trust are required first
steps to stop the brain drain, and to rebuild the path toward happiness in
Bulgaria.

Box 8.2 Occupy Movement in Sofia, Bulgaria

While the old may reminisce the communist past, the young too harbor their
frustrations. Inspired by the Occupy Wall Street movement, college students
at Sofia University in Bulgaria took part in an Occupy Movement in 2013.
They occupied the main building of the University, and launched an antigov-
ernment movement protesting the widespread corruption in government and
politics. The students demanded, among other things, government transparency and accountability and the resignation of the (then) prime minister.
Their icon, a fist of solidarity reminiscent of the communist past, could be
seen around the streets of Sofia as supporters of the movement joined the
cause. The students explained their position in a statement read to the public
on October 25, 2013:

> [We are] angered by the systemic violations of constitutional order in the
> country by the current government led by Plamen Oresharski. . . . [Our]
> ultimate goal is for Bulgaria to become a country with governance,
> grounded in moral values rather than personal benefits.

Source: Thomas Seymat, "Bulgarian Students Join Anti-Government Protests, Occupy
University Buildings." *Euronews*, October 28, 2013.

Although the protests did not become violent, the students were palpably
frustrated at the blocked opportunities and unattainable goals that their generation confronted, and impatient at the lack of response and action taken by
the government toward reform. For the students, clean politics and government transparency were the core foundations of a moral society, and a path to
true happiness.

UNHAPPINESS IN CHINA

Like the other communist countries, data on happiness and well-being from China are scant. But based on what we know, the trend in well-being following China's transition to market capitalism is largely consistent with the Easterlin paradox—that is, there is a disconnect between life satisfaction and economic performance over time. In fact, life satisfaction in China actually declined during the same period that the country experienced unprecedented economic growth and significant improvements in quality of life measures such as the Human Development Index (Graham et al. 2015). Citing data from the Gallup Organization, Kahneman and Krueger (2006) show that the proportion of individuals responding "satisfied" declined and the proportion responding "dissatisfied" increased from 1994 to 2005, a period during which China's average real income rose by 250 percent (see Figure 8.4).[11] Graham et al. (2015) explain that the declines in life satisfaction were accompanied by increases in suicide rates and incidence of mental illness. Easterlin et al. (2012) show a similar decline in life satisfaction using data from the World Values Survey, with recent trends showing some recovery after 2005. They surmise that "China's life satisfaction over the last two decades has largely followed the trajectory seen in the central and eastern European transition countries" (p. 9778).

What are the sources of unhappiness in China? Unlike the former Soviet states, China did not suffer from an economic collapse following the transition. But like the former Soviet states, China did experience a deterioration

Figure 8.4 Life Satisfaction in China, 1994 to 2005

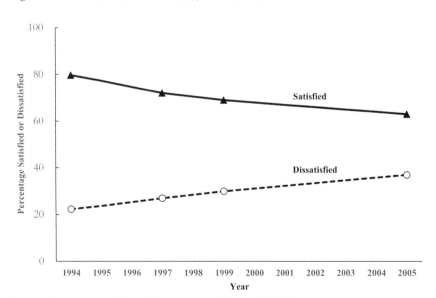

Source: Reconstructed from Kahneman and Krueger (2006).

of the social safety net and increasing inequality in its path to market capitalism. Like the former Soviet states, people were guaranteed employment under communist China. Invariably, the transition from command economy to market economy resulted in a significant increase in unemployment. Owing to rapid industrialization and privatization, approximately 70 percent of the Chinese population (mostly rural area residents) was not covered by health insurance prior to the health care reform of 2011. As Easterlin (2010) explains, these devastating conditions following the transition "have exerted in both China and Europe a similar drag on life satisfaction" (p. 95).

Speaking about the point of rising inequality, we now know that the transition benefited the upper crust of Chinese society compared to the rest (see Figure 8.5). When broken down into income categories, life satisfaction in China between 1990 and 2007 declined for the middle-third and lower-third income groups, but actually increased (albeit marginally) for the upper-third (Easterlin et al. 2012). Income inequality increased due to the greater economic disparities between urban and rural areas, in terms of wages, wealth, employment opportunities, and so on. (Graham et al. 2015). The deteriorating safety net compounded by the movement toward privatization also generated greater inequality. The transition toward a more market-driven system widened the gap between those who can afford certain services versus those who cannot. It is unsurprising then that the transition resulted in the increased dissatisfaction of the poor in post-communist China.

Figure 8.5 Life Satisfaction in China by Income Categories, 1990 and 2007

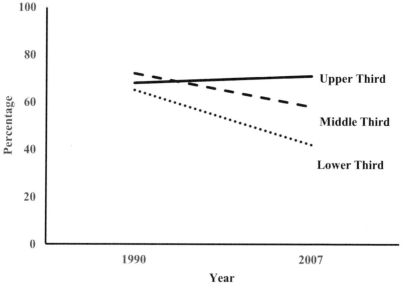

* Vertical axis shows percent responding 7–10 on a scale of 1–10.
Source: Easterlin et al. 2012.

Finally, it is worth noting that the deteriorating safety net unduly coincided with the timing of improved economic performance and rising aspirations. As discussed previously, relative deprivation is a probable cause of people's frustrations and anxiety.[12] People had high aspirations toward a better society in post-communist China but were disillusioned by the realities that emerged. Relative deprivation was presumably stronger among the large population who migrated from rural to urban areas, but were unable to secure jobs because of rising unemployment in urban areas. Life satisfaction in China is now significantly lower in urban areas compared to rural areas (Graham et al. 2015). Easterlin et al. (2012) describe the growing disconnect between economic well-being and life satisfaction in China, and conclude by emphasizing the importance of examining life satisfaction as a more comprehensive measure of well-being.

> The GDP measure registers the spectacular average improvement in material living conditions, whereas the measure of life satisfaction demonstrates that among ordinary people, especially the less-educated and lower income segments of the population, life satisfaction has declined noticeably as material aspirations have soared and concerns have arisen about such critical matters as finding and holding a job, securing reliable and affordable health care, and providing for children and the elderly. Clearly, life satisfaction is the more comprehensive and meaningful indicator of people's life circumstances and well-being. (p. 9779)

DISCUSSION

In this chapter, we examined the sources of unhappiness in post-communist countries. Although these countries were unhappy places under communism, what is more surprising is that they became even less happy after the transition. Many of the countries struggled to implement effective market mechanisms. The political void following the collapse of communism led to opportunistic behavior, widespread corruption and most crucially, the deterioration of the safety net. The transition to market capitalism altered the demand for human capital, and many workers suffered from a devaluation of their skills.

The deterioration of the social safety net is a consistent source of dissatisfaction in the post-communist countries, among the former Soviet states and in contemporary China. Communism may not have provided a high quality of life, but the people were fully insured in important life domains such as healthcare, education, and work. For the people, the market was clearly not the solution, at least in these life domains. As services that were formerly provided through public means were replaced by privatized markets, inequality widened between those who have access to the services and those who do not. Since these countries operated under virtually full employment, joblessness invariably resulted in lower aspirations and will to work. The deteriorating conditions following the transition led to a growing sense of injustice, powerlessness, and longing for the communist past. These sentiments combined have resulted in an overall negative impact on life satisfaction.

A lesson in happiness learned from the transition economies, if any, is that the social safety net plays an important role in sustaining our well-being. Following our discussion from Chapter 6, this safety net is especially important in preserving the well-being of the less privileged and high-risk demographic groups. What made the experiences of post-communism bittersweet especially for the older generation is that their lives were fully insured under communism. Many are nostalgic for the communist past because they felt more secure under the communist regime. Ironically, having experienced life under communism may have been worse than never having experienced it at all.

9

Conclusions

WHAT IS HAPPINESS AND HOW DO WE STUDY IT?

We have made the case in this book that happiness is a measurable outcome and that individuals are their own best judge of their happiness. In the introduction, we discussed how this claim alone is still controversial for some scholars. Some will insist: How can something as ephemeral and subjective as happiness be reliably captured using our social science methods? In anticipation of this critique, we have discussed the various ways of measuring happiness that social scientists employ: survey questions asking individuals to rank their happiness on a scale at one point in time, panel (or longitudinal) studies that follow individuals over time tracking variation in their happiness that occur along with their major life events as well as historical and economic events, daily diaries that ask respondents to report how happy they are feeling at various times during the day. Each of these ways of measuring happiness has its strengths and weaknesses and ultimately each can be used to answer different types of questions about happiness. The cross-sectional survey measures we used in our analyses from the ISSP dataset are not ideal for tracking change in an individual's happiness over time but they are well-suited to our comparative questions about happiness in different cultural contexts.

WHAT DO WE KNOW ABOUT WHAT MAKES PEOPLE HAPPY OR UNHAPPY?

In Chapter 2, we reviewed previous research on the individual characteristics associated with happiness, largely based on the work of psychologists. We discussed how optimistic and extraverted individuals tend to be happier and that this may be connected to certain genetic predispositions. We looked at how friends can boost our happiness (and in fact, even the friends of a friend's friends can!), and reviewed research shows that married people are happier than cohabiting people (a point we return to in Chapter 5). We talked about children, how although they may bring us a sense of meaning and purpose, they generally are associated with unhappiness, particularly for women. We talked in more depth about children and unhappiness in Chapter 7 and explored how the association between children and happiness might vary depending on the social-institutional context in Chapter 6. We reviewed the research showing that, overall, women, religious people, white people, wealthy people, highly educated people, and older people tend to be happier.

In Chapter 3, we discussed the sources of happiness at the societal level. These include macro-economic indicators such as national income and gross domestic product, and social-institutional features such as religious context and gender climate. Using a simple correlation table, we showed that many of these societal-level features are not strongly correlated with aggregate happiness. But, we also returned to the point that as sociologists we cannot take these associations at face value. The individual characteristics that we studied in Chapter 2 must be analyzed in the particular social-institutional context, which we lay out in Chapter 3. These chapters laid the groundwork for us to study the interplay of individual- and societal-factors in predicting happiness.

In Chapters 4, 5, and 6, we presented our own cross-national research on happiness. Building on the happiness literature reviewed in Chapters 2 and 3, we selected the individual and social-institutional factors that we hypothesized were the key predictors of happiness cross-nationally. In Chapter 4, we started with a narrowly focused investigation of just one type of happiness in two countries. We examined marital happiness in the United States and Japan and found that because of differences in the social norms and workplace policies of these two countries, the factors associated with marital happiness for men and women are quite different. Surprisingly, we found that the sources of marital happiness were compatible between U.S. men and Japanese women.

In Chapters 5 and 6, we broadened our analysis to look at general happiness in an international context. In Chapter 5, we set out to analyze the happiness gap between married and cohabiting individuals that we first introduced in Chapter 2. We hypothesized that social-institutional factors like the gender beliefs or religious beliefs in a society would play an important role in shaping the relative happiness of these two groups. That was exactly what we found: although married people report significantly greater happiness in more gender traditional and religious societies, there is no measurable happiness gap between married and cohabiting people in countries with more progressive gender beliefs and weaker religious beliefs. We argued that this suggests the happiness benefits of marriage are not something intrinsic to marriage as an institution but rather stem from the greater social and institutional support provided to married couples than cohabiting couples. In Chapter 6, we set out to examine the possibility that the redistributive properties of the social democratic welfare states may generate an alternate form of "happiness inequality" by transferring resources from low-risk to high-risk groups. We found that transfers and public social expenditures on welfare do not make everyone happier. Instead, redistribution raises the happiness of women with small children, cohabiting people, and the poor, while lowering it for single persons and the rich. The welfare state not only redistributes income from rich to poor, but it also reduces the happiness gap between them.

In Chapters 7 and 8, we shifted our focus from happiness to unhappiness. In Chapter 7, we examined the key predictors of unhappiness for individuals. We returned to the question of children and why they are so consistently associated with lower happiness. We also looked at divorce, widowhood, nonemployment, poor health, and disability as predictors of unhappiness. We asked to what extent people recover from negative life events and return to their previous levels of happiness and also asked to what extent we should be relentless in our pursuit of happiness—should happiness be the ultimate goal? In Chapter 8, we examined sources of unhappiness in the unhappiest countries of the world, namely the post-communist countries. Following our discussion in Chapter 6, we emphasize the importance of a social safety net as an important means to sustain people's well-being and quality of life.

HOW DOES THIS RELATE TO SOCIOLOGY?

Throughout this book, we have emphasized that happiness must be studied in context. This builds on Mills's (1959) discussion of the sociological imagination as being attuned to the intersection of history and biography. As sociologists, this is what we do. We look at behaviors and attitudes and even happiness as shaped and constrained by the social-institutional context in which the individual is living. The same individual characteristics (income, gender, marital status, parental status etc.) have different consequences for our happiness depending on where we live. Therefore, it does not make sense to study these characteristics in a vacuum, nor does it make sense to analyze the association between these individual characteristics and happiness in a particular cultural context and assume that the same association exists everywhere. If we are to understand what makes people happy, or unhappy, we must study how an individual's characteristics matter differently depending on the laws, norms, and societal beliefs associated with his or her context.

Chapters 4, 5 and 6 demonstrated the effectiveness of the sociological approach empirically. For example, we found that cohabiting persons are less happy than married persons in some places, but this happiness gap is larger for women. Moreover, the happiness gap disappears in a social context that embraces a more egalitarian view toward gender and marriage. In other words, whether a woman can achieve happiness in cohabitation depends on social norms, and on the behavior of others. They are less happy in traditional societies that enforce the institution of marriage that may stigmatize cohabitation as a threat to marriage. They are happier in more egalitarian and progressive societies where cohabitation is widely accepted and receives institutional support.

It is worth noting that our research for the most part shows that women are more sensitive to the context than are men's. The effect of cohabitation just mentioned is one example. Another example is the negative effect of children on happiness, which has been a consistent theme throughout our book. The negative effect of children applies mostly to women, and less to men but it also depends on the social context. It affects most the women who live in countries with low institutional support for families, presumably because of the disproportionate burden of childbearing that women shoulder in these countries (see discussion under "Happiness and Fertility Policy"). It does not affect women who live in the Scandinavian welfare states. In contrast, men's happiness is not affected by the presence of children, regardless of context. For all intents and purposes, and quite literally to its meaning, the universal model of man (or the universal model of happiness) as proposed by economists may apply to "men," but does not apply to women.

The one exception where men's well-being is sensitive to the context is in the area of employment. It appears that men around the world still aspire to and identify with the male breadwinner model. Full-time employment has a positive effect on happiness for men, but has no effect for women. Moreover, the positive effect of being employed is much stronger for men in societies that embrace more traditional gender roles. From the women's perspective, our analysis revealed that wives find happiness in marriage by being supported by their husbands in a more gender-traditional society such as Japan but not so in a more gender equal society such as the United States (Chapter 4). The closer attention to gender roles and the cultural milieu underscores the role of social context in shaping happiness.

HOW DOES THIS INFORM PUBLIC POLICY?

Some scholars have argued that the goal for public policy is to maximize happiness (Layard, 2005). Brooks (2008) argues that in order to protect America's overall level of happiness, policy makers must prioritize the defense of religious traditions, family life, freedom, and economic opportunity (over economic equality). While we applaud the attention to subjective well-being (and not just economic well-being) in the formulation of policy, we wonder what it means to maximize the happiness of a society. We have shown that happiness for some may come at the cost of unhappiness for others. The same norms or policies have different implications for the happiness of different groups. We can imagine social policies that boost the happiness of the wealthy by a lot while reducing the happiness of the poor only a little.

Other scholars have suggested that making everyone happy is not a desirable goal. Nettle (2005) and Ehrenreich (2009) both make the case that a society in which unhappiness is eliminated and people face no struggle, no challenge, no uncertainty, no pain, is the subject of many dystopian science fiction novels. Nettle (2005, p. 172) claims, "It is necessary to have the possibility of unhappiness for happiness to have any meaning." There is a concern that without the threat of becoming unhappy, we would become complacent, unwilling to strive for a better life.

Our analyses call for an attention to who wins and who loses in terms of happiness when a policy is implemented; this is different than advocating for policies that make everyone happy or even ones that maximize happiness. (See Box 9.1 for a discussion of the critiques of the policy intended

---

Box 9.1 Gross National Happiness as a Measure of National Progress?

In 1972, the mountain kingdom of Bhutan adopted a policy that would bring global attention to this small country. Instead of using gross national product (GNP) as the primary measure of the welfare of its citizenry, Bhutan's fourth king declared that national policy and development plans would be oriented to fostering gross national happiness (GNH). Even the 2008 Constitution of Bhutan was drafted to include a statement that the State should "promote those conditions that will enable the pursuit of Gross National Happiness" (Ura et al. 2012). This attention to measures of well-being that transcend economic well-being and include spiritual and emotional well-being was applauded by the international community, including the UN's declaration of an "International Day of Happiness," in support of a more holistic understanding of human welfare.

But what does GNH actually measure? And what is left out when GNH is used as the measure of the welfare of an entire country? There is evidence that although Bhutanese citizens scored highly on measures of values, showing high levels of agreement on key social issues in Bhutan, on other measures such as happiness with "literacy, employment opportunities, government services and schooling," citizens reported considerably less happiness (Beattie 2014).

Policies that promise to maximize the happiness of the population as a whole in reality usually benefit certain groups in the population while taking away from others. For example, although the measure of GNH prioritizes common values in society, this potentially further ostracizes the country's Nepali-speaking minority who have been forcefully displaced since the 1980s (Beattie 2014). Some also argue that in prioritizing happiness maximization, much-needed initiatives to improve literacy and employment opportunities are neglected.

to maximize happiness in Bhutan.) A policy may have good intentions, but any disturbance to the status quo will generate a new type of "happiness inequality."

Layard (2005) goes on to suggest that in our quest to maximize human happiness, the happiness of different groups should be weighted differently—it is more important to reduce suffering than to generate extreme happiness. While we do not privilege the happiness of certain groups over the happiness of other groups on moral grounds, we do agree with the mindset that this is a zero-sum game. Policies that allocate resources to particular groups are necessarily going to make some people happier and others less happy. When creating policy, policymakers must take into consideration this trade-off. When some groups win, others lose. Depending on the goals of the policy, that may be an acceptable trade-off. For example, a pro-family policy that favors families with small children may leave single people less happy, but it may have the overall effect of encouraging marriage and family formation. If the policy objective is to eliminate poverty, imposing high taxes on the rich may lower their happiness, but it may lift the happiness of the poor through redistribution.

Next, we detail the implications of our research for policy addressing economic inequality, declining marriage, and declining fertility rates. Throughout our discussion, we highlight the winners and losers from each policy and, in some cases, challenge existing policies that serve to further reinforce disparities in happiness between groups and that offer little hope of addressing the social problem at hand.

Economic Inequality and Happiness Inequality

Income inequality has been growing in most OECD countries since the 1980s. Figure 9.1 shows the change in the Gini coefficient in OECD countries between 1985 and 2008. The Gini coefficient is a measure of income inequality that we discussed in earlier chapters; it ranges from 0 in a country where everyone has the same income to 1 in a country where all the income goes to one person. There is considerable variation in inequality across the OECD countries, with the highest levels in Mexico, Chile, Israel, Turkey, and the United States and lower levels in the Nordic countries and many continental European countries. As the figure shows, inequality increased in many countries between 1985 and 2008 and it grew the most in countries with some of the lower levels of inequality in the 1980s: Germany, Denmark, and Sweden.

The United States is an example of a country with a particularly high level of inequality. The growing economic inequality in the United States since the late 1970s has been a hot topic of conversation among politicians,

Figure 9.1 Change in Income Inequality, 1985–2008

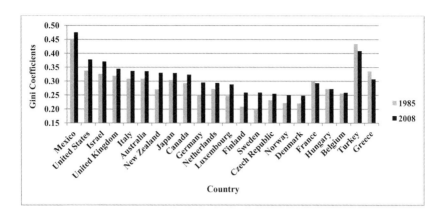

Source: OECD Database on Household Income Distribution and Poverty.

journalists, and scholars. Economist and *New York Times* columnist Paul Krugman (2007) has referred to this period of growing economic inequality as "the Great Divergence," pointing to the fact that between 1979 and 2005 the real income of the median household rose only 13 percent, but the income of the richest 0.1 percent of Americans rose 296 percent. In his 2015 *Economic Report of the President*, President Barack Obama focused on the challenges of rising income inequality. Scholars have tried to explain what is driving the overall trend toward increased inequality. Family scholars in particular have highlighted that inequality has grown fastest among families with children. Between 1975 and 2005, families with children experienced at least twice the growth in income inequality experienced by all other workers over this period (McCall and Percheski 2010; Western et al. 2008).

In response to the growth of income inequality in the United States, there has been a call for greater redistribution of wealth. In his 2015 state of the union address, President Barack Obama advocated for wealth redistribution as a means of addressing this growing inequality, in particular by funding affordable, high-quality childcare and two years of free community college through taxes levied on the wealthy. Former secretary of labor, Robert Reich, similarly argues that economic redistribution is the only way to fix the economy. Our research sheds light on who will benefit, and who will not, from policies to further the redistribution of wealth.

Scholars have made arguments on both sides of the political aisle regarding the effect of social welfare spending on happiness. Brooks (2008) argues that "happiness is easiest to find in limited government," citing research that as public social spending increases, the proportion of the population reporting they are happy declines. Rothstein (2010), on the other hand, argues that a more "generous and encompassing" welfare state makes people happier. Our argument is somewhere in between. We argued in Chapter 6 that under the redistribution policy of the social democratic welfare states, the happiness of the poor is raised and the happiness of the wealthy is lowered. If resources are redistributed to families through universal childcare programs and parental leave programs (as suggested under the Obama administration), then it is plausible to foresee that the happiness of families will increase while the happiness of single people will decline, as we demonstrated in our study. Redistribution creates both winners and losers. We think it makes sense to analyze which groups are advantaged and which groups are disadvantaged, rather than making claims about the impact of public expenditures on society as a whole.

We, therefore, advocate for a more nuanced understanding of the implications of redistribution policies for the happiness of different social and economic groups. Policymakers must consider the trade-offs in designing policies to address economic inequality, rather than relying on claims that social spending either makes everyone better, or worse, off.

Finally, our study of unhappiness in post-communist countries (Chapter 8) reveals an important lesson that underscores the importance of the social safety net. Contrary to conventional views, happiness declined among post-communist countries following their transition to capitalism. A key reason for their unhappiness was the deterioration of the social safety net. Life under communism may not have been optimal, but the people were fully insured and protected in the essential life domains such as education, work, and healthcare. On the contrary, the transition to market capitalism resulted in the dissolution of the social safety net, and left the people exposed to social risk. Their experience thus teaches us that the market is not always a viable substitute for sustaining the well-being of their citizens.

Happiness and Marriage Promotion Programs

Happiness research can also be used to challenge the assumptions on which policy is based. There is evidence to suggest that there may be a decline in marriage around the world. Cohen (2013) estimates that 87 percent of the world's population lives in a country in which the marriage rate has fallen since the 1980s. Government officials are worried. They are worried about the implications for the fertility rate, they are worried about the implications for morality and family values, and they are worried about the implications for child well-being. State governments of several countries have incentives in place to encourage couples to choose to marry. From the tax breaks for married couples that were instituted in 2015 in England to housing policies that privilege married home buyers in Singapore, many governments are trying to promote marriage as the best way to settle down and start a family. At least part of this concern is based on the notion that marriage makes people happier and our research in Chapter 6 challenges that assumption.

In the United States in particular, there has been growing concern that marriage as an institution is dying out. Some are worried that marriage is a relic of the past, a past when stable two-parent families, that were a haven in a heartless world, were the context in which most children grew up. In this romanticized version of the past, families were close-knit with little geographic mobility—kids grew up not only with two devoted parents but within a network of extended kin just down the block. Of course, they had a stay-at-home mother, who was devoted to her family and who found fulfillment in caring for them, and a breadwinning father, who provided economic stability and allowed the family to be financially independent.

Becker (1991) argued that there was a decrease in the incentive to form or maintain these "traditional" families as women increasingly started working outside the home in the second half of the 20th century. In Chapter 4, we discussed Becker's argument about the decline in the "gains to marriage." As he saw it, the stability of marriage was based on the give and take inherent in a traditional division of labor. Women were dependent on men for their paycheck, and men were dependent on women for performing unpaid household labor—cooking, cleaning, caring for children and elders. Neither could survive very well on their own. This idea that a specialized division of labor is fundamental to the functioning of the family was not new, but built on the work of earlier scholars, in particular Talcott Parsons, who argued that mothers' work socializing small children was a crucial function of the family. However, as women began working outside the home in growing numbers in the postwar period, they no longer needed a husband to rely on financially, and family life as we knew it seemed less appealing. Without a specialized division of labor, there was little reason to get married or to stick it out and stay married when the going got tough, resulting in declining marriage rates, unstable marriages, and subsequently rising divorce rates.

Not everyone agreed with Becker's interpretation of how and why families were changing in the 20th century, however. One critique is that, in arguing that the benefits of marriage were declining, he compared the American family of the 1970s and 1980s to the family of the 1950s. Family scholars have argued that the 1950s were a historical anomaly in family history, and therefore, should not be used as a benchmark against which to measure family change. In particular, Coontz (1992) details how in the 1950s we saw a decrease in the age at marriage and motherhood, an increase in fertility, a decrease in divorce, and a decrease in the proportion of adults who never married. She says the 1950s were a historical fluke, "based on a unique and temporary conjuncture of economic, social, and political factors" (Coontz

1992, p. 28). But even in this unusually pro-family, prosperous decade, the reality of family life was much more complicated than the sitcom portrayals of the era. In many cases, women did not freely choose to become house-wives but instead had been downgraded from fulfilling jobs during the war to unchallenging jobs once the soldiers returned. In the face of these limited job opportunities, women returned to domestic roles. There were striking income disparities in the 1950s, with little public assistance available. There was also greater repression of alternative family forms and lifestyles, with people pres-sured to follow the traditional family norm. Family scholars argue that, for all of these reasons, we should not use the 1950s family as our standard of comparison, nor should we romanticize the family of this period as the ideal family form to which we should strive to return.

Most of the federal money used to finance marriage promotion programs is directed to programs that teach enrollees relationship skills as a way to encourage marriage formation and stability (Randles 2012). In addition to reinforcing a model of a heterosexual two-parent married family in a time of great diversity in family forms, these programs are not necessarily hav-ing their intended impact on participants. Research evidence suggests that among low-income, unmarried parents, participation in relationship skills programs was not associated with higher rates of marriage (Randles 2012) and also raises questions about marriage promotion as an effective means of combating poverty (Heath 2012).

Our research contributes to this debate over marriage promotion programs by challenging the argument that marriage, in and of itself, makes people better off. In Chapter 5, we show that the happiness benefits of marriage are culture-specific. Although in the United States married people do report greater happiness than cohabiters, this is not the case in countries with more progressive gender ideology and weaker religious beliefs. We argue that mar-riage promotion programs are not the best use of federal money because (1) there is limited evidence in the literature that marriage promotion actu-ally promotes marriage or reduces poverty and (2) such programs could poten-tially further stigmatize cohabiting and single-parent families, contributing to the happiness inequality between married and single parent or cohabiting families. Instead, if policymakers are interested in promoting stable house-holds for children to grow up in, then programs to boost the well-being of single parent and cohabiting families by providing them with social support in addition to programs that provide poor families with access to "educa-tion, jobs, mental healthcare, and other key resources that can support both greater financial security and higher relationship quality" are what is most needed (Randles 2012, p. 679). These types of programs have the great-est potential to improve child outcomes and also reduce the happiness gap between married households and all other households as well. For example, according to Hook (2010): "Policy support for female employment and generous welfare benefits in the Nordic countries greatly reduce the risk of child poverty in both single- and two-parent households" (p. 526). When more generous social supports are available for families, children in all family types are better off. Of course, as we discussed in Chapter 6, such social welfare programs benefitting families redistribute happiness from single people to families. Policymakers should weigh the benefits and costs of these policies.

Happiness and Fertility Policy

One final area of policy discussion that happiness research can contribute to is the declining birthrate, particularly in advanced economies. According to the Population Reference Bureau (2014), total fertility rates declined between 1970 and 2013 in all regions of the world, dropping below the replacement level in North America, Europe, and in many countries of Asia (e.g., Taiwan, South Korea, and Japan). The literature on happiness and children might offer some clues for governments concerned about the declining birthrate. Much of the scholarly literature has explained fertility decline by pointing to the rising costs of children (Becker 1991) as well as ideological shifts toward individualism and secularism (Lesthaeghe 1983). But without also considering how children impact the happiness of women in particular, policies intended to increase fertility are likely to be ineffective.

Becker's quantity-quality trade-off hypothesis predicts that as the "quality" of children desired increases, the quantity of children demanded will decrease. In other words, as preferences for higher "quality," more educated, more intensely cultivated children have developed over time, parents have wanted to have fewer children. Becker (1991) also argued in his female cost of time hypothesis that women's rising earning power increased the opportunity cost of being a housewife (in other words, the value of the time in the labor force women would be giving up to stay at home increased), and reduced the demand for children.

Based on these explanations of fertility decline, state policies to increase fertility have focused on incentives to offset the rising costs of childbearing. In particular, countries like Singapore have offered couples baby bonuses ($6,000 for the first or second child and $8,000 for the third or fourth in Singapore) and Germany has instituted paid childcare leave (up to $35,000 a year) to offset the cost of childbearing. It is not clear, however, that these policies have had the intended consequence of raising fertility rates. Perhaps this suggests we need to look beyond the cost of children in explaining fertility decline and in creating policies to address it.

Other family scholars have argued that declining fertility across the 20th century is not driven solely by economic factors (namely the rising cost of children). Ideological shifts across the 20th century are also part of the story of declining fertility. Lesthaeghe (1983; 1998) points to the changes in family formation, fertility, and union dissolution in the West in the postwar period and connects these changes in families to ideational shifts, in particular the "long-term trends toward greater individual autonomy in ethical, religious, and political domains" (Lestheghe 1998, p. 6). According to these scholars, if we are to understand declining fertility, we should consider women's changing economic roles but also growing egalitarianism, antiauthoritarianism, and a greater emphasis on self-actualization (Lesthaeghe and Neidert 2006).

Building on the Second Demographic Transition literature, we argue that, in addition to considering the rising costs of children as driving fertility decline, we should consider the link between ideology, happiness, and child-bearing. Throughout the book, we discussed that children are not associated with greater happiness and, in fact, for women, the effect of children on happiness is negative. If children are acting as a drain on happiness, and there has been a shift in economically developed countries toward higher-order, self-actualization needs in the postwar period, then it is not surprising that people are increasingly choosing to forego childbearing or to stop after just one child.

We argue that women's happiness is disproportionately affected by children because they are the ones to shoulder the unpaid family labor associated with childbearing. We know from other research that, around the globe, women perform more of the time-inflexible household tasks such as cooking meals, cleaning bathrooms, washing clothes, and shopping for groceries. This unequal burden shouldered by women increases when children are born. More specifically, in the United States in 2009–2010, married women performed 1.7 times the amount of housework as married men but married mothers performed 1.9 times more (Bianchi et al. 2012). Analyzing Australian data, Craig (2006) found that mothers spend more time with children, particularly in time-inflexible tasks, and have more overall responsibility for managing the care of children. Of course, there is some variation cross-nationally in the extent to which men and women share household responsibilities, and this variation is intimately connected to both the cultural conceptions about the appropriate roles for men and women and the state supports for working families.

In the United States, work-family scholars have documented the "ideal worker norms" that characterize the American workplace. Employers expect workers to devote themselves entirely to their jobs, with the flexibility to work full-time, travel, and relocate for work, assuming that someone else will be shouldering the responsibilities of home. As women have increasingly entered the labor force across the 20th century, these intense expectations of complete devotion to the workplace have become increasingly unsustainable.

At the same time, expectations of good parenting have similarly increased to the point where working moms in 2000 were spending as much time with their children as the stay-at-home moms of the 1970s (Bianchi et al. 2006). The conflict between the demands of the workplace and the demands of intensive parenting has left many parents, and mothers in particular, feeling stressed and unhappy. Sociologists have found that work-family conflict is more closely associated with well-being for mothers because they are culturally responsible for creating a happy family life (Nomaguchi et al. 2005). In this context of work-family conflict, it is no wonder that couples may be reconsidering having children or may be choosing to stop after having one.

If social policy could intervene to make the household division of labor more equal and to lessen work-family conflict and consequently break the link between children and unhappiness for women, perhaps this could increase the fertility rate. Instead of focusing on the costs of childbearing by offering baby bonuses and benefits like paid childcare leave and part-time work options that in many cases serve to further reinforce gendered labor divisions, governments should focus on policies that make mothers in particular happier, because they are the ones disproportionately reporting unhappiness after having children. Hook (2010) argues, for example, that policies or collective agreements that reduce the length of the standard or maximum workweek have the potential to increase the amount of time breadwinners have to spend with their family as well as to change cultural conceptions about the appropriate balance between work and family. Similarly, paternal-leave policies could give couples the chance to establish more equal divisions of household labor early on in the child's life, lifting some of the burden from women and potentially contributing to cultural change in conceptions of men's involvement in domestic and nurturing labor. However, it is important to distinguish such paternal-leave policies that are available only to fathers from general extended parental-leave policies with no incentive built in for men to take advantage of them that oftentimes serve to reinforce gendered divisions of labor because women are much more likely to take them than men (Hook 2010).

What about countries where women report greater happiness when they have a specialized division of labor? Would policy interventions intended to decrease work-family conflict be ineffective in increasing fertility in these countries? In Chapter 4, we discussed our research on marital satisfaction in the United States and Japan that found Japanese women were happier in their marriages when they did not work outside the home and their husbands earned more money. We argue that this is because of persisting traditional gender norms in Japan. However, there is evidence of uneven change in beliefs about gender in Japan. Nemoto (2008) argued that Japanese women are experiencing ambivalence resulting from the conflict between their desire for equality and the structural barriers preventing them from achieving it. This ambivalence has led Japanese women to postpone marriage and may ultimately be part of the reason for the low levels of fertility in Japan today.

State policies providing paternal leave, universal childcare, and even maximum workweek limits not only provide concrete resources to families in trying to balance work and family but can also contribute to changing cultural expectations about who is most suited to care for young children and what kind of balance between work and family is appropriate. Over time, cultural conceptions of appropriate gender roles begin to change. Of course, these changes come with a cost. In making families happier, single people are less happy. In making mothers happier, we may also be making fathers less happy. We argue that such trade-offs may be necessary in order to increase fertility and also in order to change cultural conceptions about gender and care. As Glenn (2000) argued, care should be a right of citizenship, rather than a private responsibility or something only the most dependent and weakest members of our society are in need of. By extending social welfare supports to all families, we not only provide families with much-needed resources in balancing work and family, but also begin to change these cultural conceptions of care. Ultimately, we argue, such changes in cultural conceptions of care could weaken the negative association between children and unhappiness for women and could help to increase the fertility rate.

The Promise of the Sociology of Happiness

We end this book where we began, with the promise of the sociology of happiness. A sociological perspective on happiness holds particular promise because it sheds light on not just the sources of happiness but how the opportunity to achieve happiness is socially constrained. Our opportunity to achieve happiness is of course connected to individual characteristics like our personality, gender, work and family, and it is also connected to the characteristics of the context in which we live—the average income of our neighborhood, the social norms and the government policy in our country. But as sociologists, we have tried to emphasize how it is the interplay of the personal and the social that really matters in understanding what determines happiness. It matters if you are cohabiting with a romantic partner in a country with strong religious beliefs or in a country that is fairly secular. It matters if you are poor and living in a country with little economic redistribution or in a social democratic welfare state. We cannot make conclusions about the importance of marriage or the importance of kids to our happiness without considering the social context and family support policies in which those marriages are formed and those kids are born. Similarly, statements about maximizing happiness in a country or claims about which country's citizens are the most miserable tell us little about the level of happiness inequality that exists within any particular nation. This is the promise of a sociological approach to happiness: An understanding of not just how happiness varies across individuals or between nation states but of how the interplay of the personal and the social matters in shaping our happiness.

Appendix: Technical Analyses

The empirical work that we presented in Chapters 4, 5, and 6 is based on our previous research that we published in more technical form (see Lee and Ono 2008; Lee and Ono 2012; and Ono and Lee 2013). This appendix provides the technical analyses and the estimation results that were abbreviated from the corresponding chapters.

CHAPTER 4: MARRIAGE AND HAPPINESS IN THE UNITED STATES AND JAPAN

Estimation Results

The main objective of our analysis in this chapter is to identify the determinants of marital happiness in the United States and Japan. We estimate happiness equations separately for the two countries. In the United States, we use the General Social Survey (GSS) that records marital happiness in three categories ranging from 1 = not too happy to 3 = very happy. In Japan, we use the Japanese General Social Survey (JGSS) that records marital happiness in five categories. For each country, we estimated ordered logistic regression to predict marital happiness using other observable characteristics. Table A.1 shows the regression results from the United States. Table A.2 shows the regression results from Japan. Table A.3 shows the estimation results relating to different specifications of income in both countries.

The Relationship between Wife's Contribution to Household Income and Men's Happiness in Marriage in the United States

Our regression results suggest that men in the United States are less happy in marriage if their wives are working. But they are also happy as long as their

Table A.1 Ordered Logit Regression Models Predicting Marital Happiness in the United States

	(a) Married Persons				(b) Married and Working				(c) Married and Both Spouses Working			
	Full	Men	Women	M vs. W	Full	Men	Women	M vs. W	Full	Men	Women	M vs. W
Female	−0.163 (0.110)				−0.251 (0.123)				−0.063 (0.131)			
Education	0.038 (0.021)	0.055 (0.029)	0.022 (0.034)		0.041 (0.025)	0.054 (0.031)	0.026 (0.044)		0.036 (0.027)	0.048 (0.035)	0.015 (0.045)	
Working	−0.088 (0.143)	0.254 (0.296)	−0.131 (0.166)									
Spouse working	−0.342* (0.142)	−0.506** (0.178)	0.014 (0.241)		−0.383* (0.164)	−0.499** (0.190)	0.065 (0.309)					
Children	−0.402** (0.145)	−0.174 (0.210)	−0.629** (0.207)		−0.536** (0.171)	−0.196 (0.223)	−0.953** (0.274)	*	−0.592** (0.187)	−0.325 (0.257)	−0.843** (0.281)	
Health[a] Good	0.457** (0.176)	0.705** (0.255)	0.206 (0.250)		0.777** (0.217)	0.600* (0.279)	0.966** (0.350)		0.752** (0.242)	0.555 (0.332)	0.858** (0.355)	
Excellent	1.108** (0.193)	1.180** (0.276)	1.079** (0.275)		1.412** (0.233)	1.127** (0.298)	1.869** (0.378)		1.482** (0.259)	1.174** (0.352)	1.820** (0.385)	
Missing	0.375* (0.184)	0.155 (0.270)	0.565* (0.258)		0.554* (0.225)	0.094 (0.298)	1.161** (0.350)	*	0.589* (0.251)	0.024 (0.357)	1.071** (0.357)	*
Log HH income	0.116 (0.145)	0.096 (0.211)	0.182 (0.203)		0.204 (0.181)	0.218 (0.231)	0.323 (0.296)		0.130 (0.202)	0.150 (0.274)	0.263 (0.310)	

λ	0.046	0.370	-0.091		-0.004	0.575	-0.376		-0.098	0.499	-0.371
	(0.325)	(0.492)	(0.440)		(0.408)	(0.534)	(0.646)		(0.462)	(0.631)	(0.689)
N	1,811	865	946		1,336	763	573		1,098	569	529
Log-likelihood	-1,348	-612	-717		-976	-538	-423		-816	-415	-391

* $p < .05$ ** $p < .01$. Robust standard errors are in parentheses. All models include controls for age, age squared, race, and survey year dummies. Ordered logit cut-points are suppressed from the output. The column "M vs. W" indicates whether the differences in the coefficients between men and women are significant or not.

[a] Reference (or omitted) category is the combined category of poor health and fair health.

Source: Reprinted from Lee and Ono (2008).

Table A.2 Ordered Logit Regression Models Predicting Marital Happiness in Japan

	(a) Married Persons				(b) Married and Working				(c) Married and Both Spouses Working			
	Full	Men	Women	M vs. W	Full	Men	Women	M vs. W	Full	Men	Women	M vs. W
Female	-0.324** (0.057)				-0.362** (0.064)				-0.269** (0.070)			
Education	0.032** (0.011)	0.033* (0.016)	0.033 (0.017)		0.033* (0.013)	0.031 (0.016)	0.042 (0.023)		0.050** (0.016)	0.046* (0.022)	0.054* (0.025)	
Working	-0.160* (0.067)	0.094 (0.183)	-0.229** (0.073)									
Spouse working	-0.013 (0.058)	-0.084 (0.073)	0.227* (0.113)	*	-0.043 (0.067)	-0.093 (0.076)	0.280 (0.178)					
Children	-0.292** (0.092)	-0.328* (0.139)	-0.284* (0.125)		-0.361** (0.110)	-0.257 (0.153)	-0.468** (0.170)		-0.519** (0.135)	-0.417* (0.204)	-0.531** (0.188)	
Health[a] Fair	0.171 (0.166)	0.052 (0.248)	0.261 (0.229)		0.081 (0.207)	0.318 (0.285)	-0.177 (0.311)		0.096 (0.277)	0.373 (0.463)	-0.067 (0.339)	
Average	0.293 (0.157)	-0.024 (0.236)	0.517* (0.218)		0.199 (0.196)	0.249 (0.273)	0.169 (0.293)		0.272 (0.264)	0.292 (0.448)	0.315 (0.322)	
Good	0.887** (0.159)	0.621** (0.239)	1.080** (0.220)		0.823** (0.198)	0.889** (0.276)	0.778** (0.296)		0.882** (0.266)	0.900* (0.450)	0.937** (0.324)	
Excellent	1.535** (0.162)	1.257** (0.242)	1.725** (0.223)		1.436** (0.201)	1.514** (0.278)	1.349** (0.298)		1.516** (0.268)	1.530** (0.454)	1.534** (0.326)	
Log HH income	0.309** (0.064)	0.295** (0.101)	0.317** (0.085)		0.391** (0.077)	0.376** (0.109)	0.443** (0.117)		0.390** (0.100)	0.447** (0.154)	0.405** (0.136)	

λ	−0.240 (0.352)	−0.824 (0.645)	0.114 (0.430)	0.194 (0.414)	0.183 (0.799)	0.647 (0.530)	−0.418 (0.711)	0.539 (1.492)	−0.404 (0.826)
n	6,740	2,947	3,793	4,899	2,750	2,149	3,461	1,522	1,939
Log-likelihood	−8,176	−3,397	−4,743	−5,892	−3,153	−2,709	−4,203	−1,768	−2,417

* $p < .05$ ** $p < .01$. Robust standard errors are in parentheses. All models include controls for age, age squared, and survey year dummies. Ordered logit cut-points are suppressed from the output. The column "M vs. W" indicates whether the differences in the coefficients between men and women are significant or not.

[a] Reference (or omitted) category is poor health.

Source: Reprinted from Lee and Ono (2008).

Table A.3 Ordered Logit Regression Models Predicting Marital Happiness under Different Specifications of Income

	United States			Japan		
	Men	Women	M vs. W	Men	Women	M vs. W
(a) Log HH income (ln Y)	0.218 (0.231)	0.323 (0.296)		0.376 (0.109)**	0.443 (0.117)**	**
λ	0.575 (0.534)	−0.376 (0.646)		0.183 (0.799)	0.647 (0.530)	
Log-likelihood	−538	−423		−3,153	−2,709	
(b) Log R income (ln Y)	−0.270 (0.139)	0.224 (0.110)*	**	0.241 (0.073)**	0.004 (0.049)	**
λ	−0.285 (0.396)	−0.654 (0.398)		−0.781 (0.634)	−0.946 (0.349)**	
Log-likelihood	−537	−421		−3,154	−2,715	
(c) Log R income (ln Y)	−0.192 (0.152)	0.248 (0.121)*		0.252 (0.073)**	0.010 (0.049)	**
Spouse income						
Quintile 1	−0.608 (0.226)**	0.278 (0.767)		−0.151 (0.131)	0.111 (0.203)	
Quintile 2	−0.820 (0.289)**	0.809 (0.790)		−0.182 (0.117)	0.412 (0.190)*	**
Quintile 3	−0.518 (0.257)*	0.529 (0.822)		−0.072 (0.126)	0.490 (0.216)*	*
Quintile 4	−0.574 (0.291)*	0.606 (0.840)		0.067 (0.141)	0.471 (0.211)*	
Quintile 5	0.223 (0.342)	0.732 (0.893)		0.145 (0.115)	0.814 (0.208)**	**
Λ	0.122 (0.461)	−0.314 (0.604)		−0.490 (0.645)	−0.467 (0.366)	
Log-likelihood	−532	−419		−3,150	−2,706	

(d) Log HH income	0.205 (0.232)	0.350 (0.295)	0.408 (0.110)**	0.443 (0.118)**
Share of HH income = Y/Y_{HH}	−0.984 (0.377)**	0.592 (0.444)**	0.316 (0.179)	−0.152 (0.208)
Λ	0.634 (0.533)	−0.418 (0.641)	0.183 (0.802)	0.727 (0.543)
Log-likelihood	−534	−422	−3,151	−2,709
(e) Log HH income (Y_{HH})	0.182 (0.239)	0.229 (0.312)	0.200 (0.117)	0.284 (0.123)*
Relative standing				
Below average	−0.051 (0.570)	−0.136 (0.592)	0.063 (0.167)	0.155 (0.188)
Average	−0.070 (0.533)	−0.128 (0.560)	0.279 (0.166)	0.482 (0.186)**
Above average	0.130 (0.530)	0.156 (0.620)	0.451 (0.195)*	0.841 (0.222)**
Far above average	−0.100 (0.622)	0.146 (0.774)	1.397 (0.423)**	0.618 (0.444)
Missing	0.564 (0.549)	−0.461 (0.656)	0.650 (0.216)**	0.543 (0.231)*
λ			−0.180 (0.812)	0.401 (0.537)
Log-likelihood	−538	−422	−3,139	−2,696

* $p < .05$ ** $p < .01$. Robust standard errors are in parentheses. All models include controls for variables included in Tables A.1 and A.2. Cut-points are suppressed from the output. Sample size for all models is: U.S. men (763), U.S. women (573), Japanese men (2,750), and Japanese women (2,149).

wives make a substantial contribution to the household finances. How much is a substantial contribution? Using the estimated coefficients from our regressions, we can estimate the share of household income that makes men just as happy if their wives were not working. The happiness equation to be estimated is:

$$U = \beta_1 S + \beta_2 Y_{HH} + \beta_3 Y/Y_{HH} \tag{A.1}$$

where Y is the individual's income, Y_{HH} is the household income, and $S = 0$ if the wives are not working, and $S = 1$ if the wives are working. Other co-variates are suppressed from the equation. Equation (A.1) can be rewritten:

$$U = \beta_2 Y_{HH} + \beta_3 \qquad\qquad \text{if } S = 0 \text{ (since } Y/Y_{HH} = 1) \tag{A.1'}$$

$$U = \beta_1 + \beta_2 Y_{HH} + \beta_3 Y/Y_{HH} \qquad \text{if } S = 1 \tag{A.1''}$$

The difference in happiness between men with working wives and men with nonworking wives is therefore:

$$\Delta U = \beta_1 + \beta_3 (Y/Y_{HH} - 1) \tag{A.2}$$

By setting $\Delta U = 0$, we can estimate the men's share of household finance that would make them just as happy if their wives were not working, given by:

$$\Delta U = 0 \text{ when } Y/Y_{HH} = 1 - \beta_1/\beta_3 \tag{A.2'}$$

Coefficients estimated from separate models reveal that $\beta_1 = -0.702$ and $\beta_3 = -0.984$. Therefore, $\Delta U = 0$ when $Y/Y_{HH} = 0.287$—that is, when wife's contribution to household finances exceeds (roughly) 70 percent. This relationship is illustrated in Figure 4.1.

CHAPTER 5: A HAPPY COUPLE

Multilevel Modeling

We estimated two-level ordered logistic regression models, predicting general happiness. The Level 1 (individual-level) ordinal logistic regression model is as follows:

$$\log\left(\frac{\phi_{mij}}{1 - \phi_{mij}}\right) = \beta_{0j} + \sum_{q=1}^{Q} \beta_{qj} X_{q1j} + \sum_{m=2}^{M} \delta_m \tag{A.3}$$

where $\varnothing_{mij}$ is the probability that respondent i in country j is at or above response option m in his or her response to the question of how happy he or she is with life in general, β_{0j} is the intercept for country j, β_{qj} is the coefficient for independent variable q in country j, and δ_m is a threshold that separates categories $m—1$ and m (Raudenbush et al. 2004).

The Level 2 (country-level) equations reported in Table A.4 model the intercept (see Equation A.4) and the slopes of female (Equation A.5), cohabiting (Equation A.6), and being single (Equation A.7) as randomly varying across countries. The error terms of all other independent variables are modeled as fixed across countries. For example, for our model including societal measures of gender beliefs and GDP, we have the following set of Level 2 equations with random error terms:

$$\beta_{0j} = \gamma_{00} + \gamma_{01} \,(\log \mathrm{GDP})_j + \gamma_{02} \,(\text{societal gender beliefs})_j + u_{0j} \quad \text{(A.4)}$$

$$\beta_{1j} = \gamma_{10} + \gamma_{11} \,(\text{societal gender beliefs})_j + u_{1j} \quad\quad\quad\quad\quad \text{(A.5)}$$

$$\beta_{2j} = \gamma_{20} + \gamma_{21} \,(\text{societal gender beliefs})_j + u_{2j} \quad\quad\quad\quad\quad \text{(A.6)}$$

$$\beta_{3j} = \gamma_{30} + \gamma_{31} \,(\text{societal gender beliefs})_j + u_{3j} \quad\quad\quad\quad\quad \text{(A.7)}$$

The coefficient for societal gender beliefs in Equation A.5 (γ_{11}) indicates the interaction of gender beliefs in a country and gender (female). Similarly in Equation A.6, the coefficient for societal gender beliefs indicates the interaction of gender beliefs in a country and being a cohabiter (γ_{21}), and in Equation A.7 the coefficient for societal gender beliefs indicates the interaction of gender beliefs in a country and not being married or cohabiting (γ_{31}). After estimating happiness in a single model for both men and women, we estimated separate models by gender to investigate the hypothesized gender interactions discussed earlier (e.g., interactions between gender and parenthood status, employment, income, as well as marital status and the Level 2 variables).

Estimation Results

Table A.4 shows estimation results of multilevel models predicting general happiness. In Model 1, Level 2 (country-level) covariates include GDP and traditional gender beliefs. In Model 2, Level 2 covariates include GDP and religious context. In both models, Level 1 covariates include individual-level attributes such as demographics and socioeconomic status. Table A.5 shows estimation results separated by gender.

Table A.4 Ordered Logit Regression Models Predicting General Happiness (n = 33,314)

	Model 1		Model 2	
	Coefficient	S.E.	Coefficient	S.E.
Level 2 (country-level) variables				
Intercept	−2.108***	0.092	−2.125***	0.084
Log GDP (gross domestic product)	0.146	0.199	0.298	0.168
Country-level traditional gender beliefs (TGB)	0.511	0.344		
Religious context			0.318**	0.101
Level 1 (individual-level) variables and cross-level interactions				
Female	−0.058	0.035	−0.054	0.038
Female × country-level TGB	−0.269*	0.103		
Female × religious context			−0.060	0.038
Traditional gender beliefs (TGB)	−0.064***	0.014	−0.064***	0.014
Cohabiting	−0.319***	0.048	−0.322***	0.048
Cohabit × country-level TGB	−0.221	0.128		
Cohabit × religious context			−0.105	0.052
Single	−0.942***	0.041	−0.947***	0.041
Single × country-level TGB	0.207	0.118		
Single × religious context			0.083*	0.039
Child under 18 in the home	−0.019	0.024	−0.019	0.024
Religion	0.167***	0.028	0.165***	0.028
Household income z score	0.142***	0.011	0.143***	0.011
Age	−0.109***	0.005	−0.109***	0.005
Age squared	0.001***	5.0E-05	0.001***	5.0E-05
Full-time employment	0.106***	0.024	0.106***	0.024
College education	0.100***	0.031	0.099**	0.031
Random effects				
Intercept	0.208***		0.167***	
Female	0.021***		0.026***	
Cohabiting	0.019*		0.019*	
Single	0.027***		0.026***	

*p < .05. **p < .01. ***p <.001.

Source: Reprinted from Lee and Ono (2012).

Table A.5 Ordered Logit Regression Models Predicting General Happiness, Separately by Gender

| | Women (n = 18,457) | | | | Men (n = 14,857) | | | |
| | Model 1 | | Model 2 | | Model 3 | | Model 4 | |
	Coefficient	S.E.	Coefficient	S.E.	Coefficient	S.E.	Coefficient	S.E.
Level 2 (country-level) variables								
Intercept	−2.123***	0.094	−2.138***	0.083	−2.142***	0.100	−2.166***	0.092
Log GDP (gross domestic product)	0.353	0.200	0.428*	0.168	0.017	0.211	0.194	0.179
Country-level traditional gender beliefs (TGB)	0.499	0.347			0.128	0.364		
Religious context			0.307**	0.098			0.278*	0.105
Level 1 (individual-level) variables and cross-level interactions								
Traditional gender beliefs (TGB)	−0.069***	0.018	−0.068***	0.018	−0.057**	0.021	−0.054*	0.021
Cohabiting	−0.308***	0.056	−0.317***	0.053	−0.322***	0.064	−0.313***	0.063
Cohabit × country-level TGB	−0.437**	0.148			0.004	0.162		
Cohabit × religious context			−0.214***	0.057			0.042	0.069
Single	−0.784***	0.051	−0.791***	0.049	−1.155***	0.055	−1.160***	0.056
Single × country-level TGB	0.139	0.148			0.321*	0.146		
Single × religious context			0.092	0.047			0.076	0.050
Child under 18 in the home	−0.072*	0.032	−0.074**	0.032	−0.012	0.037	−0.015	0.037
Religion	0.127***	0.039	0.126***	0.039	0.200***	0.040	0.200***	0.040
Household income z scores	0.150***	0.016	0.149***	0.015	0.145***	0.017	0.143***	0.017

(Continued)

Table A.5 (Continued)

	Women (n = 18,457)				Men (n = 14,857)			
	Model 1		Model 2		Model 3		Model 4	
	Coefficient	S.E.	Coefficient	S.E.	Coefficient	S.E.	Coefficient	S.E.
Age	-0.094***	0.006	-0.094***	0.006	-0.128***	0.007	-0.130***	0.007
Age squared	0.001***	6.7E−05	0.001***	6.7E−05	0.001***	7.8E−05	0.001***	7.8E−05
Full-time employment	-0.002	0.032	-0.003	0.032	0.198***	0.039	0.215***	0.039
Full-time employment × country-level TGB	0.035	0.090			0.299**	0.097		
College education	0.095*	0.043	0.093*	0.043	0.094*	0.046	0.095*	0.046
Random effects								
Intercept	0.208***		0.154***		0.219***		0.173***	
Cohabiting	0.011		0.003		0.016		0.013	
Single	0.038***		0.032***		0.029*		0.032**	

*p <.05. **p <.01. ***p <.001.

Source: Reprinted from Lee and Ono (2012).

CHAPTER 6: THE (RE)DISTRIBUTION OF HAPPINESS

Estimation Results

We estimated multilevel models following the procedure described in Chapter 5 (discussed previously). Results are shown in Tables A.6 and A.7. In all models, Level 2 (country-level) covariates include a dummy variable for post-communist country and public social expenditures (PSE) as percentage of GDP. In all models, the coefficient for post-communist country is found to be negative and highly significant. People who live in post-communist countries are thus significantly less happy compared to people who live in other countries (as we discuss in Chapter 8). Level 1 covariates include individual-level attributes, such as demographic characteristics and socioeconomic status. In Table A.6, Models 1 and 2 are similar but have different reference categories for the measure of marital status. In Table A.7, we estimate multilevel models separately by gender.

Modeling Income and Happiness

Let happiness (U) be a function of income (I) and taxes (T) such that:

$$U = f(I, T) \tag{A.8}$$

The change in happiness from a change in income (dU/dI) is the marginal utility of income. With taxes in the equation, the marginal utility of income can be expressed as the total derivative:

$$\frac{dU}{dI} = \frac{\partial U}{\partial T} \cdot \frac{dT}{dI} + \frac{\partial U}{\partial I} \tag{A.9}$$

$$(-) \quad (+) \quad (+)$$

Here, dT/dI is the marginal tax rate that is always positive. $\partial U/\partial T$, the pure effect of taxes on happiness, is negative because people prefer lower (rather than higher) taxes. Finally, $\partial U/\partial I$, the pure effect of income on happiness, is positive since higher income is associated with higher happiness.

Equation (A.9) thus leads to several predictions. First, dU/dI is *always lower* in countries with high (versus low) marginal tax rates. Since Scandinavian countries have the highest marginal tax rates in the world, equation (A.9) would predict that dU/dI in Scandinavia is smaller compared to other countries. Note that this condition holds true even if $\partial U/\partial I = 0$. Second, if the indirect effect $\left(\frac{\partial U}{\partial T} \cdot \frac{dT}{dI} \right)$ was sufficiently negative, then this may offset the positive effect of $\partial U/\partial I$, in which case the total effect of income on happiness (dU/dI) may be zero or even negative. And third, under an unlikely scenario, there may be no taxes, or all citizens face the same lump sum tax regardless of income level. In this case, $dT/dI = 0$ and equation (A.9) would collapse, such that $dU/dI = \partial U/\partial I$. The effect of taxes on happiness can be disregarded, and dU/dI would be the same in all countries.

Empirically, happiness as a function of income (I) is:

$$U_{ij} = \beta_{0j} + \beta_{1j} I_{ij} + r_{ij} \qquad (A.10)$$

where r_{ij} is the observation- and group-specific residual. If we allow the intercept (β_0) and coefficient (β_1) to vary by country-level TAX, we get:

$$\beta_{0j} = \gamma_{00} + \gamma_{01} TAX_j + u_{0j} \qquad (A.11a)$$

$$\beta_{1j} = \gamma_{10} + \gamma_{11} TAX_j + u_{1j} \qquad (A.11b)$$

where the u's are the residual terms. Combining equations (A.10) and (A.11), we get:

$$U_{ij} = (\gamma_{00} + \gamma_{10} I_{ij} + \gamma_{01} TAX_j + \gamma_{11} I_{ij} TAX_j) + (u_{0j} + u_{1j} I_{ij} + r_{ij}) \qquad (A.12)$$

From rearranging equation (A.12), we can see that the expected value of happiness (U) is:

$$U_{ij} = (\gamma_{00} + \gamma_{01} TAX_j) + (\gamma_{10} + \gamma_{11} TAX_j) I_{ij} \qquad (A.13)$$

The marginal utility of income is the change in happiness from a change in income:

$$dU/dI = \gamma_{10} + \gamma_{11} TAX_j \qquad (A.14)$$

where γ_{10} is the main effect of income on happiness. γ_{11} is the indirect effect manifested through taxes that is expected to be negative. Note that the same predictions hold true if we were to substitute TAX with PSE, since these two measures are highly correlated, and they move in the same direction.

Table A.8 shows the results of our analysis on income and happiness. In both models, we confirm that income is positively associated with happiness ($\gamma_{10} = 0.111$). More interestingly, we find that the interaction between income and PSE (−0.005), and the interaction between income and taxes ($\gamma_{11} = -0.003$) are both negative and highly significant. These findings suggest that the marginal utility of income becomes significantly smaller in the high-PSE/tax countries than in the low-PSE/tax countries.

Table A.6 Ordered Logit Regression Models Predicting General Happiness

	Model 1		Model 2	
Level 2 (country-level) variables				
Intercept	−2.428***	(0.109)	−2.423***	(0.057)
Post-communist country	−0.805***	(0.108)	−0.786***	(0.124)
Public social expenditures (PSE) as % of GDP	−0.013	(0.009)	−0.013	(0.008)
Level 1 (individual-level) variables and cross-level interactions				
Female	0.009	(0.039)	0.026	(0.041)
Female × Country-level PSE	0.102	(0.005)	0.009	(0.006)
Cohabiting	0.627***	(0.057)	−0.340***	(0.048)
Cohabit × Country-level PSE	0.042***	(0.008)	0.027**	(0.008)
Married	0.991***	(0.051)		
Married × Country-level PSE	0.020***	(0.004)		
Divorced/Separated			−1.139***	(0.081)
Widowed			−0.989***	(0.094)
Single			−0.874***	(0.063)
Single × Country-level PSE			−0.010*	(0.005)
Child under 18 in the home	−0.022	(0.024)	0.0001	(0.024)
Child × Country-level PSE	0.007	(0.003)	0.010*	(0.004)
Age	−0.108***	(0.010)	−0.100***	(0.010)
Age squared	0.001***	(0.0001)	0.001***	(0.0001)
College education	0.154**	(0.052)	0.151**	(0.051)
Full-time employment	0.055	(0.032)	0.060	(0.032)
Income Z score	0.109***	(0.013)	0.112***	(0.012)
Random effects				
Intercept	0.086***		0.086***	
Female	0.036***		0.035***	
Child under 18	0.014**		0.020***	
Cohabit	0.039**		0.023*	
Married	0.018***			
Single			0.020**	

* $p < .05$, ** $p < .01$, *** $p < .001$ (two-tailed tests). Robust standard errors in parentheses.
Source: Reprinted from Ono and Lee (2013).

Table A.7 Ordered Logit Regression Models Predicting General Happiness by Gender

	Women		Men	
Level 2 (country-level) variables				
Intercept	−2.405***	(0.103)	−2.477***	(0.123)
Post-communist country	−0.789***	(0.120)	−0.905***	(0.104)
Public social expenditures (PSE) as % of GDP	−0.008	(0.008)	−0.020	(0.010)
Level 1 (individual-level) variables and cross-level interactions				
Cohabiting	0.495***	(0.074)	0.798***	(0.072)
Cohabit × Country-level PSE	0.050***	(0.011)	0.033***	(0.009)
Married	0.863***	(0.056)	1.156***	(0.065)
Married × Country-level PSE	0.022***	(0.004)	0.018**	(0.005)
Child under 18 in the home	−0.085*	(0.035)	0.006	(0.034)
Child × Country-level PSE	0.011*	(0.005)	0.0001	(0.004)
Age	−0.092***	(0.010)	−0.130***	(0.013)
Age squared	0.001***	(0.0001)	0.001***	(0.0001)
College education	0.160**	(0.060)	0.156**	(0.060)
Full-time employment	−0.015	(0.034)	0.148**	(0.058)
Income Z score	0.083***	(0.017)	0.116***	(0.017)
Random effects				
Intercept	0.101***		0.082***	
Child under 18	0.020**		0.017*	
Cohabit	0.085**		0.033	
Married	0.027**		0.028*	

* $p <.05$, ** $p <.01$, *** $p <.001$ (two-tailed tests). Robust standard errors in parentheses.
Source: Reprinted from Ono and Lee (2013).

Table A.8 Ordered Logit Regression Models Predicting General Happiness

	(1) Income Z-Score × Country-Level PSE		(2) Income Z-Score × Country-Level Tax	
Level 2 (country-level) variables				
Intercept	−2.426***	(0.110)	−2.431***	(0.106)
Post-communist country	−0.814***	(0.107)	−0.781***	(0.098)
Public social expenditures (PSE) as % of GDP	−0.010	(0.009)		
Tax revenue as % of GDP			−0.011	(0.006)
Level 1 (individual-level) variables and cross-level interactions				
Income Z score	0.111***	(0.015)	0.111***	(0.014)
× Country-level interaction	−0.005***	(0.001)	−0.003***	(0.001)
Random effects				
Intercept	0.085***		0.079***	
Income Z score	0.004**		0.003**	

* $p <.05$, ** $p <.01$, *** $p <.001$ (two-tailed tests). Robust standard errors in parentheses.

Models also control for the same variables shown in Model 1 of Table A.6 minus the interaction effects. These control variables are suppressed from the output.

Source: Reprinted from Ono and Lee (2013).

Notes

CHAPTER 1

1. For example, the pursuit of happiness is written in the Declaration of Independence of the United States, and in the constitutions of Japan and Vietnam.

2. For a comprehensive list of objective and subjective measures of well-being, see Sen, Stiglitz, and Fitoussi (2009).

3. Economists are particularly skeptical of using subjective data in empirical research. See a brief review of critiques in Bertrand and Mullainathan (2001).

4. Hirsch et al. (1987) write with sarcasm that economists often revert to psychic costs and benefits as a "way out" if their economic models fall short of predictions:

> On the micro level, economists' assumption of rationality can be restated as psychological hedonism, at which point the proposition becomes irrefutable. If a person chooses a job with lower pay, the economist will add that his or her utility function must include variables besides pay—you just have to include them in the formulas to show that utility was maximized. If a samurai in feudal Japan commits hara-kiri, the economist can argue that if you add the cost of shame to the man's utility function it is obvious that this choice maximized his utility. (p. 331)

5. Contingent valuation (or stated preferences) is the alternative to revealed preferences in economics. This model assumes that non-market goods can be valued and priced. In the example of an environmental problem, contingent valuation tries to estimate the price that the public is willing to pay to clean the environment. Some economists discredit such a valuation method because the question is hypothetical, and discrepancies can arise between how much the public is willing to pay and how much they actually end up paying. People may, for example, disregard income constraints when responding to the question, and protest that the price is too expensive when the policy is actually implemented.

6. Adding yet another variation to the discussion on utility and happiness, Becker and Rayo (2008) explain that the two are distinct concepts. Specifically, they claim that utility is a broader concept that subsumes happiness:

> [H]appiness is a commodity in the utility function in the same way that owning a car and being healthy are. . . . On this interpretation, happiness may be an important determinant of utility, but that does not mean that both coincide. (p. 89)
>
> Under this formulation, happiness (H) is but one of many factors included in the utility function (U) along with other commodities (Z), such that: $U = U(Z, H)$.

7. I am grateful to Ruut Veenhoven and the World Database of Happiness for providing me with data to construct Figures 1.1a and 1.1b (*Source:* Veenhoven, Ruut. *World Database of Happiness*. Erasmus University Rotterdam, the Netherlands, Accessed on April 15, 2016, at: http://worlddatabaseofhappiness.eur.nl).

8. In the economics jargon, Abramowitz (1959, cited in Easterlin 1974) explains that "there is a clear presumption that changes in economic welfare indicate changes in social welfare in the same direction, if not in the same degree" (p. 90).

9. Cited from Wilbur and Jameson (1983).

10. Paul Krugman (1994) also pokes fun at the distinction between economists and sociologists. Quoting his adviser Jagdish Bhagwati from graduate school, he explains the theory of reincarnation as follows: "If you are a good economist, a virtuous economist, you are reborn as a physicist. If you are an evil, wicked economist, you are reborn as a sociologist" (Krugman 1994, p. xi). While Hirsch et al. (1987) use the expression *clean versus dirty*, Krugman uses the expression "hard": "Economics is *harder* than physics; luckily it is not quite as hard as sociology" (p. xi). Sociology is complex because the discipline involves the study of human beings (and society), and human being do not always behave in predictable ways.

11. More sophisticated versions of multilevel models can involve three or more levels of analysis. For example, if we want to estimate student achievement, we may have a three-level model where the student is nested within a class, which is nested within a school. See Raudenbush and Bryk (2002) for discussion of models that involve three or more levels of analysis.

CHAPTER 2

1. AAUW (2015).
2. Center for American Progress (2015).

CHAPTER 3

1. The World Bank data are the most widely used source for the international comparison of Gini indices. However, the World Bank (2007) also points out a number of shortcomings, owing to the difficulties of obtaining directly comparable data across a large number of countries. In some countries, consumption is used instead of

income, and it may be measured among individuals rather than households. These shortcomings are described in greater detail in Alesina et al. (2004).

2. Scheherazade Daneshkhu, "The 'Dismal Science' Turns Its Attention to Happiness." *Financial Times*, January 10, 2004.

3. Paul Krugman, "More Thoughts on Equality of Opportunity." *The New York Times*, January 11, 2011.

CHAPTER 4

1. Statistical Survey Department, Statistics Bureau, Ministry of Internal Affairs and Communications, Japan.

2. See Ono and Rebick (2003) for a review of the barriers to women's labor force participation in Japan.

3. The average across the 26 OECD countries included in the study was 139 minutes for men and 274 minutes for women. The best performing country in terms of equity between the sexes was Norway, which recorded 184 minutes for men and 215 minutes for women (OECD Nation Time Use Surveys 2014).

4. In the 2014 OECD study (see previous endnote entry), the time spent on housework in the United States was 161 minutes for men and 248 minutes for women.

5. The Japanese General Social Surveys (JGSS) are designed and carried out at the Institute of Regional Studies at Osaka University of Commerce in collaboration with the Institute of Social Science at the University of Tokyo under the direction of Ichiro Tanioka, Michio Nitta, Hiroki Sato, and Noriko Iwai with project manager Minae Osawa. The project is financially assisted by Gakujutsu Frontier Grant from the Japanese Ministry of Education, Culture, Sports, Science and Technology for 1999–2003 academic years, and the datasets are compiled and distributed by SSJ Data Archive, Information Center for Social Science Research on Japan, Institute of Social Science, the University of Tokyo.

6. Because the responses are recorded in different categories between the United States and Japan, we cannot directly compare marital happiness between the two countries. In other words, we cannot, for example, compare the marital happiness of women in the United States versus women in Japan, and claim which is lower or higher.

CHAPTER 5

1. To create the religious context factor, we conducted a factor analysis of the correlation matrix of 12 measures of religion in a society, estimated using principal components analysis as the factor extraction method.

CHAPTER 6

1. See for example, Kostigen, Thomas Kostigen, 2009. "The Happiest Taxes on Earth: More People Are Satisfied in Heavily Tariffed Nations." *Market Watch*, as well as a number of blog entries—for example, "Study Shows 'Socialist' Highly Taxed

Countries Have Happiest People." *Oprah.com*, May 18, 2009; and "High Taxes Lead to Happiness." *TaxProf Blog*, July 7, 2010. It should be noted that the original study by Deaton (2008) using the same data did not make any reference to the role of taxes.

2. See, for example, CATO Institute report titled "In Pursuit of Happiness Research: Is It Reliable? What Does It Imply for Policy?"

3. A common critique of using PSE as a proxy for the welfare state is that social expenditures may not adequately capture the state's commitment to welfare (Esping-Andersen and Korpi 1987; Pacek and Radcliff 2008). Indeed, Esping-Andersen (1999) and others have proposed alternative measures to approximate the quality of the welfare state. However, these alternative measures are usually limited in scope and coverage of countries. The advantage of the PSE measure, in spite of its shortcomings, is that the data are available for all countries included in the ISSP dataset.

4. See Jonsson and Collins (2004) for collection of articles that analyzes how the welfare state influences the lifecycle dynamics of individuals and families in Sweden.

5. This is based on OECD's comparison between single persons with no children, and married one-earner couples with two children.

6. Exceptions include Diener et al. (2000), Soons and Kalmijn (2009), and Stack and Eshleman (1998) who examine happiness among cohabiters and married couples cross-nationally, and Margolis and Myrskylä (2011) who study how happiness varies across countries depending on the family support system.

7. We acknowledge that there are cross-cultural variations in subjective well-being. The positivity score as described by Diener et al. (2000), described in Chapter 3, may be one method to address these variations.

8. Note here that married persons are not necessarily happier in the high-PSE countries than are their counterparts in the low-PSE countries. In fact, married persons actually report lower happiness in the social democratic welfare states.

9. We note here that since PSE and GDP per capita are correlated, it may be difficult to distinguish the association between PSE and income from that between GDP and income. It is possible that PSE and GDP per capita are both proxies for the standard of living, thus leading to similar predictions. Our results should be interpreted with this alternative explanation in mind.

CHAPTER 7

1. See for example, "Raising Kids Makes Married People Happier: New Study." *Medical News Today*, October 28, 2009; and "Child-Rearing Improves Married Happiness." *PsychCentral*, October 27, 2009.

2. Estimation results (which show the U-shape with respect to age of youngest child) are identical when we predict general happiness instead of marital happiness.

3. "Women's Happiness Levels Increase after Divorce, According to New Research." *Huffington Post*, July 11, 2013.

4. See for example, Gallup study that shows that only 13 percent of employees worldwide are "actively engaged" at work. In contrast, 24 percent are "actively disengaged," which indicates that employees are unhappy and unproductive at work, and liable to spread negativity to coworkers (Gallup 2013).

5. For example, Clark et al. (2003, cited in Kahneman and Krueger 2006) show that changes in life satisfaction before and after marriage resemble a short-lived "honeymoon effect" among a sample of German women. On average, life satisfaction increases during the time period leading up to marriage, peaks at the time of marriage, then drops immediately following marriage, and returns to baseline. This illustrates an example of adaptation (Kahneman and Krueger 2006)—that is, people adapt to and internalize life events rather quickly such that their effects on happiness equalize over time.

CHAPTER 8

1. Easterlin (2010) uses the World Values Survey from 1990 onward for the 13 transition countries: former German Democratic Republic, Poland, Hungary, Estonia, Latvia, Lithuania, Belarus, Russian Federation, Slovenia, Czech Republic, Slovakia, Bulgaria, and Romania.

2. Ono is grateful to comments and suggestions from the participants of the "Conference on the Middle Class," which was organized by Sofia University and the Bulgarian Academy of Sciences in December 2013. The discussions here on post-communism and happiness are based largely on conversations with experts and scholars from the conference in Bulgaria, and the literature that we acquired following the conference.

3. Zsuzsanna Clark, "Oppressive and Grey? No, Growing Up under Communism Was the Happiest Time of My Life." *Daily Mail*, October 17, 2009.

4. Stephen Gowans, "We Lived Better Then." *What's Left*. December 20, 2011.

5. "How Satisfied Are People with Their Lives in the European Union? A New Multi-Dimensional Data Collection." Eurostat News Release, March 20, 2015.

6. The trust index is tabulated by various organizations based on the trust-related questions from the World Values Survey. See for example: http://www.wikiprogress. org/index.php/Trust.

7. Based on Ono's interview notes from Bulgaria. The economics professor from Romania now works as a taxi driver.

8. "Why Is Bulgaria the EU's Most Unhappy Country?" *Euronews*, March 20, 2015.

9. For example, BBC News ("New Border Controls: Does Bulgaria Face a 'Brain Drain'?" November 21, 2013) explains that the average pay is about eight times higher in the United Kingdom than in Bulgaria.

10. Ivan Krastev, "Britain's Gain Is Eastern Europe's Brain Drain." *The Guardian*, March 24, 2015.

11. We are grateful to David Schkade for providing us with the data that we used to reconstruct this graph.

12. Interestingly, the Graham et al. (2015) report that working in the public sector is negatively associated with the odds of experiencing economic relative deprivation in China, presumably because of the better job security provided by the public sector.

References

Aaberge, Rolf, Anders Bjorklund, Markus Jantti, Mårten Palme, Peder J. Pedersen, Nina Smith, and Tom Wennemo. 2002. "Income Inequality and Income Mobility in the Scandinavian Countries Compared to the United States." *Review of Income and Wealth* 48: 443–469.

Aldous, Joan and Rodney F. Ganey. 1999. "Family Life and the Pursuit of Happiness—The Influence of Gender and Race." *Journal of Family Issues* 20: 155–180.

Alesina, Alberto, Edward Glaeser, and Bruce Sacerdote. 2001. "Why Doesn't the United States Have a European-Style Welfare State?" *Brookings Papers on Economic Activity* 2: 187–277.

Alesina, Alberto, Rafael Di Tella, and Robert J. MacCulloch. 2004. "Inequality and Happiness: Are Europeans and Americans Different?" *Journal of Public Economics* 88: 2009–2042.

American Association of University Women. 2015. *The Simple Truth about the Gender Pay Gap*. Washington, DC: AAUW.

Anderton, Douglas L. and Deborah E. Sellers. 1989. "A Brief Review of Contextual Effect Models and Measurement." *Historical Methods* 22: 106–115.

Argyle, Michael. 1999. "Causes and Correlates of Happiness," in *Well-Being: The Foundations of a Hedonic Psychology*. New York: Russell Sage.

Arulampalam, Wiji. 2001. "Is Unemployment Really Scarring? Effects of Unemployment Experiences on Wages." *The Economic Journal* 111: F585–F606.

Balon, Richard. 2008. "In Pursuit of (Sexual) Happiness and Well-Being: A Response." *Journal of Sex & Marital Therapy* 34: 298–301.

Barger, Steven D., Carrie J. Donoho, and Heidi A. Wayment. 2009. "The Relative Contributions of Race/Ethnicity, Socioeconomic Status, Health, and Social Relationships to Life Satisfaction in the United States." *Quality of Life Research* 18: 179–189.

Bartels, Meike. 2015. "Genetics of Wellbeing and Its Components Satisfaction with Life, Happiness, and Quality of Life: A Review and Meta-Analysis of Heritability Studies." *Behavior Genetics* 45: 137–156.

Bartram, David. 2012. "Elements of a Sociological Contribution to Happiness Studies." *Sociology Compass* 6: 644–656.

Bauer, Daniel J. and Patrick J. Curran. 2005. "Probing Interactions in Fixed and Multilevel Regression: Inferential and Graphical Techniques." *Multivariate Behavioral Research* 40: 373–400.

Beattie, Alan. 2014. "Gross National Happiness: A Bad Idea Whose Time Has Gone." The Financial Times. *Beyondbrics*. Accessed on August 3, 2015, at: http://blogs.ft.com/beyond-brics/2014/09/04/gross-national-happiness-a-bad-idea-whose-time-has-gone/.

Becker, Gary S. 1976. *The Economic Approach to Human Behavior*. Chicago: University of Chicago Press.

Becker, Gary S. 1991. *A Treatise on the Family*. Cambridge: Harvard University Press.

Becker, Gary S. and Luis Rayo. 2008. "Comments on 'Economic Growth and Subjective Well-Being: Reassessing the Easterlin Paradox.'" *Brookings Papers on Economic Activity* 39: 88–95.

Berkowitz, Eric. 2012. *Sex and Punishment: Four Thousand Years of Judging Desire*. Berkeley, CA: Publishers Group West.

Bernard, Jessie S. 1972. *The Future of Marriage*. New Haven, CT: Yale University Press.

Bertrand, Marianne and Sendhil Mullainathan. 2001. "Do People Mean What They Say? Implications for Subjective Survey Data." *American Economic Review* 91: 67–72.

Bianchi, Suzanne M., Melissa A. Milkie, Liana C. Sayer and John P. Robinson. 2000. "Is Anyone Doing the Housework? Trends in the Gender Division of Household Labor." *Social Forces* 79(1): 191–228.

Bianchi, Suzanne M., John P. Robinson, and Melissa A. Milkie. 2006. *Changing Rhythms of American Family Life*. New York: Russell Sage Foundation.

Bianchi, Suzanne M., Liana C. Sayer, Melissa A. Milkie, and John P. Robinson. 2012. "Housework: Who Did, Does or Will Do It, and How Much Does It Matter?" *Social Forces* 91: 55–63.

Binder, Martin and Alex Coad. 2013. "I'm Afraid I Have Bad News for You . . . Estimating the Impact of Different Health Impairments on Subjective Well-Being." *Social Science & Medicine* 87: 155–167.

Bjørnskov, Christian, Axel Dreher, and Justina A. V. Fischer. 2007. "The Bigger the Better? Evidence of the Effect of Government Size on Life Satisfaction around the World." *Public Choice* 130: 267–292.

Blair-Loy, Mary. 2003. *Competing Devotions: Career and Family among Women Executives*. Cambridge, MA: Harvard University Press.

Blalock, Hubert. 1984. "Contextual-Effects Models: Theoretical and Methodological Issues." *Annual Review of Sociology* 10: 353–372.

Blanchflower, David G. and Andrew J. Oswald. 2004a. "Money, Sex and Happiness: An Empirical Study." *The Scandinavian Journal of Economics* 106: 393–415.

Blanchflower, David G. and Andrew J. Oswald. 2004b. "Well-Being over Time in Britain and the USA." *Journal of Public Economics* 88: 1359–1386.

Blanchflower, David G. and Andrew J. Oswald. 2008. "Is Well-Being U-Shaped over the Life Cycle?" *Social Science & Medicine* 66: 1733–1749.

Boyadjieva, Pepka and Petya Kabakchieva. 2015. "Inequality in Poverty: Bulgarian Sociologists on Class and Stratification." *East European Politics & Societies* 29: 625–639.

Brickman, P., Dan Coates, and Ronnie Janoff-Bulman. 1978. "Lottery Winners and Accident Victims: Is Happiness Relative?" *Journal of Personality and Social Psychology* 36: 917–27.

Brines, Julie and Kara Joyner. 1999. "The Ties That Bind: Principles of Cohesion in Cohabitation and Marriage." *American Sociological Review* 64: 333–355.

Brooks, Arthur C. 2008. *Gross National Happiness: Why Happiness Matters for America—and How We Can Get More of It.* New York: Basic Books.

Budig, Michelle J. and Paula England. 2001. "The Wage Penalty for Motherhood." *American Sociological Review* 66: 204–225.

Bukodi, Erzsebet and John H. Goldthorpe. 2010. "Market versus Meritocracy: Hungary as a Critical Case." *European Sociological Review* 26: 655–674.

Buss, David. M., Shackelford, Todd K., Kirkpatrick, Lee A., and Larsen, Randy. J. 2001. "A Half Century of Mate Preferences: The Cultural Evolution of Values." *Journal of Marriage and the Family* 63: 491–503.

Campbell, Angus, Philip E. Converse, and Willard L. Rodgers. 1976. *The Quality of American Life: Perceptions, Evaluations, and Satisfactions.* New York: Russell Sage.

Cha, Ariana Eunjung. 2015. "It Turns Out Parenthood Is Worse Than Divorce, Unemployment—Even the Death of a Partner." *The Washington Post*, August 11. Accessed on August 12, 2015, at: http://www.washingtonpost.com/news/to-your-health/wp/2015/08/11/the-most-depressing-statistic-imaginable-about-being-a-new-parent/?tid=pm_pop_b.

Cherlin, Andrew J. 1979. "Work Life and Marital Dissolution," in *Divorce and Separation*, edited by G. Levinger, 151–166. Basic Books.

Cherlin, Andrew J. 1992. *Marriage, Divorce, Remarriage.* Cambridge: Harvard University Press.

Cherlin, Andrew J. 2010. *The Marriage-Go-Round: The State of Marriage and the Family in America Today.* New York: Alfred A. Knopf.

Clark, Andrew, Ed Diener, Yannis Georgellis, and Richard Lucas. 2003. "Lags and Leads in Life Satisfaction: A Test of the Baseline Hypothesis." German Institute for Economic Research. Discussion Paper No. 371.

Clark, Andrew E. and Yannis Georgellis. 2013. "Back to Baseline in Britain: Adaptation in the British Household Panel Survey." *Economica* 80: 496–512.

Clark, Andrew E. and Andrew J. Oswald. 1996. "Satisfaction and Comparison Income." *Journal of Public Economics* 61: 359–381.

Cohen, Philip N. 2013. "How to Live in a World Where Marriage Is in Decline." *The Atlantic*, June 4, 2013.

Coleman, James S. 1990. *Foundations of Social Theory.* Cambridge: Belknap Press of Harvard University Press.

Coontz, Stephanie. 1992. *The Way We Never Were: American Families and the Nostalgia Trap.* New York: Basic Books.

Craig, Lyn. 2006. "Does Father Care Mean Fathers Share?: A Comparison of How Mothers and Fathers in Intact Families Spend Time with Children." *Gender & Society* 20: 259–281.

Cunningham, Michael R. 1988. "What Do You Do When You're Happy or Blue? Mood, Expectancies, and Behavioral Interest." *Motivation and Emotion* 12: 309–331.

Czismady, Adrienne. 2003. "Poverty and Ethnicity in Six Post-Socialist Countries." *Forum* 19: 3–10.

Deaton, Angus. 2008. "Income, Health, and Well-Being around the World: Evidence from the Gallup World Poll." *Journal of Economic Perspectives* 22: 53–72.

Deaton, Angus and John Muellbauer. 1994. *Economics and Consumer Behavior*. Cambridge: Cambridge University Press.

Delhey, Jan and Georgi Dragolov. 2014. "Why Inequality Makes Europeans Less Happy: The Role of Distrust, Status Anxiety, and Perceived Conflict." *European Sociological Review* 30: 151–165.

Demır, Melıkşah and LesleyA Weitekamp. 2007. "I Am So Happy 'Cause Today I Found My Friend: Friendship and Personality as Predictors of Happiness." *Journal of Happiness Studies* 8: 181–211.

DeNeve, Jan-Emmanuel, Nicholas A. Christakis, James H. Fowler, and Bruno S. Frey. 2012. "Genes, Economics, and Happiness." *Journal of Neuroscience, Psychology, and Economics* 5: 193–211.

Di Tella, Rafael, Robert J. MacCulloch, and Andrew J. Oswald. 2003. "The Macroeconomics of Happiness." *Review of Economics and Statistics* 85: 809–827.

Diener, Ed and Robert Biswas-Diener. 2002. "Will Money Increase Subjective Well-Being?" *Social Indicators Research* 57: 119–169.

Diener, Ed, Carol L. Gohm, Eunkook Suh, and Shigehiro Oishi. 2000. "Similarity of the Relations between Marital Status and Subjective Well-Being across Cultures." *Journal of Cross-Cultural Psychology* 31: 419–436.

Diener, Ed, Shigehiro Oishi, and Richard E. Lucas. 2003. "Personality, Culture, and Subjective Well-Being: Emotional and Cognitive Evaluations of Life." *Annual Review of Psychology* 54: 403–425.

Diener, Ed, Christine K. N. Scollon, Shigehiro Oishi, Vivian Dzokoto, and Eunkook Mark Suh. 2000. "Positivity and the Construction of Life Satisfaction Judgments: Global Happiness Is Not the Sum of Its Parts." *Journal of Happiness Studies* 1: 159–176.

Diener, Ed and Martin E.P. Seligman. 2002. "Very Happy People." *Psychological Science* 13: 81–84.

Diener, Ed and Eunkook M. Suh. 2003. *Culture and Subjective Well-being*. Cambridge: MIT Press.

Diener, Ed, Eunkook M. Suh, Richard E. Lucas, and Heidi L. Smith. 1999. "Subjective Well-Being: Three Decades of Progress." *Psychological Bulletin* 125: 276–302.

Dolan, P., T. Peasgood, and M. White. 2008. "Do We Really Know What Makes Us Happy? A Review of the Economic Literature on the Factors Associated with Subjective Well-Being." *Journal of Economic Psychology* 29: 94–122.

D'Onofrio, Brian M. and Benjamin B. Lahey. 2010. "Biosocial Influences on the Family: A Decade Review." *Journal of Marriage and Family* 72: 762–782.

Durkheim, Emile. 1951. *Suicide: A Study in Sociology*. New York: Free Press. (Original work published 1897)

Easterlin, Richard A. 1974. "Does Economic Growth Improve the Human Lot?," in *Nations and Households in Economic Growth: Essays in Honor of Moses Abramovitz*, edited by P. A. David and M. W. Reader, 89–119. New York: Academic Press.

Easterlin, Richard A. 1987. "The Argument." *Birth and Fortune*. University of Chicago Press.

Easterlin, Richard A. 2001. "Income and Happiness: Towards a Unified Theory." *Economic Journal* 111: 465–484.

Easterlin, Richard A. 2010. *Happiness, Growth, and the Life Cycle*. Oxford: Oxford University Press.

Easterlin, Richard A., Robson Morgan, Malgorzata Switek, and Fei Wang. 2012. "China's Life Satisfaction, 1990–2010." *Proceedings of the National Academy of Sciences* 109: 9775–9780.

Ehrenreich, Barbara. 2009. *Bright-Sided: How the Relentless Promotion of Positive Thinking Has Undermined America*. New York: Metropolitan Books.

Eichhorn, Jan. 2013. "Unemployment Needs Context: How Societal Differences between Countries Moderate the Loss in Life-Satisfaction for the Unemployed." *Journal of Happiness Studies* 14: 1657–1680.

Einstein, Albert. 1949. "Why Socialism?" *Monthly Review* 1: 9–15.

England, P. and G. Farkas. 1986. *Households, Employment, and Gender*. Aldine de Gruyter.

Esping-Andersen, Gosta. 1990. *The Three Worlds of Welfare Capitalism*. Princeton, NJ: Princeton University Press.

Esping-Andersen, Gosta. 1999. *Social Foundations of Postindustrial Economies*. Oxford: Oxford University Press.

Esping-Andersen, Gosta. 2007. "Equal Opportunities and the Welfare State." *Contexts* 6: 23–27.

Esping-Andersen, Gosta and Walter Korpi. 1987. "From Poor Relief to Institutional Welfare States: The Development of Scandinavian Social Policy," in *The Scandinavian Model: Welfare States and Welfare Research*, edited by Robert Erikson, Erik Jorgen Hansen, Stein Ringen, and Hannu Uusitalo, 39–74. Armonk, NY: M.E. Sharpe.

Evenson, Ranae J. and Robin W. Simon. 2005. "Clarifying the Relationship between Parenthood and Depression." *Journal of Health and Social Behavior* 46: 341–358.

Farmer, Melissa M. and Kenneth F. Ferraro. 2005. "Are Racial Disparities in Health Conditional on Socioeconomic Status?" *Social Science & Medicine* 60: 191–204.

Ferriss, Abbott L. 2002. "Religion and the Quality of Life." *Journal of Happiness Studies* 3: 199–215.

Firebaugh, Glenn and Matthew B. Schroeder. 2009. "Does Your Neighbor's Income Affect Your Happiness?" *American Journal of Sociology* 115: 805–831.

Fowler, James H and Nicholas A Christakis. 2008. "Dynamic Spread of Happiness in a Large Social Network: Longitudinal Analysis over 20 Years in the Framingham Heart Study." *BMJ* 337: 1–9.

Frawley, Ashley. 2015. "Happiness Research: A Review of Critiques." *Sociology Compass* 9: 62–77.

Freedman, Vicki A., Frank Stafford, Norbert Schwarz, Frederick Conrad, and Jennifer C. Cornman. 2012. "Disability, Participation, and Subjective Wellbeing among Older Couples." *Social Science & Medicine* 74: 588–596.

Frey, Bruno S. and Alois Stutzer. 2002. "What Can Economists Learn from Happiness Research?" *Journal of Economic Literature* 40: 402–435.

Fujita, Frank and Ed Diener. 2005. "Life Satisfaction Set Point: Stability and Change." *Journal of Personality and Social Psychology* 88: 158–64.

Gallup. 2013. *State of the Global Workplace.* Washington, DC: Gallup Inc.

Gangl, Markus. 2006. "Scar Effects of Unemployment: An Assessment of Institutional Complementarities." *American Sociological Review* 71: 986–1013.

George, Linda K. 2010. "Still Happy after All These Years: Research Frontiers on Subjective Well-Being in Later Life." *Journal of Gerontology B Psychological Sciences and Social Sciences* 65B: 331–339.

Glenn, Evelyn Nakano. 2000. "Creating a Caring Society." *Contemporary Sociology* 29: 84–94.

Glenn, Norval D. 1990. "Quantitative Research on Marital Quality in the 1980s: A Critical Review." *Journal of Marriage and Family* 52(4): 818–831.

Graham, Carol. 2005. "The Economics of Happiness: Insights on Globalization from a Novel Approach." *World Economics* 6: 41–55.

Graham, Carol. 2008. "Happiness and Health: Lessons—and Questions—for Public Policy." *Health Affairs* 27: 72–87.

Graham, Carol, Lucas Higuera, and Eduardo Lora. 2011. "Which Health Conditions Cause the Most Unhappiness?" *Health Economics* 20: 1431–1447.

Graham, Carol, Shaojie Zhou and Junyi Zhang. 2015. "Happiness and Health in China: The Paradox of Progress." Global Economy and Development Working Paper Series No. 89. Washington, DC: Brookings Institution.

Gruber, June, Iris B. Mauss, and Maya Tamir. 2011. "A Dark Side of Happiness? How, When, and Why Happiness Is Not Always Good." *Perspectives on Psychological Science* 6: 222–233.

Guriev, Sergei and Ekaterina Zhuravskaya. 2009. "(Un)Happiness in Transition." *Journal of Economic Perspectives* 23: 143–168.

Hansen, Thomas and Adam Shapiro. 2007. "Relational and Individual Well-Being among Cohabitors and Married Individuals in Midlife—Recent Trends from Norway." *Journal of Family Issues* 28: 910–933.

Haring-Hidore, Marilyn, William A. Stock, Morris A. Okun, and Robert A. Witter. 1985. "Marital Status and Subjective Well-Being: A Research Synthesis." *Journal of Marriage and Family* 47: 947–953.

Hayashi, Takeshi. 1990. *The Japanese Experience in Technology: From Transfer to Self-Reliance.* The United Nations University.

Hays, Sharon. 1996. *The Cultural Contradictions of Motherhood.* New Haven, CT: Yale University Press.

Heath, Melanie. 2012. "Making Marriage Promotion into Public Policy: The Epistemic Culture of a Statewide Initiative." *Qualitative Sociology* 35: 385–406.

Heuveline, Patrick and Jeffrey M. Timberlake. 2004. "The Role of Cohabitation in Family Formation: The United States in Comparative Perspective." *Journal of Marriage and Family* 66: 1214–1230.

Hicks, M. and M. Platt. 1970. "Marital Happiness and Stability: A Review of the Research in the Sixties." *Journal of Marriage and Family* 32: 553–574.

Hirsch, Paul M., Stuart Michaels and Ray Friedman. 1987. "'Dirty Hands' versus 'Clean Models': Is Sociology in Danger of Being Seduced by Economics?" *Theory and Society* 16: 317–336.

Hook, Jennifer L. 2010. "Gender Inequality in the Welfare State: Sex Segregation in Housework, 1965–2003." *American Journal of Sociology* 115: 1480–1523.

Hughes, Michael and Melvin E. Thomas. 1998. "The Continuing Significance of Race Revisited: A Study of Race, Class, and Quality of Life in America, 1972 to 1996." *American Sociological Review* 63: 785–795.

Idler, Ellen L. and Stanislav V. Kasl. 1992. "Religion, Disability, Depression, and the Timing of Death." *American Journal of Sociology* 97: 1052–1079.

Inglehart, Ronald and Hans-Dieter Klingemann. 2000. "Genes, Culture, Democracy and Happiness," in *Culture and Subjective Well-being*, edited by Ed Diener and Eunkook M. Suh, 165–183. Cambridge: MIT Press.

Inglehart, Ronald. 2004. "Subjective Well-being Rankings of 82 Societies (Based on Combined Happiness and Life Satisfaction Scores)." World Values Survey Paper Series.

Inglehart, Ronald, Roberto Foa, Eduard Ponarin, and Christian Welzel. 2013. "Understanding the Russian Malaise: The Collapse and Recovery of Subjective Well-Being in Post-Communist Russia." Higher School of Economics Research Paper No. WP BRP 32/SOC/2013.

International Social Survey Programme (ISSP). 2004. *ISSP 2002 Codebook: Family and Changing Gender Roles III*. Koeln: Zentralarchiv fuer Empirische Sozialforschung.

Iwao, Sumiko. 1993. *The Japanese Woman*. The Free Press.

Iyengar, Sheena. 2011. *The Art of Choosing*. New York: Twelve.

Jonsson, Jan O. and Colin Mills. 2001. "Introduction: Family, Work and Inequality in a Life-course Perspective," in *Cradle to Grave: Life-course Change in Modern Sweden*, edited by Jan O. Jonsson and Colin Mills. Durham: Sociology Press.

Kahneman, Daniel and Alan B. Krueger. 2006. "Developments in the Measurement of Subjective Well-Being." *Journal of Economic Perspectives* 20: 3–24.

Kahneman, Daniel, Alan B. Krueger, David A. Schkade, Norbert Schwarz, and Arthur A. Stone. 2004. "A Survey Method for Characterizing Daily Life Experience: The Day Reconstruction Method." *Science* 306: 1776–1780.

Kangas, Olli and Joakim Palme. 1993. "Statism Eroded? Labor-Market Benefits and Challenges to the Scandinavian Welfare States," in *Welfare Trends in the Scandinavian Countries*, edited by Erik Jorgen Hansen, Stein Ringen, Hannu Uusitalo, and Robert Erikson. 3–24. Armonk, NY: M.E. Sharpe.

Kenworthy, Lane. 1999. "Do Social-Welfare Policies Reduce Poverty? A Cross-National Assessment." *Social Forces* 77: 1119–1139.

Kenworthy, Lane. 2004. *Egalitarian Capitalism: Jobs, Incomes, and Growth in Affluent Countries*. New York: Russell Sage Foundation.

Kim, Hyoun K. and Patrick C. McKenry. 2002. "The Relationship between Marriage and Psychological Well-Being—A Longitudinal Analysis." *Journal of Family Issues* 23: 885–911.

Kimura, Kiyomi. 2001. "Kakei No Kyoudousei to Huhukankei" (Cooperation of Household Finances in Marital Relationships). *Kakei Keizai Kenkyu* 49: 14–24.

Korpi, Walter and Joakim Palme. 1998. "The Paradox of Redistribution and Strategies of Equality: Welfare State Institutions, Inequality, and Poverty in the Western Countries." *American Sociological Review* 63: 661–687.

Kravdal, Oystein. 2008. "Why Is Fertility in Norway So High?" in *Complexity: Interdisciplinary Communications 2006/2007*, edited by O. Willy, 66–71. Oslo: Center for Advanced Study.

Krugman, Paul. 1994. *Peddling Prosperity: Economic Sense and Nonsense in the Age of Diminished Expectation*. New York: W.W. Norton.

Krugman, Paul. 2007. *The Conscience of a Liberal*. New York: W.W. Norton.

Lareau, Annette. 2003. *Unequal Childhoods: Class, Race, and Family Life*. Berkeley: University of California Press.

Layard, Richard. 2005. *Happiness: Lessons from a New Science*. New York: Penguin Press.

Lebra, Takie Sugiyama. 1984. *Japanese Women: Constraint and Fulfillment*. University of Hawaii Press.

Lee, Kristen Schultz and Hiroshi Ono. 2008. "Specialization and Happiness in Marriage: A U.S.-Japan Comparison." *Social Science Research* 37: 1216–1234.

Lee, Kristen Schultz and Hiroshi Ono. 2012. "Marriage, Cohabitation, and Happiness: A Cross-National Analysis of 27 Countries." *Journal of Marriage and Family* 74: 953–972.

LeMasters, E. E. 1957. "Parenthood as Crisis." *Marriage and Family Living* 19: 352–355.

Lesthaeghe, Ron. 1983. "A Century of Demographic and Cultural Change in Western Europe: An Exploration of Underlying Dimensions." *Population and Development Review* 9: 411–435.

Lesthaeghe, Ron J. and Lisa Neidert. 2006. "The Second Demographic Transition in the United States: Exception or Textbook Example?" *Population and Development Review* 32: 669–698.

Lim, Chaeyoon and Robert D. Putnam. 2010. "Religion, Social Networks, and Life Satisfaction." *American Sociological Review* 75: 914–933.

Lindbeck, Assar. 1997. "The Swedish Experiment." *Journal of Economic Literature* 35: 1273–1319.

Lindbeck, Assar. 2004. "Improving the Performance of the European Social Model: The Welfare State over the Individual Life Cycle," in *Building a Dynamic Europe: The Key Policy Debates*, edited by Jordi Gual, 39–69. West Nyack: Cambridge University Press.

Lindert, Peter H. 2004. *Growing Public: Social Spending and Economic Growth since the Eighteenth Century. Volume 1*. Cambridge: Cambridge University Press.

Locksley, Anne. 1980. "On the Effects of Wives' Employment on Marital Adjustment and Companionship." *Journal of Marriage and Family* 42(2): 337–346.

Lucas, Richard E. 2007. "Adaptation and the Set-Point Model of Subjective Well-Being: Does Happiness Change after Major Life Events?" *Current Directions in Psychological Science* 16: 75–79.

Lucas, Richard E., Ed Diener, Alexander Grob, Eunkook M. Suh, and Liang Shao. 2000. "Cross-cultural Evidence for the Fundamental Features of Extraversion." *Journal of Personality and Social Psychology* 79: 452–468.

Lykken, David and Auke Tellegen. 1996. "Happiness Is a Stochastic Phenomenon." *Psychological Science* 7: 186–189.

Major, Aaron. 2015. "Is Parenthood Really Worse Than Divorce? Demographic Clickbait in the *Washington Post*." The Society Pages. *Scatterplot*. Accessed on August 14, 2015, at: https://scatter.wordpress.com/2015/08/13/is-parenthood-really-worse-than-divorce-demographic-clickbait-in-the-washington-post/.

Mankiv, N. Gregory. 2012. *Principles of Economics* (6th Edition). Mason: South-Western Cengage Learning.

Margolis, Rachel and Mikko Myrskylä. 2011. "A Global Perspective on Happiness and Fertility." *Population and Development Review* 37: 29–56.

Margolis, Rachel and Mikko Myrskylä. 2013. "Family, Money, and Health: Regional Differences in the Determinants of Life Satisfaction over the life Course." *Advances in Life Course Research* 18: 115–126

Märtinson, Vjollca K. 2007. "Families in Different Contexts: A Comparison of European, British, and U.S. Union Formation and Family Patterns," in *The Family in the New Millennium, Volume 1*, edited by Scott A. Lovell and Thomas B. Holman, 124–152. Westport: Praeger.

McCall, Leslie and Christine Percheski. 2010. "Income Inequality: New Trends and Research Directions." *Annual Review of Sociology* 36:329–347.

McLanahan, Sara and Julia Adams. 1987. "Parenthood and Psychological Well-Being." *Annual Review of Sociology* 13: 237–257.

Merton, Robert K. 1968. *Social Theory and Social Structure*. New York: Free Press.

Michalos, Alex C. 1985. "Multiple Discrepancies Theory." *Social Indicators Research* 16: 347–413.

Mills, C. Wright. 1959. *The Sociological Imagination*. New York: Oxford University Press.

Ministry of Finance. 2000. *An Outline of Japanese Taxes 1999*. Tokyo: Printing Bureau, Ministry of Finance.

Mogilner, Cassie. 2010. "The Pursuit of Happiness: Time, Money, and Social Connection." *Psychological Science* 21: 1348–1354.

Mueller, Charles W., Toby L. Parcel, and Fred C. Pampel. 1979. "The Effects of Marital-Dyad Status Inconsistency on Women's Support for Equal Rights." *Journal of Marriage and Family* 41(4): 779–791.

Myers, David G. 2000. "The Funds, Friends, and Faith of Happy People." *American Psychologist* 55: 56–67.

Myrskylä, Mikko and Rachel Margolis. 2014. "Happiness: Before and After the Kids." *Demography* 51: 1843–1866.

Nelson, S. Katherine, Kostadin Kushlev, and Sonja Lyubomirsky. 2014. "The Pains and Pleasures of Parenting: When, Why, and How Is Parenthood Associated with More or Less Well-Being?" *Psychological Bulletin* 140: 846–895.

Nemoto, Kumiko. 2008. "Postponed Marriage: Exploring Women's Views of Matrimony and Work in Japan." *Gender & Society* 22: 219–237.

Nettle, Daniel. 2005. *Happiness: The Science behind your Smile*. New York: Oxford University Press.

New York Times Correspondents. 2005. *Class Matters*. New York: New York Times.

Ng, Yew-Kwang. 1997. "A Case for Happiness, Cardinalism, and Interpersonal Comparability." *The Economic Journal* 107: 1848–1858.

Nock, Steven L. 1995. "A Comparison of Marriages and Cohabiting Relationships." *Journal of Family Issues* 16: 53–76.

Noddings, Nel. 2003. *Happiness and Education*. Cambridge, UK: Cambridge University Press.

Nomaguchi, Kei M., Melissa A. Milkie, and Suzanne M. Bianchi. 2005. "Time Strains and Psychological Well-Being: Do Dual-Earner Mothers and Fathers Differ?" *Journal of Family Issues* 26: 756–792.

Ochiai, Emiko. 1997. *The Japanese Family System in Transition: A Sociological Analysis of Family Change in Postwar Japan*. Japan: LTCB International Library Foundation.

OECD. 2008. *Growing Unequal? Income Distribution and Poverty in OECD Countries*. Paris: OECD.

OECD. 2009. *Taxing Wages 2009*. Paris: OECD.

OECD. various years. *OECD Factbook*. Paris: OECD.

Ogasawara, Yuko. 1998. *Office Ladies and Salaried Men*. University of California Press.

Olah, Livia. 2003. "Gendering Fertility: Second Births in Sweden and Hungary." *Population Research and Policy Review* 22: 171–200.

Ono, Hiromi. 1998. "Husbands' and Wives' Resources and Marital Dissolution." *Journal of Marriage and Family* 60: 674–689.

Ono, Hiromi and James M. Raymo. 2006. "Housework, Market Work, and 'Doing Gender' When Marital Satisfaction Declines." *Social Science Research* 35(4): 823–850.

Ono, Hiroshi and Kristen Schultz Lee. 2013. "Welfare States and the Redistribution of Happiness." *Social Forces* 92: 789–814.

Ono, Hiroshi and Marcus E. Rebick. 2003. "Constraints on the Level and Efficient Use of Labor," in *Structural Impediments to Japan's Economic Growth*, edited by M. Blomstrom, J. Corbett, F. Hayashi, and A. Kashyap, pp. 225–257. NBER and University of Chicago Press.

Oppenheimer, Valerie Kincade. 1997. "Women's Employment and the Gain to Marriage: The Specialization and Trading Model." *Annual Review of Sociology* 23: 431–453.

Oswald, Andrew J. and Nattavudh Powdthavee. 2008. "Does Happiness Adapt? A Longitudinal Study of Disability with Implications for Economists and Judges." *Journal of Public Economics* 92: 1061–1077.

Pacek, Alexander and Benjamin Radcliff. 2008. "Assessing the Welfare State: The Politics of Happiness." *Perspectives on Politics* 6: 267–277.

Parsons, Talcott. 1942. "Age and Sex in the Social Structure of the United States." *American Sociological Review* 7: 604–616.

Perelli-Harris, Brienna and Nora Sánchez Gassen. 2012. "How Similar Are Cohabitation and Marriage? Legal Approaches to Cohabitation across Western Europe." *Population and Development Review* 38: 435–467.

Pollmann-Schult, Matthias. 2014. "Parenthood and Life Satisfaction: Why Don't Children Make People Happy?" *Journal of Marriage and Family* 76: 319–336.

Popenoe, David and Barbara Dafoe Whitehead. 2002. *Should We Live Together? What Young Adults Need to Know about Cohabitation and Marriage*. New Brunswick, NJ: The National Marriage Project.

Population Reference Bureau. 2014. *2014 World Population Data Sheet*. Washington, DC: PRB.

Powdthavee, Nattavudh. 2009 (April). "Think Having Children Will Make You Happy?" *The Psychologist* 22: 308–310.

Prescott, Edward C. 2004. "Why Do Americans Work So Much More Than Europeans?" *Federal Reserve Bank of Minneapolis Quarterly Review* 28: 2–13.

Presser, Harriet B. 1994. "Employment Schedules among Dual-Earner Spouses and the Division of Household Labor by Gender." *American Sociological Review* 59(3): 348–364.

Preston, Samuel H. and Alan Thomas Richards. 1975. "The Influence of Women's Work Opportunities on Marriage Rates." *Demography* 12(2): 209–222.

Radcliff, Benjamin. 2001. "Politics, Markets, and Life Satisfaction: The Political Economy of Human Happiness." *American Political Science Review* 95: 939–952.

Radcliff, Benjamin. 2013. *The Political Economy of Human Happiness: How Voters' Choices Determine the Quality of Life*. Cambridge: Cambridge University Press.

Randles, Jennifer M. 2012. "Marriage Promotion Policy and Family Inequality." *Sociology Compass* 6: 671–683.

Raudenbush, Stephen W. and Anthony. S. Bryk. 2002. *Hierarchical Linear Models: Applications and Data Analysis Methods*. Thousand Oaks, CA: Sage Publications.

Raudenbush, Stephen W., Anthony S. Bryk, Yuk Fai Cheong, Richard Congdon, and Mathilda du Toit. 2004. *HLM 6: Hierarchical Linear & Nonlinear Modeling*. Lincolnwood, IL: Scientific Software International.

Raymo, James M. and Miho Iwasawa. 2005. "Marriage Market Mismatches in Japan: An Alternative View of the Relationship between Women's Education and Marriage." *American Sociological Review*: 70: 801–822.

Rodgers, Willard. 1982. "Trends in Reported Happiness within Demographically Defined Subgroups, 1957–78." *Social Forces* 60: 826–42.

Rogers, Stacy J. and Danelle D. DeBoer. 2001. "Change in Wives' Income: Effects on Marital Happiness, Psychological Well-Being, and the Risk of Divorce." *Journal of Marriage and Family* 63: 458–472.

Riley, Matilda White. 1987. "On the Significance of Age in Sociology." *American Sociological Review* 52: 1–14.

Rizzo, Kathryn M., Holly H. Schiffrin, and Miriam Liss. 2013. "Insight into the Parenthood Paradox: Mental Health Outcomes of Intensive Mothering." *Journal of Child and Family Studies* 22: 614–620.

Rogers, Stacy J. 2004. "Dollars, Dependency, and Divorce: Four Perspectives on the Role of Wives' Income." *Journal of Marriage and Family* 66(1): 59–74.

Rosen, Raymond C. and Gloria A. Bachmann. 2008. "Sexual Well-Being, Happiness, and Satisfaction, in Women: The Case for a New Conceptual Paradigm." *Journal of Sex & Marital Therapy* 34: 291–297.

Rossi, Alice S. 1968. "Transition to Parenthood." *Journal of Marriage and Family* 30: 26–39.

Rothstein, Bo. 2010. "Happiness and the Welfare State." Social Research 77: 441–468.

Ryan, Richard M. and Edward L. Deci. 2001. "On Happiness and Human Potentials: A Review of Research on Hedonic and Eudaimonic Well-Being." Annual Review of Psychology 52: 141–66.

Samuels, David. 2012. "Lottery Winner Jack Whittaker's Losing Ticket." Businessweek, December 13. Accessed on June 24, 2015, at: www.businessweek.com/articles/2012–12–13/lottery-winner-jack-whittakers-losing-ticket.

Samuelson, Paul and William Nordhaus. 2005. Economics (18th Edition). New York: McGraw-Hill/Irwin.

Sandstrom, Gillian M. and Elizabeth W. Dunn. 2014. "Social Interactions and Well-Being: The Surprising Power of Weak Ties." Personality and Social Psychology Bulletin 40: 910–922.

Save the Children. 2015. The Urban Disadvantage: State of the World's Mothers 2015 Executive Summary. Fairfield: Save the Children.

Sayer, Liana C. and Suzanne M. Bianchi. 2000. "Women's Economic Independence and the Probability of Divorce." Journal of Family Issues 21(7): 906–943.

Schnittker, Jason. 2008. "Happiness and Success: Genes, Families, and the Psychological Effects of Socioeconomic Position and Social Support." American Journal of Sociology 114: S233–S259.

Schoen, Robert, Nan Marie Astone, Kendra Rothert, Nicola J. Standish, and Young J. Kim. 2002. "Women's Employment, Marital Happiness, and Divorce." Social Forces 81(2): 643–662.

Schyns, Peggy. 2002. "Wealth of Nations, Individual Income and Life Satisfaction in 42 Countries: A Multilevel Approach." Social Indicators Research 60: 5–40.

Sen, Amartya, Joseph E. Stiglitz, and Jean-Paul Fitoussi. 2009. Report by the Commission on the Measurement of Economic Performance and Social Progress. Paris: The Commission on the Measurement of Economic Performance and Social Progress.

Simon, Robin W. 2008. "The Joys of Parenthood, Reconsidered." Contexts: Understanding People in Their Social Worlds 7: 40–45.

Simpson, Ida Harper and Paula England. 1981. "Conjugal Work Roles and Marital Solidarity." Journal of Family Issues 2(2): 180–204.

Soons, Judith P.M. and Matthijs Kalmijn. 2009. "Is Marriage More Than Cohabitation? Well-Being Differences in 30 European Countries." Journal of Marriage & Family 71: 1141–1157.

Sorensen, Annemette and Sara McLanahan. 1987. "Married Women's Economic Dependency, 1940–1980." American Journal of Sociology 93: 659–687.

South, Scott J. and Glenna Spitze. 1994. "Housework in Marital and Nonmarital Households." American Sociological Review 59(3): 327–347.

Spanier, Graham B., Robert A. Lewis. 1980. "Marital Quality: A Review of the Seventies." Journal of Marriage and Family 42(4): 825–839.

Spitze, Glenna. 1988. "Women's Employment and Family Relations: A Review." Journal of Marriage and Family 50(3): 595–618.

Stack, Steve and J. Ross Eshleman. 1998. "Marital Status and Happiness: A 17-Nation Study." Journal of Marriage and the Family 60: 527–536.

Stark, Rodney and Jared Maier. 2008. "Faith and Happiness." Review of Religious Research 50: 120–125.

Steinmo, Sven. 1989. "Political Institutions and Tax Policy in the United States, Sweden, and Britain." *World Politics* 41: 500–535.

Stevenson, Betsey and Justin Wolfers. 2008. "Happiness Inequality in the United States." *The Journal of Legal Studies* 37: S33–S79.

Sugihara, Yoko and Emiko Katsurada. 2002. "Gender Role Development in Japanese Culture: Diminishing Gender Role Differences in a Contemporary Society." *Sex Roles* 47: 443–452.

Tokyo Metropolitan Government. 1994. *International Comparative Survey Concerning Issues Confronting Women*. Tokyo Metropolitan Government.

Twenge, Jean M., W. Keith Campbell, and Craig A. Foster. 2003. "Parenthood and Marital Satisfaction: A Meta-Analytic Review." *Journal of Marriage and Family* 65: 574–583.

Ueno, Chizuko. 2001. "Modern Patriarchy and the Formation of the Japanese Nation State," in *Multicultural Japan: Palaeolithic to Postmodern*, edited by Donald Denoon, Mark Hudson, Gavan McCormack, and Tessa Morris-Suzuki, 213–223. Cambridge: Cambridge University Press.

Umberson, Debra and Walter R. Gove. 1989. "Parenthood and Psychological Well-Being: Theory, Measurement, and Stage in the Family Life Course." *Journal of Family Issues* 10: 440–462.

Umberson, Debra, Tetyana Pudrovska, and Corinne Reczek. 2010. "Parenthood, Childlessness, and Well-Being: A Life Course Perspective." *Journal of Marriage and Family* 72: 612–629.

Ura, Karuma, Sabina Alkire, Tshoki Zangmo, and Karma Wangdi. 2012. *A Short Guide to Gross National Happiness Index*. Thimphu, Bhutan: The Centre for Bhutan Studies.

VanLaningham, Jody, David R. Johnson and Paul Amato. 2001. "Marital Happiness, Marital Duration and the U-Shaped Curve: Evidence from a Five-Wave Panel Study." *Social Forces* 79: 1313–1341.

Varian, Hal R. 2010. *Intermediate Microeconomics: A Modern Approach* (8th Edition). New York: W.W. Norton and Company.

Veenhoven, Ruut. 2000. "Well-Being in the Welfare State: Level Not Higher, Distribution Not More Equitable." *Journal of Comparative Policy Analysis* 2: 91–125.

Wadsworth, Tim. 2014. "Sex and the Pursuit of Happiness: How Other People's Sex Lives Are Related to Our Sense of Well-Being." *Social Indicators Research* 116: 115–135.

Waite, Linda J. and Maggie Gallagher. 2000. *The Case for Marriage: Why Married People Are Happier, Healthier, and Better Off Financially*. New York: Doubleday.

Weber, Max. 1976 (1904). *Protestant Ethic and the Spirit of Capitalism*. New York: Scribner.

Western, Bruce, Deirdre Bloome, and Christine Percheski. 2008. "Inequality among American Families with Children, 1975 to 2005." *American Sociological Review* 73: 903–920.

Westley, Sidney B. 1998. "What's Happening to Marriage in East Asia?" *Asia-Pacific Population and Policy* 46: 1–4.

White, Lynn and Stacy J. Rogers. 2000. "Economic Circumstances and Family Outcomes: A Review of the 1990s." *Journal of Marriage and Family* 62(4): 1035–1051.

White, Merry Isaacs. 2002. *Perfectly Japanese: Making Families in an Era of Upheaval.* University of California Press.

Wilbur, Charles K. and Kenneth P. Jameson. 1983. *An Inquiry into the Poverty of Economics.* Notre Dame: University of Notre Dame Press.

World Bank. 2007. *World Development Indicators 2007.* Washington, DC: World Bank.

Yamaguchi, Kazuo. 2006. "Fuufu Kankei Manzokudo to Work-Life Balance" (Marital Satisfaction and Work-Life Balance). RIETI Discussion Paper Series 06-J-054.

Yang, Yang. 2008. "Social Inequalities in Happiness in the United States, 1972 to 2004: An Age-Period-Cohort Analysis." *American Sociological Review* 73: 204–226.

Yavorsky, Jill E., Claire M. Kamp Dush, and Sarah J. Schoppe-Sullivan. 2015. "The Production of Inequality: The Gender Division of Labor across the Transition to Parenthood." *Journal of Marriage and Family* 77: 662–679.

Index

Page numbers followed by (b) or (t) indicate a box or table. *Italicized* page numbers indicate a figure.

About the Authors

HIROSHI ONO (PhD in sociology, University of Chicago) is Professor of Human Resources at Hitotsubashi University, Graduate School of International Corporate Strategy. He has extensive international experience, having held professional and academic positions in the United States, Japan, and Sweden. His research integrates sociology and microeconomics to study the causes and consequences of stratification and inequality, with applications in the areas of gender, family, education, and labor markets. His current work examines the determinants of happiness in an international context and career mobility in the Japanese labor market. His papers have appeared in the *American Sociological Review*, *Social Forces*, *Social Science Quarterly*, and *Social Science Research*, among others.

KRISTEN SCHULTZ LEE (PhD in sociology, Cornell) is Associate Professor of Sociology at the University at Buffalo, SUNY. She specializes in the areas of gender, family, the life course, and happiness, and her current research examines families and happiness in an international context, elder care in Japan, and children's educational trajectories in the United States. Her research has been supported by the Fulbright Foundation and the Japan Foundation, and her papers have appeared in *Social Forces*, *Social Problems*, *Journal of Marriage and Family*, and *Social Science Research*, among others.